JIM
BREUER

I'M NOT HIGH

(But I've Got a Lot of Crazy Stories about
Life as a Goat Boy, a Dad,
and a Spiritual Warrior)

GOTHAM
BOOKS

GOTHAM BOOKS
Published by Penguin Group (USA) Inc.
375 Hudson Street, New York, New York 10014, U.S.A.
Penguin Group (Canada), 90 Eglinton Avenue East, Suite 700, Toronto, Ontario M4P 2Y3, Canada
(a division of Pearson Penguin Canada Inc.); Penguin Books Ltd, 80 Strand, London WC2R 0RL,
England; Penguin Ireland, 25 St Stephen's Green, Dublin 2, Ireland (a division of Penguin Books Ltd);
Penguin Group (Australia), 250 Camberwell Road, Camberwell, Victoria 3124, Australia (a division of
Pearson Australia Group Pty Ltd); Penguin Books India Pvt Ltd, 11 Community Centre, Panchsheel
Park, New Delhi—110 017, India; Penguin Group (NZ), 67 Apollo Drive, Rosedale, North Shore 0632,
New Zealand (a division of Pearson New Zealand Ltd); Penguin Books (South Africa) (Pty) Ltd, 24
Sturdee Avenue, Rosebank, Johannesburg 2196, South Africa

Penguin Books Ltd, Registered Offices: 80 Strand, London WC2R 0RL, England

Published by Gotham Books, a member of Penguin Group (USA) Inc.

First printing, October 2010
1 3 5 7 9 10 8 6 4 2

Gotham Books and the skyscraper logo are trademarks of Penguin Group (USA) Inc.

LIBRARY OF CONGRESS CATALOGING-IN-PUBLICATION DATA

Breuer, Jim, 1967–
I'm not high : but I've got a lot of crazy stories about life as a goat boy,
a dad and a spiritual warrior / Jim Breuer.
p.   cm.
ISBN 978-1-592-40575-6 (hardcover)
1. Breuer, Jim, 1967– 2. Comedians—United States—Biography. I. Title.
PN2287.B68555A3   2010
792.7'028'092—dc22
[B]   2010019123

Printed in the United States of America
Set in Goudy Old Style
Designed by Sabrina Bowers

Penguin is committed to publishing works of quality and integrity.
In that spirit, we are proud to offer this book to our readers;
however, the story, the experiences, and the words are the author's alone.

To my soul mate, best friend,
and dearest wife, Dee.
You have stood in the shadows,
supporting my every move
and keeping me grounded.

Contents

Introduction: Vegas **1**

Chapter 1: Nearly Aborted **13**

Chapter 2: Getting the Bug **33**

Chapter 3: Florida Bound . . . and Gagged **49**

Chapter 4: A Lesson from Steve Harvey . . . and a Few Others, Too **64**

Chapter 5: Engaged **79**

Chapter 6: From Harlem, It's the *Uptown Comedy Club* **100**

Chapter 7: It's a Breuer Family Wedding **115**

Chapter 8: Babysitting Billy **118**

Chapter 9: God Fired Me from *Buddies* So I Wouldn't Cheat on Dee **127**

Chapter 10: Joining *Saturday Night Live* . . . and Becoming Joe Pesci **143**

Chapter 11: Birth of Goat Boy **172**

Chapter 12: Finding Farley **175**

Chapter 13: Meeting the Mayor **187**

Chapter 14: Chris Kattan, Heavy Metal Man, and the End of *SNL* Days **194**

Chapter 15: *Half Baked,* Dave Chappelle, and Monk the Pooping Dog **204**

Chapter 16: Birth of Gabrielle **216**

Chapter 17: Saving Steve-O **222**

Chapter 18: Life in the Jersey Burbs **227**

Chapter 19: Partying Like a Rock Star **233**

Chapter 20: Getting Sirius **238**

Chapter 21: Dad Moves In **246**

Epilogue: RV Tour **253**

Acknowledgments **261**

Introduction

Vegas

In late fall 2008, I decided to write a book. This book. The whole thing really started on a flight. My wife, Dee, and I were headed to the Comedy Festival in Las Vegas for the weekend, and I was amped about performing all-new material. For years, I'd been thinking about my message, my act, and what I really wanted to say.

I began doing a daily show on Sirius satellite radio back in 2004, when Dee and I had just started our family. It let me connect with people while still having a normal life as a dad. But over the course of doing my radio show, it occurred to me that the grind—going out and doing stand-up every week—was what really made me happy. It also occurred to me that my message had changed. Or maybe just evolved. What inspires me and what I want to share is what's most important to me now: the ups and downs of family life—like alternating between changing my kids' diapers and my dad's.

I wanted to see other families brought together by my comedy, by the little annoyances of our day-to-day that really end up being the best things about being alive. Most people, though, see me as the guy with sleepy eyes and a goofy laugh who played a stoner in *Half Baked* and a goat on *Saturday Night Live*. But I'm not that guy—I wasn't then and I'm especially not now. So after a long break from stand-up, I thought, "If I'm going to get back into it with a whole new, more honest point of view, I'll do it in Vegas in front of a bunch of other comedians." They'd tell me if it was any good or not. And on the flight there I'd start putting down some thoughts on paper.

Once Dee and I got into our seats on the plane in Newark, I took out my notebook and started writing. And magic happened. I felt like my hand was moving across the page on its own. I've written my whole life, but never before had stuff just spilled out of me like that. The next thing I heard was the voice of the flight attendant telling us to get ready for landing four and a half hours later. I'd written fifty pages, front and back, and my hand was killing me. I showed it to Dee, and she couldn't believe that I'd done it all on the flight.

We landed and checked into the monumentally extravagant Caesars Palace, and the next night I did my set at the Palace Ballroom. I crushed and got a standing ovation, validating what my gut had been telling me for a long time. The security guard who walked us into the venue was waiting for me when I came off the stage. He looked just like Mark McGwire back in his steroid days. I couldn't help but ask if he'd dabbled in performance-enhancing substances, too.

"It gave me a competitive advantage in my field," he said matter-of-factly. He was tossing a water bottle back and forth between his hands and when he'd catch it, it would just disappear into his giant paw. "Now, though, the whole thing doesn't appeal to me anymore."

"Why not?"

"Let me ask you something," he said, not answering my question. "You had a really awesome, powerful set tonight. Are you a godly man?"

"I pray," I said. "I try to lead a life I can be proud of."

"Have you been born again?"

"Nope," I said, then nodded toward Dee. "But she has."

"So have I," he said.

At that, I feared that I was going to get dragged into a discussion about accepting Jesus Christ as my savior. But instead he simply told me that he really liked my set, and I guess he just wanted to learn more about me.

Dee interjected. "I'm just upset that he dropped five F-bombs on the crowd." Then she looked at me and said, "That wasn't necessary."

"I can see through the cursing," the security guy said, "and still totally get Jim's message. You know, Jesus hung out with all kinds of people and never sat in judgment of them. It's good to keep an open mind. A message can be delivered in any medium. We can't ignore it just because we don't like how it arrives."

Then the juicehead with the big heart, Dee, and I just started sharing stories in that back hallway. We must have sat there for two or three hours.

"You should really write these stories down, bro," the security guy said. "They're like testimonies. You need to share them."

"It's funny that you're saying that," I told him. "Because the whole flight out here, that's exactly what I was doing—writing them all down."

We eventually parted ways and Dee and I went back to our suite. I was fired up about the progress I'd made on writing the book and about the response I'd received for doing stand-up material that was true to my heart. The next day Dee and I both worked out in the morning, and then I was going to meet her in the lobby in the early afternoon.

While Dee was out running errands, I continued to write and stare out of our giant window down at the Las Vegas Strip. Something overtook me, and I took a break and walked closer to the window. I felt untouchable. Life could not have been going any better. And I felt like it was time to address all of the negative energy out there, to literally tempt fate.

"I know you're out there, but you can't stop me from touching people's lives," I said out loud, addressing the Devil, and any other as yet unannounced evil forces out there. "And I'm going to do it without being a preacher. I'm not a shrink, either. I'm just an everyday, ordinary guy with some deep-ass stories. I'm a modern-day prophet warrior. Try and stop me. If you have any power at all, come and destroy this notebook." I held it up to the window, sneering and laughing at the same time.

Immediately the rational, sober part of me told me not to push it. Sure, I was raised in Long Island and I loved to bust balls. But as an adult you have to take your good fortune with humility and grace. It's great to hit the home run, but if you make fun of the pitcher as you're rounding the bases you're going to get put on your ass the next time you're at the plate. There was no good reason to start taunting Satan.

I stepped away from the window and now I was feeling a little paranoid. I looked around the room, thinking it would be wise to put the notebook in a drawer or something, just to be safe. But all of the drawers seemed to be unprotected, just begging a thief or a vengeful spirit to steal from them. I walked over to the safe, but it was tiny. If you had a Rubik's Cube that you really wanted to protect, this would have been the perfect safe for it. But a notebook? It didn't really fit without getting all crinkled up and wedged. I forced it in there for a second, like a taco, and tried to close the door. It wasn't happening, despite repeated slammings. Now I was starting to freak out. I even had Yoda's voice inside of my head, growling, "Never underestimate the power of the dark side." Fate, the Devil, or whoever was messing with me already.

Then I stopped and realized how pathetic I was acting. I got mad at myself for cowering like a baby and defiantly pulled the notebook out of the safe. I put it back on the desk and said to the room, "It's right here. In plain view. And there's nothing you can do about it."

By now I was running late to meet Dee. She was down in the fancy Caesars spa getting a manicure and pedicure. Unbelievably, she'd talked me into getting one, too. Weren't these things generally reserved for chicks? "Yes," I thought, "but Vegas is about indulgence and trying new things. And Dee and I could just sit and talk without a care in the world."

So I got on the elevator and took it to the lobby. Because of the festival, it felt like the red carpet at the Oscars down there. The floor was packed with famous comedians rubbing elbows. I hadn't really expected to see so many people I knew, but as I got closer to the nail spa, I could see Jerry Seinfeld and Chris Rock standing a few feet in front of its entrance, inside of which Dee was patiently waiting for me.

"What's happening, Jim?" Jerry said just as I walked up.

"We're getting something to eat," Chris added.

"Oh, I'm just hanging out," I said, gazing around the lobby. "Taking it all in."

Just then Eddie Izzard walked by and stopped to say hello, just as Dee poked her head out the spa's doorway. She had little wads of tissue between each finger, protecting her newly painted nails.

"I thought I heard you out here," she said, smiling. "They're waiting for you! Hurry up!"

Then she ducked back in.

Now the guys looked confused. "Actually, I'm getting a, uh, procedure, ah, too," I explained sheepishly.

I believe Jerry made a face as if I'd just told him I was going to walk in and ask for a vasectomy. Here I was in Vegas, home of flashing lights, high rollers, and showgirls, and I was going to sit in a spa with my wife, listen to Kenny G, and get my toenails painted. It was emasculating, even if that's the one thing I wanted to do most at that moment.

"Bonding," I said. The guys nodded, piecing it together.

I babbled on. "You guys are all married, right? You know how it is."

"That's cool, Jim," Chris said, backing slowly away. "Sounds like a nice afternoon."

So then I went into the spa. A big Jamaican woman gave me my first and only pedicure, and it was amazing. All the women in there were gossiping about the festival, wanting to get tickets or meet a star, not knowing that Jerry Seinfeld, Chris Rock, and Eddie Izzard had just been standing not more than ten feet away from them. I soon forgot all about not wanting my guy friends to know what I was up to. And I also forgot about the notebook up in our suite.

When we finished, I was just ready to go back up to the room and take a quick nap before dinner. Between spending the whole flight writing, then performing, then staying up until nearly dawn talking to the security guard, I was wiped out. I was relishing lying down without being awoken by the screams of my children. When you're a parent of young kids, you soon learn that every time you try to steal a nap, just when you start to drift off, you'll inevitably hear a blood-curdling shout or wake up to discover that someone's given the cat a haircut or used a Sharpie to decorate a piece of furniture.

When we got back upstairs we saw the maid's cart in front of our door. I heard her vacuuming inside, and I didn't want to scare her, so I opened the door slowly while knocking loudly. Maybe I wouldn't even take a nap, I thought. Maybe I'd write a few more pages while I was on a roll.

As we walked in, I heard the vacuuming coming from the bedroom. The noise stopped, and then the maid wheeled the machine back out into the living room. Her eyes bugged out when she saw us.

"I'm sorry," I said, laughing. "I tried to knock. I didn't want to scare you."

The maid had dark, dark circles under her eyes. I don't make a practice of judging people on looks—probably because I've had people assume I'm a degenerate pothead my whole life—but this woman was creepy. She was thin, in her late forties, with a head of jet-black hair. I assumed she was maybe from somewhere in South America. Or maybe from the blackest pits of hell. I wasn't sure.

"I apologize about your candy," she said nervously. "I'm so sorry."

"What do you mean?" I asked. The festival had sent a package of gifts to the participating comedians—a briefcase filled with candy and coffee mugs. But now I just saw the briefcase on the kitchen table with nothing inside of it.

"I thought you had checked out," she said timidly. "So I gave the candy to a friend. To another maid. I can get it back. I'm sorry. I'm sorry."

I had no idea why she thought we checked out when all of our clothes and luggage were still in the room. To me it sounded crazy, but I didn't want to make a big deal of it. Accidents happen. I'm sure she had a lot of rooms to clean, and I bet people leave them in complete disarray—especially in Vegas. Plus, in the bigger picture, we were given this amazing suite with a view of the whole Strip for the weekend. If this was the worst thing that was going to happen, big deal. I looked over at Dee, who shrugged and grinned. It was just candy.

"No," I said to the maid. "Don't worry about it. I don't think I'll miss the extra five pounds I would've gained eating it." I laughed, letting her know there were no hard feelings.

"No biggie," Dee added.

The maid nodded silently, then quickly started pushing the vacuum toward the door. She seemed in a hurry to leave. I figured she was embarrassed and wanted the situation to be over. But I wanted to make sure nothing else had gone missing.

"Is that all you gave away was the candy?" I asked. I figured now was my only chance to check. Once the maid left the room, it would be all but impossible to get anything back. It was a giant hotel, she didn't speak English very well, and it would just be a convoluted ordeal. But it wasn't money or jewelry I was thinking about. It was my notebook, which I was relieved to see was still on the desk.

"No," the maid said, shaking her head. "Just candy. That's all."

"Great," I said. "Let's not worry about that."

"Thank you," she said, smiling, and walked back out to her cart in the hallway.

Dee went into the bedroom, and I walked over to the desk. I had no sane reason to pick up the notebook and thumb through it. I mean, it was sitting there just as I'd left it. Opening it up would be proof that I was paranoid. I get that the candy—so tempting and delicious, spilling out of a wide-open briefcase—was an obvious target to be snapped up. But a $3.59 notebook? All of the hotel rooms were furnished with stationery. And the maid probably had extra supplies of it on her cart to replenish any that had been used. If she needed paper, she had access to tons of it.

But I had a peek anyway. And I couldn't believe my eyes. Every page I had written on was gone, ripped out, and what remained were only blank pages. I closed it. What was happening wasn't real. I reopened it again, and still the pages were nowhere to be found. I flipped page after page. This was impossible.

I began to sweat. I took a deep breath.

"Dee," I called out. This time there would be a logical explanation. "Where did you set all the pages I was working on?"

"What are you talking about?" she answered.

"From my notebook," I said.

"I thought it was there."

"It is," I said. "But it's empty."

She came out of the bedroom and looked over at me. "What are you talking about?"

"So, you didn't touch this?" I said, holding up the notebook. "There's only blank pages in here."

"You must have put them in your suitcase," she said calmly. She didn't seem too concerned. "Wait, are you sure you didn't take them into the bathroom, Jim?" She made a face indicating that working on the can was exactly the sort of thing I'd do.

"No!" I yelled. "What are you, crazy? I kept them in the notebook. There was no reason to tear them out."

"Stop panicking and take another look."

"Dee," I said, "the notebook is way thinner. The only pages left in it are blank. Everything I've written is gone."

"Why don't you go ask the maid then?" she said. "There's got to be some reasonable explanation."

"Why would the maid have them?"

"Why would she have cleaned out all our chocolate, Jim?" Dee said, shrugging. "None of it makes any sense."

I took the notebook, bolted from the room, and saw the maid's cart a few doors down. I poked my head in the room she was cleaning, and she came out into the hallway. She took a look at the notebook and started shaking her head and apologizing again.

"Sorry," she said. "Sorry."

"What happened?" I asked. I was close to losing it, but I did feel slightly relieved that at least I knew who was responsible for the missing notebook. "I thought you said the candy was the only thing that went haywire in there."

"Sorry. I thought was garbage," she mumbled in broken English.

"*Garbage?*" I said, exasperated. I shook the notebook. "You went in *this* and ripped out the pages and threw them *away*? Why? Why would you do that?"

"Sorry. Sorry."

"Well, where's the garbage?" I thought it might be on her cart. That seemed logical. I thought we could just dig through her trash can and fish them out, and then I'd go and stuff the pages in the safe or keep them in my pocket for the rest of the trip. Before she answered I dug into the garbage and started flipping through it.

"All gone," she said, shaking her head again. "Not in there."

"Come on!" Now I really felt like this might be a big prank. Maybe the comedians at the festival were behind it. But how would anyone know that this was the most important property I had on the trip?

"He come and take garbage from hallway," she explained. "I set papers in hallway."

"Who is he?" I asked. "What are you saying?"

"Janitor," she said. "He remove."

"Oh, man!" I yelled. "We gotta find this stuff. Don't move a muscle, okay? Please, lady, just stay right where you are."

I went into my room and called the front desk. They said they'd send a manager right up. Then the maid hurried into our room and said, "I think I can go find them. I'm sorry. I will go look." She wandered off before the manager arrived. I doubted she'd ever come back. I was thinking with all that had happened, maybe she'd just flee into the Vegas night with some free candy and the handwritten scribbles of my life story.

If I hadn't dared the universe to mess with that notebook, I wouldn't have been so worked up about losing the pages. There was no explanation for what had happened. Why would the maid have removed all the pages I'd written stuff on and left the rest of it intact and on the table? Apparently the hospitality pledge at the hotel went something like: "At Caesars Palace, our maid service is so good, whenever you leave the room, you can be sure we will go through all of your handwritten documents and notebooks, remove any and all soiled pages, and leave what remains of your unused paper supply right where you left it. Promise!"

After a few minutes, a manager knocked on our door. I told her what happened, and she was naturally dumbfounded. "I'm very sorry," she said earnestly. "This makes no sense. I don't know where the maid got the notion that you were checking out. The first people to know that would be us. If you left, we'd let her know. Otherwise, she's got to believe that you're still a guest. She knows that. There's a chart right on her cart that says so. It's really puzzling."

"I just want to get my writing back," I said. Soon enough the maid came back holding the missing pages. As she handed them over to me, I noticed that they weren't crinkled. There were no food stains or coffee grounds on them. They were pristine. None of this added up.

"Thank you so much," I said. "I'm truly grateful." I flipped through them and discovered that there were a bunch of pages missing. "Where's the rest?" I asked. Panic returned. "Tell me where you found these! We've gotta keep looking."

So the maid, the manager, and I went down into the bowels of Caesars Palace, to the garbage chute.

"I'll scoop all the garbage by hand," I said. "I don't care. I just need to find my papers." We looked and looked and didn't find any more pages. I resigned myself to the fact that (a) I had gotten a big chunk of them back and (b) I had also been a dumbass who basically begged for trouble. The maid apologized and somberly returned to her work. Caesars Palace officials apologized again and again, and called our room a few times asking what they could do for me. I was tempted to say, "How about you start with comping that overpriced pedicure for me?" but I didn't.

In the end, I'd done a great set, had a nice getaway with Dee, and committed to paper a lot of the stories that make up my life. As I said, I don't get overly tangled up in religion. In the pages to come, you'll read about my views on the church, organized religion, and the concept of being born again. All my life I've bickered with people who say I should know the Ten Commandments, or take communion, or worship a certain way. I don't have much patience for any of that. I'm spiritual on my terms and have my own relationship with God. And what went down in Vegas was definitely spiritual.

After I left Vegas, I often thought about having my writing disappear that weekend, and for a long time I was certain it was because I mouthed off and challenged evil forces. The maid was just a conduit. You could call it karma or whatever you like. As time has passed though, I've changed my thinking on this. The maid had taken the pages somewhere and had not destroyed them. Maybe she needed them. Maybe something compelled her to take them, and once her shift was over she'd read through them. And maybe she found something in them. (Perhaps something as delicious as the candy she also stole from me.)

Who knows? The book is once again intact. And there are messages in it. I've had a big bank account and a tiny one, and I've been spiritually rich and poor, too. In between playing stickball on the streets of Long Island, having loved ones taken from me at the worst times, meeting the woman of my dreams when I wasn't even having dreams, and getting big breaks and also getting broken, I've figured out a lot. I'd never claim to have all the answers to the test, but I've looked over the shoulders of some great people and have cribbed the most important one: We all have a mission to honor ourselves and those around us.

(And, by the way, yeah: There's plenty of stuff about weed in here, too, Meatball.)

Chapter 1

Nearly Aborted

As a boy, I used to sit and talk for hours with my best friend Phil out in the street on Jefferson Avenue in Long Island. We lived in Valley Stream, a beautiful community near Queens that lies directly underneath about twelve thousand flight paths to and from JFK airport, which is just a few miles away.

So maybe Phil couldn't always hear much of what I said, but on one summer night we were hanging out, stargazing and discussing what our lives would be like in the year 2000.

"Man, we're going to be old," Phil said, cringing at his own imagination. "Like over thirty."

"By then," I said with all the confidence of youth, "I will have met all of the New York Mets. I will have hung out with AC/DC. And I will have acted with Joe Pesci, Robert De Niro, and Jack Nicholson." I didn't know how it was going to happen, but I was certain fame was coming my way.

Even by age fifteen, Joe Pesci was already my favorite actor and my inspiration. I watched him act in everything, from movies like *Raging Bull*, where he had a huge role, to *Easy Money* (which to me is a classic) to a bunch of films where he had bit parts. He just had such electricity. I was captivated by him and had started doing impressions of him when my friends and I played stickball in the street. "Come aaaahhhn," I'd moan in my best Pesci-ese. "Pitch da bawl. It ain't gonna bite ya. Jeez. Hey. Whatsa matta witch yoo? Ya trow like ya take it up the wazoo." Doing Pesci impressions was where it all started for me, and the reaction I got for it told me that I'd make a living at performing someday.

Phil had heard my Pesci and knew that I was committed to my dream, so on that night when I predicted I'd have it all, he said simply, "I believe it." And that's what I loved about him. He never said much, but he always had my back, and that was about the best endorsement of a dream a guy could get in Valley Stream.

"Yep," I blathered on. "I am definitely going to be famous one day."

Back then, in addition to my big dreams, I also felt like the world was looking out for me, and that if I stayed true to myself I'd someday be able to share my talents with everyone. And when I say the world was looking out for me, I mostly mean that I've always been blessed and lucky. That goes all the way back to before I was born, as I almost didn't even make it into the world. I was nearly aborted.

Let me explain.

By the time my mom, at age forty, wandered into the Rock Front Tavern, in Valley Stream, in the mid-1960s and met my dad, a garbage man moonlighting as a bartender, she had already had enough kids. There were Eddie, Bobby, Dorene, and Patti, and they came from an array of different fathers, one of whom was dead and one of whom was a crazy maniac who almost killed them all before Mom made a midnight escape, driving from Florida to Long Island in one straight shot with her young brood.

So life hadn't worked out the greatest for Mom. But she found a way to get through it and even had some fun along the way. She was usually the life of the party, and she loved to flirt and carouse. I figure that if she had been born a decade or two earlier she would have been a burlesque dancer. She still likes to kick up her heels, belt out tunes, dance around, and laugh from the bottom of her belly. Even into her golden years now, sometimes I'll catch her batting her eyes at a strange man after she's had a few martinis, and I'll have to tell her to knock it off. That's just who she is—and I inherited a lot of that from her. But I also think that some of her partying was an attempt to take the edge off a rough life.

Mom was born in the mid-1920s, grew up on Long Island, and as a teenager fell in love with a man named Edwin "Lefty" Troy. He was her first love, and he was great to her. He'd take her dancing and was always a gentleman, doing all of the chivalrous stuff that made Mom believe that love was a wonderful thing. She and Edwin had big plans to build a life together. There were only a couple of small problems.

The first was that Edwin's family hated her. The Troys were Catholics and Mom was Lutheran. To me that doesn't seem like a big deal, but to them, in that era, it was bitter like a race war. It crushed my mom that they couldn't get married in Edwin's church. And his family certainly wouldn't attend a wedding in her Lutheran church. So they ended up having a simple civil service at city hall. And Edwin's family still wouldn't attend. It was completely out of the question. So she doesn't have a wedding day memory of smiling in-laws looking on as their son placed a ring on her finger. Instead she remembers that in the days leading up to the wedding, Edwin's father told her father, "I'd rather my son be dead than married to a Lutheran."

And there was the second problem: Edwin's father soon got his wish. Edwin was sent off to fight the Nazis in World War II under General Patton. Two months before he was to be discharged, he was killed in action.

Mom tells me of knowing it was coming. Of feeling it for a few days. She was pregnant when Edwin left, and losing the father of her child was what she dreaded most. And sure enough, one sunny afternoon, she was looking out the window of their little Long Island home—their baby, Eddie, who would never meet his father, cooing in a basinet behind her—and saw two soldiers walking somberly and purposefully up the sidewalk. They knocked on the door and Mom could barely open it. She dropped to her knees, sick with the knowledge of what they were about to tell her. She knew that as soon as she let them in, her life would change forever.

"Mrs. Troy?" the taller one inquired. To her he didn't look much older than her Lefty. "We're here today to regretfully inform you . . ."

They handed her the official documents and left. She was the first person they told. Mom pulled it together enough to call her father, who then placed a call to Edwin's father. When he answered, Mom's father simply told him, "Well, you got your wish. Your boy is dead."

There was a service for Eddie at his parents' beloved Catholic church, and the priest would not acknowledge Mom or baby Eddie. The whole ceremony was about a great Catholic man who left behind his parents. There was no mention of Mom or their son, who were, of course, seated in a pew right in front of the guy.

My grandfather was there, too, and he grew angrier and angrier at the callousness of the priest. Eventually he squeezed Mom's arm and said, "Get up!" through gritted teeth. Mom was mortified. She was there to mourn, not to draw attention to herself. It took her a second to gather up the baby and shuffle sideways out of the pew after her father. The priest had just finished his remarks and the organist was beginning to play when her father addressed the priest and the whole church with his booming voice.

"This man had a wife and a son, thank you very much!"

After what Mom went through with Edwin, her take on organized religion was that it was nothing but a scam and a business. To her, the church didn't represent God, it represented money and the worst kind of clannishness, and that turned her off forever. But it didn't diminish her faith, which she passed along to me when I was young.

Dad, on the other hand, was pretty much a hard-core atheist from the word go because he didn't have a lot of things to convince him otherwise. He was born in Dayton, Kentucky, the youngest boy in a family of ten kids. His mother died giving birth to his younger sister, who was stillborn, when he was four years old. His father was a massive alcoholic who'd issue beatings for small infractions like milk spills and overlooked chores. At age six he had to walk along railroad tracks to find coal every day for heat and hot water. Dad's tough childhood came to an abrupt end when he joined the navy at age seventeen and became a gunner in World War II, stationed most of the time in the Philippines.

And so that upbringing made him cynical about everything, but especially about notions that a great reward awaits those who live a virtuous life. Throughout my life, whenever a discussion of God has come up, he's been extremely dismissive, but not without a twisted touch of humor.

I'd ask him, "Do you believe in the afterlife?"

"It must be pretty good," he'd say with a wink, "because no one ever comes back."

If I asked, "Do you think that we have souls, or a spirit that lives on after us?"

He'd say, "Sure! Sure we do. They look just like Casper the Friendly Ghost. Floating around above us." Then, without fail, he'd point up in the air and say something like, "And there's your uncle now. How ya doing?" And give a sarcastic little wave.

Anyway, after three and a half years in the war, seeing a lot of combat along the way, Dad wound up back in the United States. Many of his veteran buddies now worked in sanitation on Long Island, and they hooked him up with a job as a garbage man. He got married and had three kids with his first wife, but then they got divorced and he was trying to support them by moonlighting as a bartender. That's when Mom walked into the Rock Front Tavern and batted her eyes at him. Soon they were dating, and then Mom got pregnant with me. Only she didn't know it right away.

She had been having some bad bleeding, so she went to her doctor. Pregnancy was the furthest thing from her mind. The doctor gave her a quick exam and explained that she probably just had an early miscarriage, and she wrote it off as that. The bleeding stopped and she never gave it a second thought. A couple months later, she and my father went out dancing at an Elks club. She was back to partying like crazy as usual (with my developing brain along for the ride). Dad gave her a twirl on the dance floor and she felt a kick in her stomach. She stopped mid-spin.

"What's the big idea?" he said. "I thought I was doing pretty good out here."

"I can't tell you here," she said, somewhat horrified. "But, boy, do I have some news for you."

The next day she was back at the same doctor, and he confirmed that she was pregnant, which is when all the abortion talk—due to Mom's increasing age—began. Everyone she knew tried to talk her into it, even Dad's sisters.

But from the moment he knew, my dad never wavered. He wanted her to have the baby, even though I'm sure he knew what a rough ride he had in store for himself. He was in his forties and probably thought he was done raising kids. But Mom trusted his input and she prayed. And the message she got in return was clear. "Something told me over and over again not to abort this child," she told me. I was born on June 21, 1967, the first day of summer.

To this day, if anyone ever asks Mom about me, the first thing she says is, "All the doctors said that I should abort him." Thanks, Mom. She makes sure to add that they also warned her that her baby could have physical or mental defects. Of course, many people I know think that the doctors were right.

*　　*　　*

A lot of my early life was spent at the Rock Front with my dad behind the bar. It was just a local Long Island hangout, but to me it had a smoky *Goodfellas* mystique, with regulars who had names like Tricky Dick, Whistling Dick, Dan Dan the Oil Man, Shady Pete, Lucky Lucy, and Jimmy the Rat. Not *the* Jimmy the Rat, but close enough. While my dad slung them brandy old-fashioneds, vodka sours, and longneck Miller High Lifes, these guys taught me, at age four, to play pool and shuffleboard.

And I taught them about the New York Mets. My love for the team came from my dad—baseball is one of the first things he ever shared with me. At the bar, the Mets games on TV and my baseball card collection were my babysitters when Dad got busy. He challenged customers to quiz me and I was rarely stumped. I knew the stats for any guy on the Mets' twenty-five-man roster across a three- or four-year span. To me, it was unbelievable that these gods played their games just a few miles away and had a pitching staff with guys like Tom Seaver, Jerry Koosman, Jon Matlack, *and* Tug McGraw.

If I wasn't at the Rock Front I could likely be found at the house of my sitter, an Italian American woman named Mary. She and her husband were a little older than my folks, in their fifties, and for a long time they were really like another set of parents. While my parents worked, I'd spend every afternoon with Mary playing army men, coloring, and helping her with household chores, and all the while she'd never stop singing, "Fairy tales can come true/It can happen to you."

Mary and her husband, Jimmy, lived in a modest house, not far from where life for me started out—the Fenwood Apartments, a low-income housing development in Valley Stream—and as I spent more and more time at Mary's house, her singing decreased. Her relationship with her husband took on a new wrinkle—at least to me—and it confused me. Jimmy looked a lot like Uncle Junior from *The Sopranos*, bald on the top, with a little hair on the sides. At first, I thought he was great. I even called him "Grandpa" for a long time, but I eventually saw him transform into an animal. I'd be watching *Chico and the Man* on TV or playing Matchbox cars on Mary's kitchen floor, he'd come home, and it would get ugly. He'd start chasing her around trying to slap her.

"Get over here," he'd yell menacingly, rolling up his sleeves, spittle forming at the corners of his mouth.

"No," she'd cry. "Wait! Not in front of little Jimmy." She'd push him away and scoop me up and put me in a bedroom. Then she'd take her beating from him. The closed bedroom door didn't do much to muffle the sounds and it scared the hell out of me.

When he was finished, he'd scram, and Mary would do her best to pull herself together, even though she'd often have bruises all over her body. One day at school, my teacher, Mrs. Gerdick, pulled me aside.

"Is everything okay at home?" she asked. I have no idea how I was acting, but I must have looked shell-shocked.

"Yeah," I said a bit too unconvincingly. She called my mom in for a conference.

"Something's going on with Jimmy," Mrs. Gerdick said. "He's seeing something somewhere, and he's traumatized and sad from it."

I was too nervous to spill it there and then. I didn't want to make trouble, ruin Mary's life, or worse, get Grandpa Jimmy angry with me. But when we were driving home, I couldn't keep the situation from my mom any longer.

"He's beating her, Mom," I said. "Jimmy beats Mary up all the time."

My mom's eyes welled with tears. "How long has this been going on?"

"I don't know," I said. "But I don't know if I can stay there anymore."

"You don't have to, Jimmy," my mom said. She and my dad scrambled to find another sitter, and in the meantime, things were changing at Mary's really fast.

Eventually it came out that Grandpa Jimmy and a fat neighbor were having an affair. I found out because one morning, before my new sitter could start, I had one more stint at Mary's. My mom was driving me over to her house, and as we turned onto her block, we saw it was filled with cop cars. We parked, got out of the car, and saw that the door to the neighbor lady's house was open and had been hacked to pieces, like someone had taken an axe to it.

We made our way through the police, who were coming in and out of Mary's place, and went inside. I have no idea why the cops let us in, but we soon discovered Mary sitting at her kitchen table, with a black eye, shaking.

"What happened?" my mom said.

"I was going to kill her," Mary growled. That was the only time I'd ever seen her out of control. "I brought my hammer over there and she wouldn't come out. I'm going to kill her. I'm going to kill her."

That's all she kept saying. Grandpa Jimmy went away for a year or two after that, and Mary began singing again. A couple years later, she and Grandpa Jimmy briefly tried to reconcile, and he wanted to hang out and be my friend, like nothing bad had ever happened.

"Hey, Jimmy," he'd say. "Let's take a ride or something."

"I'm good," I'd respond, no matter what he was offering. "No, thanks."

Eventually they split up for good and Mary ended up taking care of me until I was twelve. She became the lunch lady at my grade school, and afterward she'd take care of me until my folks were done working. I still think of her every day.

When I first started seeing her husband beat up on her, I started having nightmares about dying. Not me dying, but everyone. It was typical kids' stuff: What happened when you died? Where did you go? One night my mom heard me bawling and came into my bedroom.

"What's the matter?" she asked.

"Where do you go when you die?" I sat up in my Batman pajamas. "Are you just frozen? Do you have to lay in the dirt forever?"

"You go to heaven," Mom said calmly, sitting down on my bed. "God watches after you. Is that what had you so upset?"

"I just wanted to know what happens," I said, sniffling.

"Well, that's what happens," Mom explained. "It's peaceful up there. You're with all the family members you love. And it's okay to pray while you're here," Mom added. "Especially when you're scared. But, really, you can talk to God anytime and he'll listen."

She showed me how to kneel down by my little bed and pray. And that's how my relationship with God began. Of course, we never went to church. No one ever cracked a Bible. I was never baptized, and I have no idea what all of the Ten Commandments are even to this day. But Mom just impressed upon me that God was watching over me, and she made sure I knew that God helped us all if we let him into our lives.

*   *   *

At this point I should explain something about little Jim Breuer: I was eighty-two pounds in kindergarten. And I looked high. This could have been a recipe for a disastrous childhood. I guess Mary really knew how to feed me. I had cheeseburgers and fries four days a week at her house. Then, when I got home, I'd wolf down a bowl of ice cream, eat dinner, and then have something else for dessert.

The only reason I knew I weighed exactly eighty-two pounds was because they made me weigh in at school. Right in the middle of class the nurses would come and take me out into the hallway, weigh me, and try like heck to introduce me to the food pyramid and give me some grasp on nutrition. The only fruit I was eating at that time was bananas, and that was always as part of a split. Thank God there were two other kids in my class who weighed in at about a hundred pounds each. If kids started teasing me, I could always turn to my two tubby comrades and say, "Well, they're fatter."

I loved Batman, and in kindergarten, that's what I really wanted to be for Halloween. It would be my first costume ever. So my mom went to the store to buy me the getup, which was a hot vinyl, one-piece thing with no separate pants. I was five years old at the time, but she bought me the age 6–8 size just to be safe. That was even too small, but I would not admit it. I put it on and went to school, but it was so tight I couldn't even step up onto the curb. I had to be super careful about how I walked lest I split the thing. My mom tried helping me, and after four steps, she stopped cold.

"You just can't go in like this," she said.

"I'm going!" I shouted. I'd been waiting for this costume and I was going to wear it. I was on the verge of a full-on tantrum. "I'm Batman!" I shouted. So she followed behind me, trying to stuff my fat back into the costume wherever it was popping out. The mask didn't fit, either—it was sticking straight out and dripping with sweat from my fat face. As I finally made it into the classroom, I had all of the kids' attention. Everyone was staring at me. Muffled sounds came from underneath my mask. "Em Bhhhtmnnnn! Bhhhtmnnn!" I yelled. And as soon as I sat down in my desk chair, that sucker ripped from my ankle to the top of my thigh. For a while after that, my classmates serenaded me with a modified version of the *Batman* theme song: "Na-na-na-na-na-na-na-na, Fatman!"

So yeah, not surprisingly, I was self-conscious about being fat. And I feared older kids. It's not fun being called fat or told you have big tits at any age, and I got called every name in the book right from the start. For a while, I lived my life waiting for confrontation from strangers or bigger kids. In fact, that's probably what made me start studying people and mimicking them, because once they detonated the "You're fat" bomb, I had to bring a takedown quickly. By the time I was a second-grader, no one could beat me at psychological warfare. I'd start with their haircut, the way they walked, the way they talked, how they would write, anything. I was just waiting.

My comebacks were two parts wit and one part meanness. So when someone said, "You're fat," I'd say, "You're retarded. I can lose weight. You can't lose your retardation. You know, it's funny, because the teachers were just having a conversation about how stupid you are. They were talking about holding you back, but they're so tired of taking time out of their day to catch you up to everyone else, they might just pass you to get rid of you."

And yet, at the same time, I had a lot of love around me. My friends never called me fat. Maybe it's because they feared I'd throw them on the floor and sit on them. As I got closer to junior high, it dawned on me that chicks were not going to dig an obese guy. Eventually I started working out hard and burned it all off.

So that's little Jim Breuer: big in spirit and big in body. But let me tell you about Jefferson Avenue. When I was about five, we moved out of the Fenwood Apartments into our own second-floor apartment in a house on Jefferson Avenue in Valley Stream. A year or two later, we moved a few doors down and had a house all to ourselves. This was a big deal, a step closer to real middle-class life. It was me, Mom, Dad, my half sister Patti, and my half brother Bobby. Patti and Bobby were both a good decade older than me and total products of the early 1970s—they smoked, drank, and partied relentlessly. And they both did this nomad thing, where they went across the country on spiritual journeys and returned home *changed*.

I looked up to them both, and I remember being really excited one spring day when I was seven, when Patti called. She announced she was about a day away from making it home to Valley Stream. My big sister was on her way. She'd made it as far west as Ohio, winding up at some crusty free-love commune, where when people weren't having sex, they were tripping their brains out on acid. Sure enough, a mufflerless VW van dropped Patti in front of the house early the next morning. Mom greeted her at the door before I could scramble outside to hug her. I couldn't see Patti, but all I heard was Mom shouting.

"Holy cow," Mom moaned. "What's that hunk of metal stuck in your nose?"

"It's a nose ring, Mom," Patti said. "Jewelry. Relax."

"Ugh, I'm gonna throw up," Mom said. "We can't let Jimmy see you this way."

But I saw it. She also had a Jimi Hendrix–style Afro to boot, which was pretty funny on a white chick who'd always had straight, shoulder-length hair.

But that wasn't all. Patti brought home guests. Little microscopic ones that lived in her underwear. Some escaped and set up shop in our house, which Mom now scrubbed hourly. In retrospect, Patti's nose ring was a day off compared to the crabs. Mom didn't bother explaining it all to me, she just pleaded with me not to sit on the toilet seat because of the crabs. I literally would look around the toilet for ocean life and think she was losing her mind. Crabs? It didn't make sense. All of this earned my sister the nickname "Hurricane Patti," which we still call her today.

Mom and Dad had been through it all before and were sort of making new rules as they went along. They didn't bother marrying each other until I was nine years old. And I only found that out because once Mom was watching TV and called out to my dad, "Hey, there's the guy that married us." And on the screen was a recently elected city councilman.

My friends on Jefferson Avenue were like a whole other family to me, as strong as any other bond I had. Playing together out in the street with them is really where I came of age. This was my core gang:

Phil—He looked like Ben Stein, the actor/political ideologue who famously played a teacher in *Ferris Bueller's Day Off*—but with a leather jacket. He didn't say much but when he did, he was often the voice of reason.

Billy—A tall, glasses-wearing, brainy, unathletic nerd. We loved him, even though he was terrible at stickball and every other game we played. The flights in and out of JFK fascinated him, and he could tell you everything about aviation that you never wanted to know. (Now he's an engineer at Northrop Grumman.)

Jeffrey—The consummate Italian-looking Long Island kid. His hair was always slicked back, and he loved wearing mesh shirts and a gold chain.

Chris—A blond, all-American, Wonder bread–type kid. Chicks dug him. He was unassuming and wouldn't hurt a fly.

Tommy—He was five or six years younger than us and would happily jump off his Big Wheel without a second thought to sock kids in the face if asked. He was a maniac, and we loved him.

Elmo—He had big ears, was really skinny, and was named Elmo. None of that made life easy for him.

We *lived* outdoors. We played stickball all the time. When it got colder, we played street hockey on rollerskates. We'd also play asses-up handball. As guys got eliminated, they had to stand against the wall and the remaining players got to whip the ball at their butts. We built go-carts, forts, and obstacle courses, or just ghost rode old bikes (you'd get going fast on the bike, leap off, hope to land on your feet, and watch it go sailing) for distance. If it snowed, we played tackle football immediately, like it was a law. And we always tried to make each other laugh. This was where I tried out Bugs Bunny impressions, animal impressions, Pesci, De Niro, Nicholson, anything to get people laughing.

Of the group, I was the oldest kid by two years and sometimes it was like *Lord of the Flies* on our block with me as the leader. I abused this role. There were kids a few years older than me milling around Jefferson Avenue, but they weren't part of our core gang.

If I said, "We're going to be Mets fans," we were Mets fans.

If I said, "We're only going to listen to Judas Priest," we only listened to Judas Priest.

But like all kids we got into arguments. Mostly our disagreements were easily solved or forgotten, mindless bickering about rules to games or whose turn it was. One time, though, Tommy's twin cousins wandered over from their house about a mile away and took things to a deeper place.

They were probably about nine years old. One twin had dark olive skin and was roly-poly with glasses and the beginnings of a starter mustache. The other was blond, white as a ghost, and frail. They both thought they were world-class athletes. In reality, they were both little punk know-it-alls who'd always challenge us to games and refuse to quit no matter how bad we were beating them.

Their family was pretty religious. Catholics. One day, maybe out of frustration from getting trounced in a stickball game, one of them started ragging on me, right in the middle of the street.

"So, Breuer," the light-skinned one said. "I heard you never go to church."

Before I could even answer, his darker-skinned brother chimed in. "Yeah, are you even baptized?"

My friends quietly circled, waiting to see how I'd respond. It was no secret that I never went to church. It wasn't anything I bragged about, but I wasn't ashamed, either. Up until now, no one had given it a second thought. Tommy must have told them about it and they thought they'd use it against me somehow.

"Yeah," I said. "Big deal. I never go. But I love God."

"It's impossible to love Him if you don't go to church," the light-skinned cousin insisted.

"Listen . . ." I started to explain before I was interrupted with another question.

"What's Corinthians 11:14?" the dark-skinned one asked, pushing up his glasses.

"Who gives a shit?" I said indignantly.

"It's a Bible passage, which you'd know if you weren't going to hell," the light-skinned one said.

"You're always cursing," the dark-skinned twin added. "That's the kind of stuff you have to say Hail Marys for."

"Why?" I asked. Was it really possible that these twins were more annoying arguing religion than they were losing at sports?

"You say them to get forgiveness," he said.

"No, you say them to get forgiveness," I said. "I just ask God for his forgiveness without doing some goofy drill. It's like doing push-ups or something."

They simply continued on, deaf to my reason.

"Oh, you're so backed up on Hail Marys, it will take you 'til you're sixteen to even get caught up on them. And that's if you stop swearing now forever."

"I don't need to say any Hail Marys," I said. "What you little re-tards don't know is that I talk right to God. I don't need church or commandments or any little made-up Bible stories. You should try just talking to him sometime. It's pretty freakin' simple."

"But only priests can do that," the light-skinned cousin said.

"Bullshit," I said. "You bananas are morons. Let me show you something."

And then I looked up at the sky and just started talking.

"Hey, God," I said. "Can you believe these goofballs? You love me, right? And I love you. And I don't walk around judging people for how they worship. Isn't that whole don't-cast-the-first-stone thing in the Bible? Can you believe people would waste energy arguing about you when they could just be talking to you?"

"That's not how you do it!" the light-skinned one yelled.

And then Phil raised a more important question. "So," he asked, clearly bored by it all, "we gonna play stickball or anything?"

*   *   *

Jefferson Avenue was lined with simple residential houses up and down the block, and at one end of our street was the border between Nassau County and Queens. We didn't have much, but there was a real disparity between what we had and what the people in Queens had. That was my first real exposure to race and to how the system plays out in America. Our side was all white. Their side was all black. On our side the road was nicely paved, and the Queens side was all potholes. We had a candy store, they had a liquor store. Racial tension was high, if somewhat incomprehensible to me at that age. I never felt like there was going to be a brawl, but a black guy crossing Ocean Avenue/Hook Creek Boulevard and walking down our block was a rare occurrence, and if one did walk down our street, it was like a wild bear was loose. When we saw a black guy on our street, we started shaking in our boots. "Oh my God, what are we going to do? He's rampaging. He can go in our house. He can do whatever he wants. We're helpless!" As you might imagine, we never went on their side of the street.

But it wasn't black people we were most terrified of. That honor belonged to the Rizzo brothers. (I'm not going to rattle their cage by giving up their real name here. You'll soon understand why.) There must have been a half dozen of them and they were always in and out of jail. The oldest was in his early to midtwenties at that time, and the youngest was probably all of nine years old, and the kid would burn up and down the streets on a loud moped, wearing jeans and no shirt with a lit Marlboro Red dangling from his mouth.

One summer night my dad took our little elderly miniature poodle, Duffy, out for a walk. I was probably twelve at the time, up in my room, goofing off. I heard Dad come back inside and didn't think much of it. He fell asleep in his chair in the living room. I could hear him snoring and the sounds of the TV, and a while later I heard a heavy beating on our door. I was sure the glass was going to break; there was anger and urgency in the knocking. It sounded like the police. I raced down the stairs and to the door. I looked out the window and nearly crapped my pants. It was the five oldest Rizzo brothers. Dad was just coming to, rubbing his eyes and sitting up in his chair.

"Get your father, we wanna talk to your father!" one of them said, dropping his cigarette and stamping out the butt on our porch. I started crying immediately. I thought I was going to see my dad get beat to death. They were there to hurt him.

I scrambled to lock the door while trying to yell to my mom to call the police, but no sound would come out of my mouth. I felt something behind me. My dad yanked me from behind and pulled me out of his way, then went right out the front door.

"You went after our little brother," one of them said. "And we're coming after you."

"Get in the house, Dad," I said, whimpering. "The cops are coming."

"Just go inside and shut the door," my dad said disgustedly. And he turned back to the Rizzos and asked calmly, "What do we got? One, two, three, four, five of you? Against one little old man? It's gonna take five of you to kick my ass?"

He paused and they didn't respond. They just stood there looking ready to smack him. They weren't going to leave our front steps until something happened. The whole block was dark and quiet. And I'll never forget the look on Dad's face. It went from incredulous to almost giddy.

"Well, guess what?" Dad said. "One of you is gonna go down with me tonight. You may beat the shit out of me. Stomp me to death. But I'll take at least one of you with me."

One by one, they sucked their teeth, sneered, and puffed out their chests.

"Do you guys get it?" my dad asked, smiling. "I don't care if I die tonight. All I know is if I do, I'm taking one of you with me. So, which one of you is it going to be?"

Then he looked them all in the eyes. "Is it gonna be you? Is it gonna be you? Is it gonna be you?" Right down the line. He had a look in his eye and a sound in his voice that I knew that none of them could identify with. He was coming from a completely different planet. I didn't realize it then, but I know now that it was the war coming out. When you'd spent years fighting in infernal jungles knowing you could die at any time, five punk kids in Long Island aren't really going to faze you.

Not one of the Rizzos initiated any physical contact. One by one they all backed down and just seemed content to talk it out.

"Weren't you walking your dog tonight?" one of them stammered.

"Sure," Dad said. "The dog's gotta crap like everyone else."

"Well," the oldest one said, continuing on. "Our little brother says you hit him with a chain."

"A chain?" Dad asked, then started laughing. He turned back to face me and gave me a little nod. I opened the door a sliver, then tossed him a tiny leash. "You mean this? I've got an eight-pound toothless poodle. I don't need a chain to walk him. Some cretin kicked at him tonight and I barely snapped this leash in his direction."

The Rizzos began placing the blame on their little brother, who had by now joined them.

"This is what you made us come down here for?" one of them said angrily to the youngest brother. Then they started apologizing to Dad and said they'd never bother him again. He had scared the crap out of them. He scared the crap out of me, too. I'd never seen a man just not care if he lived or died, and smile about it to boot. That was about as heated as the neighborhood ever got and about as nuts as my dad ever got. He was generally happy just to keep one eye on me and one eye on the newspaper as I played out in the street. Dad never hit me. He never yelled. He never said, "I love you." But that's who he is. The most important thing is that he was always there.

My mom was the one with the emotions. She yelled, screamed, cursed, cried, blamed, laughed. She was very protective of me. Little did Dad and Mom know what the next few years would bring.

Chapter 2

Getting the Bug

Impressions came naturally to me as a kid, and I would hone my craft at school, since there was an unlimited supply of people to mimic. I also got a lot of pleasure out of writing and creating things that would make my friends laugh. For some reason, every day in fifth grade, I'd draw a comic strip of my classmate Anthony Campo and bring it in for him to read. It was called *The Adventures of Campo and His Guido Mobile*. I turned him into a superhero with a magical muscle car that people kept messing with. It wasn't exactly flattering, but he really got off on it and kept bugging me to churn out more. For weeks, every day he'd walk in and say, "Hey, Breuer, where's *The Adventures of Campo and His Guido Mobile?*"

Anthony was bored at school and the comic strip was enough of a distraction to make the place interesting for him. This encouraged me. Throughout my childhood, humor and wit got me attention and set me apart from my peers. It was my social calling card, and I was good at it in ways that other kids are good at figure skating or math or whatever. And, like I said earlier, it helped prevent kids from making fun of me for being such a lardass.

Despite the thrill I got from making people laugh, I avoided any and all dramatic productions in school. My long-standing policy was that plays were for fairies. Maybe a tiny part of me feared getting up in front of a bunch of people and making myself vulnerable to their criticism. But I'd still claim it was fear of looking like a fairy. One spring our teacher Mr. Cooper sorted out roles for the end-of-the-year play, and I experienced an awakening. As he described the roles for the play, I could now see a purpose for being funny—somewhere I could use it for good.

"We have three parts left, kids," he said. He was known for the "Cooper Clutch." If you got out of line in his class, he'd look you right in the eyes, wiggle his index finger, and say, "Come with me." If you didn't move fast enough, he knew exactly where to grab the back of your hair so he could lift you up off your feet and march you out in the hallway and do God-knows-what to you. I hadn't gotten on his bad side. In class, I was pretty docile. School was a place for me to just hide. But as Mr. Cooper listed the parts, I saw potential in one that remained—a doctor who rushed onstage from the audience to help the narrator through a coughing fit. But that role was pretty much spoken for by Chris Pascocello. He had curly hair and big nerdy glasses. Put a lab coat on him, and it was instant M.D.

"The doctor will go to Chris if no one else wants it," he said. "Anyone?"

"I'll give it a try," I said. Twenty-five heads turned to me in the back row of the classroom.

"Jim Breuer?" Mr. Cooper said, not skeptically but out of sheer surprise. "Okay, give us what you've got," he added with an encouraging smile.

I bolted from my desk and jogged toward the head of the class, saying, "Vat seemz to be ze prrroblem hee-ar? Zere iz a dohktor in ze haus!" (For some reason I thought it would be funnier if I played the doctor like a crazy German scientist.) The whole classroom howled. Mr. Cooper did a double-take. As I tried it again and again, he'd watch me with strange admiration and then laugh heartily. I had no idea where I got the balls to do it, but it was a relief taking those first steps.

When the laughing died down, Mr. Cooper looked around the class and said, "Are we okay with Jim as the doctor?" I got a huge ovation. When it came time to perform the play, all the parents and the other kids from school gave me the same reaction. Then the narrator and I got even more laughs when we couldn't find the opening in the curtain to leave the stage. People assumed we did it on purpose. After that I had the bug and would occasionally volunteer for other school plays, even taking on the role of the sergeant in *South Pacific* in eighth grade.

If faced with a choice, though, I still enjoyed spontaneously doing impressions or characters I'd made up on my own. That stayed with me through my youth. After junior year in high school, I was riding my bike around the neighborhood one summer night when I came across a pretty girl I sort of knew, sobbing on her front porch. She was about my age, and I'd never seen anyone crying that hard unless they'd experienced some physical pain, like wiping out on their bike. And even then, those were younger kids, and their crying stopped as soon as their mom hugged them or gave them cookies and milk. This was a teenage girl whose sobs were filled with pure emotion, and it made me feel lousy to see her that way. I rode up onto the sidewalk and called out to her.

"What happened?" I asked.

"My boyfriend broke up with me," she said, looking down, shielding her olive-skinned face with her hand.

"Hmmm," I said, scrambling to offer advice. "You'll meet others." I've since learned that no one ever appreciates hearing that line.

"We dated for *five* years!" She looked at me like I was completely clueless.

I sat on the porch with her for a while and got nowhere. She continued to sob and wasn't receptive to any of my clumsily offered generic advice.

"If I can't help you," I said, standing up, "maybe I should just take off and give you some privacy?"

She nodded quickly, then kept sniffling. Going down her walkway, I got an idea. I pulled the back of my T-shirt over my head, like some kind of shawl, and then turned around to face her.

"Unless, you wanna tell Grandma what's wrong, baby," I said in a crackly, brittle old-lady voice. "You know Grandma's heart is with you, child."

At first, she looked at me like I was nuts, but as I kept it up, a smile spread slowly across her face. Not a huge one, but enough to get her to stop crying.

"Now, tell me, who is this boy?" I crackled on, hobbling toward her. "He don't know you like I do, girl. Let Grandma come and sit with you a spell. Oh, my hips is achin'. Do you know where I set my Metamucil, girl?"

She started laughing. Hard. "Stop," she said, laughing even harder. "Stop it."

"You can't get Grandma to stop her love, baby. I'm sorry," I said.

I continued on for ten more minutes, just acting like a kooky old grandma.

"You're from somewhere else. This was the worst day of my life and you've made me forget all about it." She looked at me like I'd performed a voodoo ritual. Then she gave me a hug. "You have no idea what you've just done. Wow!"

Satisfied that she'd stopped crying, I got up to leave. "Grandma's got to try to ride this rickety bike and go fetch some marmalade now."

I pedaled home, feeling like God had given me a gift. I had the power to make people laugh. I could use it to communicate and help. If this was my "mission" from Him, I accepted it, gladly. I never forgot that day and how the girl recognized something deeper in me.

All of my life humor had been a natural default operating mode for me. If there was trouble? Go to humor. Pain? Go to humor. Sorrow? Go to humor. Depression? Go to humor. Anger? Go to humor. To this day, it's how I get out of arguments with my wife, and if my kids are crying, a little slapstick and humor gets them right out of it.

Sometimes Grandma and other characters would just emerge out of boredom. And they wouldn't always be so benevolent. When I was in high school I worked in the paint department at the Valley Stream Sears, and I had plenty of time and unwitting participants on whom I could really craft my material. Some of my coworkers thought I was crazy, and others were drawn to it. There was an older coworker, kind of a bully, who'd wander over to my department and say gruffly and insistently, "Do Grandma."

This usually meant jumping on the internal house phone and prank calling another department. Coworkers nearby would stand next to me and listen while I phoned Sporting Goods or any department that was super busy. The rule at Sears was that you answered the phone politely no matter what was going on. So "Grandma" would call and fire off the most annoying questions ever: "I understand you're selling a new Wilson basketball? Well, how round is it? Have you had much trouble with them being defective? Could I get a rain check on one? I'm going to be taking the bus, do you have anyone who could come out and help me get off of it? Well, could you write my name on the box? And could you write my grandson's name on the ball? My script is a little shaky." And I'd just go on and on until the person on the other end of the phone quit or turned into a shivering pile.

When the Cabbage Patch Kids dolls got really popular, on the day of a new shipment, I'd go and hide them all on different shelves in other departments and watch the mayhem as the doors opened up and customers looked futilely for the dolls in the toy department, then stumbled on them placed next to microwaves or women's skirts.

Sometimes that older coworker would come by and tell me to do "the bully and the popcorn." So I'd play two characters—right out on the open floor of Sears—a bully selling imaginary popcorn, and a kid who didn't want to buy it. Then I'd proceed to beat myself up.

"Wanna buy some popcorn?" I'd say really fast with a moronic lisp.

"Nah, I don't care for any," I'd reply meekly.

"What did you say?" I'd ask, sounding tough, then smack myself. "Just buy the freakin' popcorn. Three boxes, five dollars."

"Ouch," I'd yell. "Lay offa me!"

Pretty soon a crowd would gather around, with guys from other departments cheering me on like it was a real boxing match. "Come on, hit him. Hit him again," they'd yell. I'd throw myself into the paint cans or trip over lawn mowers. Then I'd start cowering or protecting myself from myself, dodging my own punches, flailing again all over the place.

One prank phone call I made at Sears could have easily landed me in prison. It was a federal offense, apparently. A new guy had started in hardware. He was in his late thirties, so to me, a teenager, he was already suspect. He wasn't even in commissions hardware, where the guys salivate all over the power saws and riding lawn mowers, pulling down a percentage on each one they sell. This poor guy was just peddling wrenches for a measly hourly wage.

I was standing around the paint department (by the way, to this day, I know nothing about paint), and one of my coworkers, a kid a couple years older than me, came by complaining.

"Hey, this new guy in hardware is really serious," he said. "I was looking for a lightbulb for my dad's garage, and he booted me out of his section."

"Why?"

"I dunno," he said with a shrug. "He said I ought to stay in my department."

"Oh, *really?*" I said.

I picked up the house phone and called hardware.

"Sears Valley Stream hardware," the guy said. "This is Jack, how may I help you?" I could see him right down one of the main aisles, probably fifty feet away from where I was standing.

"Jack," I said in a horrendous Middle Eastern accent. "This is Muammar Gaddafi." This was at a time when some really heavy stuff was going on between the U.S. and Libya. Gaddafi's name was as reviled and feared here as Osama bin Laden's is today.

"Okay?" he said. He had no clue.

"I am Muammar Gaddafi!" I repeated loudly.

"How can I help you, uh, Mua . . . Muammar?" he said patiently, trying to get the pronunciation right. He had no clue.

By now, I had a few coworkers around me, listening to my end of the conversation, looking down the aisle, waiting to see what would happen.

"I have just sent six missiles to hit your Sears hardware department in Valley Stream." My accent was so purposely hacky that I didn't expect anyone to believe it.

"Excuse me?" he said.

"You heard me!" I yelled frantically. "You now have five minutes to get out!" I ended the call by shouting, "Long live the paint department!"

We watched as Jack hung up the phone calmly, without flinching, and simply walked away. He didn't seem to have a care in the world. In fact, it looked like he was going back to organizing the screwdrivers. None of us could believe it. There was not much else going on, so a couple of us went and sat down in the break room, scheming about how else we could get him.

After a few minutes, we lost interest and started talking about the Mets and girls. We forgot all about Jack and Muammar. When we left the break room, we saw that the girl from the candy department was gone. The toy department people were nowhere to be found. There were no customers left on the floor. As we were looking around, wondering what was going on, an older security guard came racing out of the stockroom.

"Breuer!" he yelled. "What the heck are you guys doing here?"

"It's called working," I said cockily. "You should give it a try sometime."

He ignored me and kept yelling. "You've got to get out of the store right now! The new guy from hardware just took a bomb threat."

"What?!" I asked. I got a sinking feeling in my stomach.

"They're about to evacuate the whole damn mall," he said. Sweat beaded on his forehead. Then for dramatic effect, he added, "We don't know what we're dealing with."

Not thinking of the consequences, I said, "Wait, wait, wait. There's no bomb threat." I just wanted him to calm down.

"There sure is, Jim," he said insistently.

"No," I said. "I called this guy and said I was Muammar Gaddafi, the leader of Libya. I said I sent *missiles*. But I never said there was a bomb."

"Oh my God," the security guard said, turning pale. "You made that call?"

"Yeah, but any moron would have known it wasn't a bomb threat."

He looked down at his watch and unholstered his walkie-talkie. "False alarm! False alarm!" he shouted into it. "Don't evacuate the mall!"

"Cops are already on the way!" someone chirped back through his speaker. This wasn't going to end well. Or maybe it was. Two of my dad's sons from his first marriage were cops in Valley Stream. The mall was Gary's beat, and sure enough, he was on duty that day. Gary marched into Sears and huddled soberly with the security guard before walking over to me, shaking his head.

"Jim," he said. "Stay off the phone." I was lucky to get off without getting arrested, but an internal report was filed. And this report worked its way through the corporate bureaucracy, all the way to the top. I was soon notified that I had to meet with the president of Sears's New York district at his office in Roosevelt Field, Long Island.

One week later, I showered, combed my hair, put on my only suit, and took the train to meet with the president. I sat down in front of his desk. He tried to appear stern, but I thought I could detect a smirk.

"Let's hear your side of things," he said, standing up and pacing his office floor. Looking back, I was very fortunate that there hadn't really been any major bombings or school shootings back then.

I started to explain. "Well, I was done with all my work. I shouldn't have made a prank phone call, but every once in a while I'll admit that I call up other departments as a character, just to be silly. The fellow I called was being a little territorial about his store section. A little excessive, I felt. And I promise you, sir, with God as my witness, I said I was Muammar Gaddafi. Do you think that Gaddafi would really single out the Valley Stream Sears, go to the trouble of getting their phone number, then specifically contact the hardware department, telling whomever answered the phone that he was targeting it with missiles?"

The president scratched his chin and paced some more. "Yeah, I get that, Jim," he said. "No one in their right mind would have bought this, but even still . . ."

In the end, I didn't get canned. I had to apologize in person to Jack, and about two weeks later, he quit, because pretty much everyone else who worked at Sears would walk by him shouting, "Muammar Gaddafi!"

41

Beyond those incidents, I have to say I was a pretty good kid. Maybe even naïve, based on my age and where I lived. When I turned thirteen and kids at junior high and high school started talking about house parties, I had no idea what they were talking about. It was difficult to imagine. I was shocked they were willingly inviting people in to trash their parents' houses. The stories came mostly from jocks who'd brag about it.

"Hey, Breuer," one of the kids I played baseball with said one day after practice. He was tall and skinny, a popular guy, kind of the ringleader of the bunch. A group of our teammates gathered around us. "When's it gonna be your turn?"

"To what?" I asked.

"To start throwing parties," he said.

"Like with beer and stuff?" I said. "Never. Fat chance of that."

"You chicken?" he said, playfully taunting me.

"No. But why would you have a twenty-person party at your parents' house?" I asked. "My God, if any of you numb-nuts knocked off even one wing off my mom's Hummel figurines, I'd kill you." I said that probably because I knew I'd never hear the end of it from my mom.

"Sure you would," he said, and the kids laughed.

"Whatever," I said. "You really have that little respect for your parents?"

"Well," he said, "maybe you're just not ready yet. Maybe it's because you hang out with a bunch of younger kids watching Mickey Mouse."

"You talkin' about the kids from my block?" I asked. "They're a lot cooler than hanging out with you guys, smoking pot and hanging out in your parents' basement. That's idiotic."

Despite what you may have heard or think about me, I was completely straightedge until my senior year of high school. I didn't drink or have a girlfriend until that year (though I had my first kiss a couple years earlier), and if that meant being a late bloomer, I was one, and happily so.

My mom and dad were pretty lax when it came to disciplining me, and I wasn't going to ruin that by acting like a knucklehead. By the time I came into their lives, I figure, they'd seen it all. As such, my dad probably only intervened with me two or three times in my whole life, and that was only if I was doing something really bothersome or terrible.

I remember when I got a bit older and got my license, Dad had to step in. Remember that this was an era when it wasn't completely uncommon to go out all night, have a bit too much to drink, and then drive home. It's reprehensible, but it was a different mind-set back then. One morning after a night of drinking, Dad woke me up at five thirty A.M. before he went to work.

"Hey," he said, leaning over my bed, shaking my shoulder. "Wake your ass up. What were you, all banged up last night? Did ya have a little too much to drink?"

"No!" I said, angry to be woken up.

"Yeah?" he said. "Horseshit! The front end of the car is in the bushes. Why don't you get up and move the car before your mother wakes up, dummy."

"I wasn't drunk, Dad."

"Okay. Sure thing, hotshot. Go move the car." He'd never give me a whole speech. He'd just say, "Don't bullshit a bullshitter." That was his favorite saying.

* * *

When I got to Valley Stream Central High School, I met a kid who blew my mind: Jimmy Sciacca. He was as much into music as I was into making people laugh. He was fearless about doing what he loved and

I guess it eventually rubbed off on me. Every year, the tenth, eleventh, and twelfth grades would spend a week battling each other in sports, music, and sketches. When we were seniors, the theme of Sketch Night was for some reason the Bible. Jimmy was one of the writers for the event, and he approached me in the hallway one morning.

"Jim, you gotta be in Sketch Night."

"I can't do that, man." I was back to being somewhat shy about showing off my gift onstage. It was easy for me to be funny when it was just me with a friend one-on-one, or with a group of people in an informal setting, but I'd gotten away from organized performing and hadn't done any theater for a while. I didn't fit in with the drama kids. "I'm not into that crowd," I explained.

"Jimbo," he said, "it's not like that. Get off the sidelines. There's no egos. You just gotta come down, hang, and see what it's all about."

Jimmy had taken Bill Cosby's bit on Noah's Ark and basically rewritten it. He showed me what he had done and said, "I think you'd be perfect for this."

The bit starts while Noah is in his woodworking shop. God's voice chimes in saying, "Hello, Noah?"

Noah says, "Who is this?"

"God."

"No, really . . . *who* is this?"

"God. Listen, I need you to build an ark."

"What's an ark?"

That bit is so genius. I reluctantly went with Jimmy to a rehearsal and met the drama kids, and they turned out to be cool. They were in agreement that I should do "Noah's Ark." Still, I didn't think I could make it funny.

"You like Eddie Murphy, right?" Jimmy asked me.

"He's the best." I had just seen him at the Westbury Music Fair and would copy his routine word for word while wearing a Walkman down in my parents' basement, pretending I was onstage. He was a tremendous influence on my comedy career.

"So do it in his voice," Jimmy said. "Imagine how he would do it." This was easy because I basically spent my life imitating his laugh, the way he walked, the way he talked, and all of his bits.

So that's how I practiced it, and that's how I did it in front of the whole school. When God asked me to build the ark so many cubits by so many cubits, I said, "Say what? I don't know no darn cubit!" Today it might seem racially insensitive, but as a kid growing up on Long Island in the early 1980s, it felt like the ultimate tribute. I even copied his laugh—the one where it sounds like rapid, deep little wheezes. The crowd went bonkers and I felt the same rush I did when I made the girl on the porch laugh, only this was ten times more.

The next day at school, girls looked at me differently, stopping to say, "You were sooo funny." Guys who'd thus far ignored me said, "You're a pisser, Breuer. We gotta hang out!" It was so popular that there was an encore performance of Sketch Night, and all the kids, knowing what was coming, started chanting, "Noah! Noah!" before I went onstage. And as I stood behind the curtain and peeked out into the crowd, I saw jocks, punks, nerds, and parents all harmoniously unified. It was a rush seeing them all brought together through humor. I told myself, "I have to be a comedian."

I was voted class clown my graduating year, and that summer when Jimmy's band played gigs at little clubs on Long Island, they asked me to warm up the crowd. I'd unleash my AC/DC and Ozzy impressions, and then I would say, "And now, for a band that needs no introduction . . . ," and just walk off the stage without actually introducing them. By the end of the summer, I did my first open mic night at Governor's Comedy Club. I had bits about city pigeons who are mad at humans, how people freak out about spiders, and about sneaking into the house drunk. The crowd was small, just my friends, my sister Dorene, and her friends. But still I was shocked when I was not approached by a Hollywood agent or manager after the gig. I was certain a five-picture movie deal couldn't be far away.

Mom and Dad's plans for my future included more than just jumping onstage at rock clubs on Long Island. To appease them, I enrolled at Nassau Community College in the fall of 1985.

"You should take some bookkeeping classes," my mom said. My older half brother Eddie was a successful executive in magazine publishing in Manhattan. Looking at what he'd done, they didn't see how being a comedian was a viable job. But I dreaded even contemplating a nine-to-five life. What I'd been exposed to my senior year had stoked a fire inside of me. No one was ever going to give me a standing ovation for my bookkeeping work or chant, "Accounting! Accounting!" to me in the parking lot as I showed up for a desk job.

As my first few classes dragged by, that thought kept racing through my mind. My accounting professor surveyed the classroom one morning and offered this frank advice: "If you think you're going to fail this class, or if you don't want to be here anymore, this is the very last day you can get a 'withdrawal.' After today, you'll get an F if you don't complete your work. So, if anyone here still wants a W, please get up and leave the class."

He hadn't even finished his sentence by the time I got up and started walking toward the door. The whole class started cracking up, but I didn't care. In my heart, I had made the right decision. I went right over to the drama building and changed my major to acting. When I got home, I told my parents what I'd done.

"It's the end of the discussion," I said. "If you want me to pursue a higher education, then I'm gonna do it through acting."

My mom was concerned, but my dad was supportive. "Do it while you're young," he said, shrugging. "Get it out of your system."

The kids hanging around the theater department weren't much different from the Sketch Night kids at high school, except many of them just seemed content to be able to say, "We're in theater." I was there to become a star. I was going to get discovered, because Eddie Murphy, Billy Crystal, and Robert Klein all went to this college. In the future, they'd be saying Jim Breuer went there.

I had a Judas Priest denim jacket, I wore a lightning bolt earring, and I could act. I carried myself in a manner that said, "I'll be seeing you at the Oscars, or actually I won't, 'cause you guys will be watching me at home."

I got one of the leads in the play *Wait Until Dark*. My character was a thug who got stabbed to death while greedily rummaging through a blind woman's apartment trying to locate some stashed heroin. You might have seen the movie version, which starred Audrey Hepburn. I was psyched, because I got to roll down a flight of stairs. The next semester's play was *When You Comin' Back, Red Ryder?* The lead had to be really solid, as there was a scene in a diner that went on uninterrupted for like an hour where the character takes the place over, mentally breaking down every person there. He gets a chick to suck face with him, then makes a musician sit and write a song on the spot and perform it.

The auditions were happening during the production of *Wait Until Dark*, and I remember my major rival, a guy named Bobby Mayor, feeling me out, seeing if I was up for the challenge.

"It's a lot of work," he said. "We're so busy with this play. It's going to be really tough."

I think he was hoping I'd say, "Yeah, you're right. I'm going to sit this one out." But I wanted it. I even threw a chair in the audition. I was a violent animal in that room. And I won the lead role. It was my favorite play I did at school. In the middle of it, one of the characters, a woman, revolts against my mind games and slaps me in the face. I knew I had nailed the role because when we performed it the audience always exploded during that scene.

After I got the lead in *The Glass Menagerie*, one of the professors said I should focus on building sets because more students needed to get a shot at performing—they were becoming disillusioned. I was angry. I had no idea you could be too successful. Looking back on it, I wish someone would have just pointed me to auditions outside of the school and inspired me to keep pursuing acting in some other way. Instead, I was blackballed.

Chapter 3

Florida Bound . . . and Gagged

After I'd done about a year and a half at Nassau Community College, I got some unwelcome news. My parents decided they were ready to leave New York. They wanted to move to Florida. Our neighborhood was changing, they wanted to retire, and moving down there was the thing to do then.

When my mom told me they were going to look at homes in Florida, I thought she was kidding.

"She's serious," my dad said insistently. This was during the phase where my dad was doing whatever my mom asked him to. (Actually that phase has lasted about forty years.) But I fought them tooth and nail on it for a few days. I didn't want to go. I was a kid from Long Island. What was I gonna do in Florida?

They went down there and started looking at houses. On the second day of their trip, I was sitting around our house moping, and the phone rang. I picked it up. My mom was freaking out.

"Oh. My. God!" she shrieked. I thought maybe my dad had gone missing or they'd been robbed or something.

"What's going on?" I asked. I was panicking. I heard a shuffling of the receiver, then my dad's voice.

"We were looking at houses," he said, then he paused, like there was something he didn't quite know how to tell me.

"And?" I asked. "What happened? What happened?"

"There was an alligator in the backyard," Dad said, sounding perturbed. "This place is not for me."

When they hung up, I was like, "Nice!" I assumed they were packing their bags and coming back home, and that would be the end of the Florida business. When they came home a couple days later, Mom was all smiles. I assumed she was happy about coming to her friggin' senses.

"We bought a house!" she squealed in a singsong voice. "We're moving to Florida!" She was wearing a two-piece velour sweat suit, typical Mom-wear. And as she broke the news, she did a *Price Is Right*–contestant dance, like when they get called down for the Showcase Showdown. She was over the moon. I guess she figured she'd play the odds when it came to alligator attacks.

I couldn't believe it. I didn't know much about how banks worked, but I was skeptical that all the paperwork could be done in such a short time. And I was pissed that they'd made such a rash decision.

"What do you mean you bought a house?" I yelled. "What are you talking about?"

"You're gonna love it," my mom said. "It's right by the Gulf."

"I'm not going," I said. "I'm not a retiree."

"If you stay here," my mom asked, "where are you gonna live?"

I had no idea. I wanted independence, but I wasn't *that* independent yet. I was a student who worked at Sears part-time in the paint department. There was no way I could swing paying rent on my own while remaining in school. I was mad and I was determined not to go.

But by the middle of 1987, I found myself moving to Palm Harbor, Florida. It was just north of Tampa/St. Petersburg. So long, community college. So long, acting in plays. So long, comedy.

I didn't have much to pack except the giant chip on my shoulder. I wasn't going to give Florida a chance. Not for one second. We were moving to a little cul-de-sac. A new development on an extremely quiet, dead, boring street. It was nothing remotely like Valley Stream. There were maybe about twenty houses, tops, and some of them weren't even finished yet, including ours.

So for the first couple weeks, I had to live with my mom and dad at a Days Inn in Clearwater, Florida. I wasn't just depressed about the move. I was livid. Each night, it was either watch cable with my parents (and not have possession of the remote control), hang out by the empty swimming pool, or go out.

Well, one night, I chose going out. I went to a place called Swampwater Al's. I just sat there drinking vodka-and-cranberries trying to forget about how lame everything was. Looking back, I know that was probably the luckiest night of my life, because I *drove* back to the hotel after that. I don't remember an inch of that drive. I only remember ordering my first couple of drinks and then, a few hours later, waking up projectile vomiting from my bed, straight over onto my parents' bed in our room at the Days Inn.

My dad woke up, obviously, and emitted his own stream—of curse words. He and my mom were covered in puke. Not a chunk or two here and there. Not splattered. They were now wearing puke pajamas. You could have gone swimming in their bed. It was like *The Exorcist*. The smell was unreal. I swear the puke left my body like I was a fire hose. And there weren't enough towels to clean it up.

My dad hopped out of bed, and raced over to take me to the bathroom, like that was going to do any good. He picked me up by the back of my shirt and my hair and started to carry me as fast as he could. And as he did so, I doused him again, and everything else in the room, too. I was hitting the wall from about three feet away, so hard it was splattering back at us. Maybe 5 percent of my puke ended up in the toilet. It was the first time I got sick from drinking, and I've never been that sick again, drunk or sober. And I couldn't claim to my parents that it was the flu or food poisoning or anything. They knew that I was *wasted*. They knew I was unhappy. I couldn't believe the turn our lives—*my life*—had taken.

I passed out for the rest of the night in the bathroom. And I'd wake up only to throw up again. I remember my parents scrubbing themselves off in the bathroom, then trying to sleep on the floor, while reminding me, "You're gonna clean this up!"

"In the morning, Mom," I slurred. Like that was going to happen. And their nagging just made me mad all over again. "I don't wanna live down here . . . ," I yelled from the toilet.

And then we finally got to move into our house, and it had a swimming pool. I liked that. But still I wasn't going to give this place much of a chance. It was a foreign territory, and I had no direction. Was I going to get a job? Doing what? Over and over again, I constantly asked myself, "What am I doing here?" And I had no clue.

The only thing that made any of it bearable was the girl who lived next door, Kristen. At seventeen, she was a couple years younger than me, and we hit it off immediately. We'd sit together on her front stoop every night talking our heads off while we shared a cigarette. She was from Boston originally. She had moved down to Clearwater a year or two before we did, so she was pretty immersed socially but remained a little skeptical of Florida at the same time. She was the kind of ally I really needed, and trusted.

Only it took a while for me to realize that because my initial stint in Florida lasted just a few months. It wasn't long before I told my parents, "I'm outta here." For better or worse (and in my mind it was better), I was going to go back to Long Island and make it on my own.

I let Kristen know, and she wasn't cool with that. She had scored tickets to see Pink Floyd in concert in a few weeks and wanted me to stay at least until after the show, but I wasn't hearing that. We were becoming confidants, but that wasn't going to derail my big plans: I was going to stay at my friend's house on Long Island and work at TGI Friday's. That would show everyone.

My friend Rooster was my age, and he lived on Long Island with his mom and brother. The plan had been for me to live with them for a month, but I ended up staying for five or six. Rent-free. They were a generous, great family. Okay, Rooster's mom was a little rambunctious sometimes, but only with her kids, not me. She was a crazy Italian woman who never *discussed* things with her kids, because chasing them with a broom was much easier (not that she ever intended to really hit them). One night she chased Rooster into his room full-blast, only she had the handle raised. When it smacked the door frame, the broom went flying and she wiped out hard. Yes, it was great to be back in nice, normal Long Island.

Oh, and there's this, too: I would sleep on their living room floor, right next to the bathroom, where there was a massive cockroach infestation. When I'd go in there in the middle of the night and turn on the lights, tons of them would scurry out of the sink, running for cover. My mom would call and ask how it was going, and I'd say, "Awesome!" But really I was too grossed out to even take a shower there. I remember waking up one night and feeling something around my chest and also on my nose and mouth. I slapped at my face and saw two of them drop off and crawl across the rug. That's when I knew I had to get out of there. And as generous as Rooster's family was, I could feel that they were getting tired of having a dude crashing in their living room.

But I just couldn't make enough money to get my own place. I loved bussing tables at TGI Friday's, but when it came time to wait on people I was a disaster. The thing that really sucked about the place is that the waitstaff had to bring (and be *fluent* in) fifty-three different-shaped glasses to the bartender depending on what drinks patrons ordered. Because you really couldn't appreciate the fine palate of a Purple Rain cocktail if it came in a glass designed for a Seabreeze. Do you think I was any good at keeping the glasses straight?

I was great with a table full of kids. I would draw on their place mats and make them laugh, but if I got a table full of businessmen and they were all ordering crazy drinks? Forget it. They would never get their food orders because I was too busy trying to find out what I needed to give the bartender just to get a vodka 7UP back from him. It got to the point where I'd grovel, but the results were always the same:

"I don't get you your drinks until you get me my glasses, got it?"

Pretty soon, I was just giving my tables to other waiters and waitresses. I got great pleasure whining and complaining back and forth with this kid who worked there as a dishwasher. Once as I was icing my fingers after having slammed them in a door, he came up to me with a puzzled look and said, "Dude, what are we doing here?"

"I don't know," I said. "My parents moved to Florida, man. I'm just trying to get by."

"Yeah, but why are we working?" he asked. He was getting philosophical about bussing tables and washing dishes at TGI Friday's. "Why can't we just hang out? Life should be about hanging out, not working. We should be like the Indians, man."

"I agree!" I said, even though it was my understanding that Indians had it pretty tough. Those awesome leather pants they wore didn't make themselves. But the hanging out part of his speech resonated. My dishwasher friend had a point. My TGI Friday's career was far from fulfilling.

While he was saying all of this, we were watching an ice cream truck pulling up into the parking lot. The driver hopped out and started unloading all of these giant barrels of ice cream.

"Bro," my buddy said, eyeing them up, "I'm quitting right now."

"Yeah," I replied, "me, too." What did I have to lose, after all? "Should we tell them we're quitting or just leave?"

"No way," he said, "Let's just leave, bro."

So we quit right on the spot. And as we were sneaking away, we started looking closer at that ice cream truck. Real close. The delivery guy had gone inside the restaurant leaving a truckful of delicious ice cream unattended. We both had the same idea at the same time.

"Open your trunk," my friend said.

We quickly snagged three or four giant barrels of ice cream, and floored it over to my sister's place in Valley Stream; we were laughing our asses off the whole way. It felt like payback, I guess, to the whole Friday's infrastructure that was unfairly keeping us down. We got to her place and hauled the ice cream into her house, extremely psyched about our caper, before realizing that the barrels would not fit in any normal-sized freezer.

"Dude," I said, "what the hell are we gonna do with this ice cream?"

So we went out on the street and started giving it to all the kids in the neighborhood. We were like the Robin Hoods of pilfered chain-restaurant ice cream. Later we bought a bunch of Tupperware containers and scooped the ice cream into them to better store what was left of it. Genius idea. I'd just quit my job, I was getting kicked out of my cockroach-infested crash pad, I had very little money, and what I did have I spent on Tupperware for stolen ice cream.

Yep, clearly living in Florida was all that was keeping me from realizing my full potential. So I moved into my sister's place for a while in Valley Stream and soon enough I was ready to go back to Florida and give living with my parents a second chance. My attitude had changed. I wasn't going to be mean-spirited anymore. I would find a job. I would not puke on any relatives. And I would count my blessings, like having a swimming pool and a face free from crawling cockroaches.

Based on the extensive industry knowledge I accrued working at

TGI Friday's, I enrolled in hotel and restaurant management classes at Tampa College. It made my mom happy because my parents always were so pragmatic about my having a fallback career. At that point, having only the Long Island Governor's gigs and opening for my friends' bands under my belt, no one in my family trusted that comedy was going to do it for me.

I took a real estate class, but I cheated on the exam. My sister Patti took it with me, and the whole time, I was like, "Pssssst! What did you get for number fourteen?" She wouldn't tell me and, needless to say, I didn't get very far in that field. None of it was me.

I was dying to go into stand-up comedy. I was dying to go into acting. And I did end up taking one acting class, but it was terrible. It was leagues beneath the stuff we worked on in community college on Long Island. So I dropped out of college and I went back to waiting on tables (this time at a place with simpler glasses). I was biding my time, trying to figure it all out, but life, strangely, wasn't sucking as bad as it did in Long Island. A lot of that was because of Kristen. I was talking to her every day, but there was no romantic motivation behind it. We both just really needed to have a friend—someone else who was trying to figure everything out, too.

And besides, I was a twenty-year-old, and I thought I was a *cool* twenty who should be dating a twenty-one-year-old woman. So even though Kristen was cute—petite, with great, blond, totally eighties big hair and blue eyes—and liked the same music and TV shows as me, I wasn't looking for romance. She got the signal that I didn't see a romantic future for us, so she went out of her way to try to hook me up with different girlfriends of hers, as well as introducing me to everyone else I knew at the time. She was by far the best friend I'd had in years.

Of course, the pull of show business still lingered. One day I saw an ad in the newspaper for the Paramount Talent Agency. It said, "Models and Actors Needed." Paramount sounded familiar to me. It sounded like a name I could trust. People who knew what was going on. The agency was located in a strip mall, but it was a *nice* strip mall. When I walked in, I saw eight-by-tens of Sylvester Stallone, Eddie Murphy, and famous models. This, I thought, was show business. I had finally landed where I needed to be.

My thought was that they must be related somehow to Paramount Pictures. There was no Internet then, so it wasn't super easy for a twenty-year-old, fame-hungry guy to figure it all out. And besides, their office had posters for Paramount movies all over the walls. It seemed too good to be true. Who would have thought they'd have an outpost in my town, Clearwater, Florida!

"You definitely have the look," one of the "execs" there told me. First words out of his mouth. "Hang on a sec!" Then he summoned someone from the back room. "Ted, you gotta see this kid." Then he looked at me seriously and said, "You want to act, but have you ever thought of modeling? Why not do both?"

"W-well," I stammered.

"Well, you should," he said. "Truth is, you could model, but you're also going to be in movies really quick. I suppose you've got a head shot, right?"

"No."

"Oh, you need one. We can do that for you. And you should sign up for some of our classes, too. Things are going to start moving really fast for you."

Before I knew it, I walked out of there $1,500 poorer. I was getting pictures taken of me in a business suit, a tennis outfit, a dentist's uniform—because you never know what kind of roles might be out there. It showed my versatility. They sent me on auditions where the only people trying to get cast were other people who had signed up for the program.

Of course, I shared it all with Kristen. I'd bring all of the portraits of myself in different settings over to show her and she was my sharpest critic.

"Are you sure this isn't like some porn ring?" she would say teasingly. "Who else do you think is looking at you in those little white shorts?"

"It's all legit," I'd say. That would only make her laugh harder.

"I thought you wanted to do comedy, anyway."

"Well," I'd explain, "if I can make millions of dollars modeling should I turn it down?"

"I don't think there's any danger of that."

She didn't want to see me get taken advantage of, and I think she thought ridiculing me was the quickest way to get me to wake up or change course.

Throughout it all, Kristen never alluded to the fact that she wanted more than friendship, but her mom and stepdad would sometimes hint at it. We went out for New Year's Eve once, and her parents sat us down and talked to me about what we were going to do and how we were going to behave. I bought her a sweatshirt once at Busch Gardens because she was cold, and every once in a while her mom would pull me aside and tell me how much Kristen adored it. Their behavior seemed odd to me, and it never added up that Kristen might be into me. In fact, one night, after I'd just moved back and it was clear that I was going to be around for the foreseeable future, Kristen told me that I *had* to meet her friend.

"You're going to love Kelly," she said. "She's so *you*. She's a goofball. She's laid-back. She's funny. She's into the same music that you are. You have to meet her." She was really pushing her on me. I knew that she was trying to help me socially, but this was intense.

So I took Kristen's advice and went out with Kelly. And she was great, but she, too, was pretty much just a friend. I didn't have a whole lot of interest in pursuing anything with her. But the fact that Kelly and I hung out changed something in Kristen. For one thing, Kristen started dressing a lot hotter.

And Kristen *already* looked hot. Amazing. She had a knockout body. And she grew less and less excited to hear about my hanging out with Kelly. I thought that was weird because she was the one who pushed for it. Slowly, I came to learn that there was a bet between the two girls: Which one would get Jim to kiss her first? Typical high school stuff. And what was at stake, besides my dignity? One dollar.

I'd continued to see Kelly, partly because I was mad at Kristen for orchestrating the bet. And that made Kristen mad. Apparently she was annoyed she hadn't won the bet. The whole situation confused me. "Does she *like me* like me?" I wondered. We'd spent New Year's Eve together, gone to Busch Gardens, hung out nightly, and I never had a clue. It hadn't come up in all the nights we'd spent talking, and now we *weren't*.

We froze each other out for weeks. I stopped doing stuff with Kelly. It was just too weird, and I didn't want to be in the middle anymore. Their senior prom was coming up, and though we'd all decided long ago to go as a group of friends, that was probably not happening now, and I didn't care to find out. Still, as the days went by, I knew I was being foolish. Kristen had been my lifeline since I'd moved to Florida. It dawned on me that I should be the bigger person and not let a little drama ruin what we'd built. Something nagged me to go to her house and talk.

One night, Kristen's front door was open, and as I pulled up to my parents' house, I could see her sitting in the living room, watching TV. I got the guts together to approach her. We met in her breezeway and sat down and talked for hours.

I told her that if she was really into me, she should have let me know from the get-go. She shouldn't have felt like she had to hide anything. We reached an understanding and put the bet behind us. It was a great talk. She also told me she'd bumped into an old friend from Boston who was in town and wanted to take her to the prom.

She wanted to know if I'd take Kelly and we could still all go as a group. I figured, why not? This night felt like a resolution to me, and that was important.

As we worked things out, I felt the need to kiss Kristen so bad. I had an overwhelming feeling. Not a romantic one. Not a sexual one. It was more like this overwhelming godly soul kiss. It was unexplainable. It felt right just to kiss her on the forehead and that's what I did.

Everything was peaceful. It was one of those rare, perfectly satisfying moments, utterly calm and serene. I felt clarity, which obviously, at that time, was in pretty short supply for me.

Kristen died in a car accident the next day. She was a passenger in a car driven by one of her friends, and about a mile from where we lived, it collided with a truck.

I remember driving up to my house that day and seeing a ton of people fanned out across her lawn. Too many people at such a strange time to signify anything other than the fact that something really heavy and really bad had just gone down. My sister was outside. She grabbed me and ushered me into my parents' house and told me what happened, because she didn't want any freaked-out kids to just bum-rush me and tell me. The only friends I'd made there were through Kristen. She was the glue for all of us.

I was in a fog for a couple days until the wake. It was the first time a death had ever hit me that close. Her dad lived in Boston and he showed up at her house beforehand. He made a point of walking over to talk to me.

"I just want to thank you for being a great friend to Kristen," he said.

"You *know* me?" I asked, dumbfounded.

"She talked about you all the time," he said.

To me, Kristen's wake was so morbid. It was my first real funeral. Pictures of her were everywhere. Chairs were set up around her casket.

Everyone was looking at her. Nobody spoke. You walked in, kneeled before the coffin, then sat down. I needed to get out of there. I went out to the parking lot with some of the friends she'd introduced me to. A couple of girls, and a guy named Ed. I liked them all.

"Kristen wouldn't want this," I said, exasperated. "This is depressing."

So I just started riffing on each person who was there. I was imitating Kristen's voice. It was coming from her. I was acting as if she was in heaven, looking down at us, and what she would be saying. It was pure comedy. People gathered around and soon they were laughing.

"Is this right?" Ed asked. "Should we be laughing right now?"

I didn't know. Periodically, I would stop and people would encourage me to keep going. It was like a strange, out-of-body experience. Like I was watching myself do this while channeling Kristen's sense of humor and voice. When I was done, there was a circle of about thirty people surrounding me, and I said, "That's what Kristen would want right now. Not for us to sit around mourning. Let's celebrate her."

At her burial, I hung around until everyone left, and then I talked to her grave. "I'm sorry for not being with you that day," I said. "That was stupid." She had a class photography project that she wanted me to help with, and I blew it off. I was purposely late. She had waited around her house for me to show, then got fed up and left with a friend, and I never saw her again.

"Listen," I said to her grave. "I've got to get back into doing stand-up comedy again. I saw firsthand the healing power of comedy and it was huge."

(Now, you might be saying, "Breuer, this is getting deep and heavy," and to that I'd reply, "I'm only just getting started.")

Back at Kristen's house, family and friends had gathered, and again, the scene was too much for me. I stepped outside, right in front of her house. The sky was clear and blue, but directly above Kristen's house was a perfect circular rainbow around the sun. I know there's a term for this phenomenon, *sun dogs*, but it was like a movie scene. Why did it happen at this exact time?

I wanted to make sure I wasn't seeing things, so I asked her friends and family to come outside and take a look. Some guests, along with Kristen's mother, began weeping. Later, Kristen's mom came to me and handed me a stack of all of her handwritten poems. Only then did I realize the depths of what she felt for me. We had shared something amazing that had been built on friendship and communication, not just stereotypical, fickle teen dating. We'd made a bond that wasn't based on anything superficial, just mutual honesty and openness. I don't think I even knew that was what having a girlfriend was all about yet. I'd totally felt a similar bond at times with my family, and some of the people on my block back in Valley Stream, but here was a girl who, very quickly, I completely connected with, who never judged me. In the end, that helped me focus on what I wanted and who I was trying to become.

* * *

And here's another strange thing: I got asked to go to a surprise birthday party in Sarasota, Florida, last year. I was at home in New Jersey, making dinner with Dee when I found out about it. I turned to her and said, "I don't know why, but I feel like there's another reason that's bringing me to Florida."

"What reason?" she asked, pulling apart some broccoli spears. "I don't know," I said with a shrug. "I know the party will be a lot of fun, but something else is calling me there."

"Whatever," Dee said, smirking. She'd been down this path before with me. More than once.

A day later it hit me. It had been in my subconscious for a while. I came back to Dee said, "I need to talk to Kristen's brother. I need to reconnect with Sean and talk with him about his sister. But I have no idea how I am going to find him. And I don't know why this Florida thing is on my mind. Last I heard he was living back in Boston."

I didn't give it much more thought. I flew down to Florida. Went to the party. Had a great time. Then this Sean thing began to weigh on my mind. The next day I drove back to the Tampa airport early. I was sitting in the parking lot lamenting on how I wished I had seen Sean while I was here or at least find out for sure where he was living. My time here was almost over and I didn't do it. Then I asked God. I said, "If there's a way you can bring Sean into my life right now, just do it, God. Every time I think of something like this, it happens. So I know you can do it, God."

I turned in my rental car and went in to board my flight. At the Tampa airport, the security station and X-ray machine are right in front of the tram that takes you to other terminals. I showed my ID to the security person and started walking through security toward the tram, and I heard my name.

"Jim?"

I turned around and saw a heavyset guy whom I didn't recognize. "How are you doing?" I said, thinking it was a fan. "Nice to meet you."

And the guy looked at me and said, "Jim. It's me, Sean."

"Sean?" I asked.

"Yeah," he said with a laugh. "Kristen's brother."

I thought I was going to pass out.

"Oh, my God," I said, smiling. "What are you doing here?"

"Flying in from Boston to visit my parents," he said, nodding out toward the runways. "I just landed."

I had to laugh as I explained to him what was going on. "Dude, if you knew the events in my head going on up until this moment you'd lose your mind! I've been thinking a lot about you. I really felt, for some reason, I'd run into you down here."

Chapter 4

A Lesson from Steve Harvey . . . and a Few Others, Too

After Kristen passed, I put my mind and energy on comedy full force. I was watching TV at my parents' one night and Eddie Murphy was on *The Arsenio Hall Show*. As he sat with Arsenio, he was talking about what it took to make it. At a certain point, the words coming out of Eddie's mouth seemed to be meant for me. "Commit 100 percent to your dream, Breuer. What the hell are you doing taking hotel management classes?" That was more than enough for me. I got into the game, and made enough of a splash on the local scene that I was spending a lot of nights as the house emcee at Ron Bennington's Comedy Scene in Clearwater.

Sunday night was open mic night at the Comedy Scene, and Steve Harvey was doing the last of six shows following that. Florida, by the way, would prove to be a great training ground: In my time down there, I'd open for comics like Carrot Top, Larry the Cable Guy, Paula Poundstone, and Richard Jeni. Anyway, Steve had been the headliner since Tuesday. I was emceeing, after having opened for him a couple of nights beforehand.

I stuck around to catch his final set, and after Steve was done performing, he walked by, flashed me a smile, then paused and said stoically, "Hey, I wanna talk to you." Any time a veteran comedian cared to take a minute or two to dispense some wisdom, I was all ears. But looking at him, I could see a deep intention. Like he *had* to share something with me. I was thinking, "Oh jeez, why me? Is this another one of those heavy things? Or is he about to tell me that I totally suck at comedy, and he doesn't want to see me continue sucking in such a horrific way?"

We sat down across from one another in a booth up in the back of the club. He was wearing a beige suit, and as he hunched forward, he loosened his black patterned tie and dabbed at some residual sweat on his forehead with a napkin. He looked around at the nearly empty room and remained very serious. "Forget all those motherf-ers up there tonight, you've got something, kid," he whispered. "Being around here this week, observing you, watching your act, I can see it. I know you have it in your heart." He beat on his chest lightly with his fist. "You're in it for the long haul. I can feel your passion when you're onstage."

I was speechless. It turned out I didn't need to say much, anyway. Steve had it covered.

"Okay, okay," he said, conceding that I was not perfect. "One thing you need to work on is your pacing, you hit the stage like a roller coaster at its peak." He brought his hand up in the air, then slammed it down onto the table very fast. "Then *whoosh*, you go screaming down that track."

I nodded. I knew what he meant. I was young and full of energy, and I confidently performed with a golden cross dangling from my left ear while wearing a silk shirt, Capezio (the ultimate *Miami Vice*–meets–Bon Jovi brand) dress pants, and, you got it, Capezio shoes. I was a man on fire when I was onstage, and I wanted to slay the audience.

"You wanna bring them up here," he continued. "Get them really peaking, then you can fly down that track together. And then you slowly bring them back up again. You can't be at the peak the whole damn set! You'll burn people out.

"Keep working on your material, Jim," he said. "You've got a gift, and that means you've got as good a shot as anyone. A better shot than most. But you've got to want it."

"I do," I said.

Steve held up his closed fist. "This is where you are right now." He opened it, wiggled his fingers, pointed them in all directions, and said, "And this is where you wanna get to," before closing them again back into a fist.

One by one, he opened each finger back up. "Family," he said, sticking out his thumb. "This represents your family. Never forget your blood."

Then he opened his index finger and said, "Dedication. Dedicate yourself to your craft. Respect it. Every club you go to, you may see someone with a little more talent, someone in a better spot, whatever. Look close enough—you'll see their passion and how hard they've worked to get to where they need to be. Do the same."

Then he opened his middle finger. "This is faith. Never turn your back on your faith. God will get you through the toughest spots."

His ring finger was next. "Morals. Just because you're away from home, don't go boozing and losing your mind."

He finally got to his pinkie finger and said, "Sacrifice. It takes sacrifice to get to the top. Your time. Your life. Your family. You've got to be ready to leave stuff behind."

The whole time he spoke I couldn't figure out why Steve was singling me out. Did he see something deeper in me than just the comedian? Why me? Why not the guy in the middle of the lineup?

Or one of the open mic guys? At that time in my life, I was a deep believer in God sending messages, and I felt like this encounter with Steve Harvey was one of those messages. I'd never seen a comedian get this deep or even address anything like faith. For years, I would tell people about his speech, and what I thought it meant, and where I thought it came from (angels). Some would say, "I totally believe that," and others would say, "You're an idiot."

"You're going to think this is nuts," he said. "And maybe you can't envision it now, but there are going to be times when you're on the road by yourself in some dive-ass motel and you will not be able to do *anything* but sob like a baby, wondering what in the hell you've done with your life. Those are moments where you've got to remember this conversation and persevere. You don't gotta remember *me*. You've just gotta remember the spirit of this conversation and get through it. If you really want to get out there and change lives with your comedy, you've got to accept that you will encounter these hurdles."

What he said was a tremendous help when those feelings and emotions eventually did come my way, because, let me tell you, they did, and there's nothing more depressing and soul crushing than sitting in a Super 8 motel out in the Midwest somewhere not being sure if a gig is even gonna happen. You're fourteen or fifteen hours from home. Everyone else you know is working or in college. And you're eating three meals a day at a Waffle House because you can't afford Cracker Barrel, or you're sitting by yourself in your motel room eating microwaved frozen White Castles, wondering, "Am I gonna make it? What, exactly, am I *doing* with my life?" And then you start thinking about your family. Missing them. Bit by bit, two-week chunks of your family life go missing and then you get home and your parents have gotten a little bit older and slower, and it breeds a sense of dread inside of you.

"As for me," Steve said, "my pop lives in Cleveland, which is where I'm headed this week. He's getting older and it's my mission to make it before he passes on. I'm going to show him it was all worth it. That's why I'm out here, working my ass off."

Gradually the conversation got lighter, but what he said stuck with me my whole career. All I wanted to do for about a decade and a half was meet up with him again so I could tell him what a tremendous influence he was.

When I got on TV later on, I kept figuring we'd run into each other. We both worked in Harlem at the same time—me at the *Uptown Comedy Club* show and he hosting *Showtime at the Apollo*. But it never happened. When I got on *SNL*, I assumed he'd host at some point and we'd talk. That, too, never came to be. But I was always hoping he was somewhere watching me.

Three or four years ago, I took my sister Dorene to Los Angeles for the first time. The minute we landed, I insisted that we drive over to Burbank, to a great little hole-in-the-wall restaurant near NBC Studios called Ribs USA. Driving there from the airport, I told Dorene the whole Steve Harvey story for probably the forty-fifth time.

We parked and walked inside Ribs USA. It was nearly empty. I ordered my ribs and iced tea and insisted Dorene do the same. As we ate, who walks in with an entourage and sits down two tables away from us but Steve Harvey? He and his whole crew were wearing these amazingly tailored pinstripe suits and fedoras.

"Dorene," I said, dropping my rib bone onto my plate. "Guess who just walked in?"

"Mel Gibson," she said, her eyes dancing at the thought of it.

"Steve Harvey," I whispered.

"Come on," she said with a frown. "Are you messing with me? For real?" She turned around and had a look. "That's not him, Jimbo," she said, shaking her head.

"It sure is," I said. "And now's my chance." I got up and walked over to where he'd sat down. There wasn't room for me to squeeze into his booth—that might have been presumptuous anyway—so I crouched down next to it. The guys in his entourage shot me some funny looks, wondering what I was up to. Steve set his menu down and looked over at me. I smiled.

"Mr. Harvey," I began. "I know you're probably not going to remember this, but I met you a long time ago in Clearwater, Florida, at the Comedy Scene."

"Oh, yeah?" he said, raising an eyebrow.

"Yeah," I said. "Maybe 1989 or '90."

"Okay . . ."

And I told him who I was and repeated what he'd told me that night. I did the fist, opening and closing it. I told him that what he'd said had touched my life. He had no idea who I was, but I could see that he was really putting his brain to work trying to remember me.

"You talked a lot about your father that night," I said. "I was curious, did he ever get to see your success before he passed away?"

"Yeah!" he said. That hit him like a revelation. "He did. You know, I do remember the club you're talking about. And I don't remember the exact moment, but I feel you. Do you still do comedy?"

"Yeah," I said. "I've been on TV. I did a movie. I tour."

"That's great," he said. Again, the wheels in his head started turning. "You know, I've got a little project I'm working on—"

"Oh, no, no, no." I cut him off. I didn't need him to throw me a bone, and I didn't want him to think that was what this was about. "Listen, I'm not here to get work. I'm just here to say thank you."

Then one of his friends took off his hat and started laughing. "Oh, I know you. You got a special on Comedy Central!" He looked at the rest of his group. "Yo, he funny. The white boy really funny." Steve still couldn't place me, even as the rest of his buddies caught on. "You were in *Half Baked* with Chappelle," another one added, and started reciting lines from the movie.

It didn't matter that Steve didn't know who I was. Point is, I got to tell him what I'd been waiting to tell him for fifteen years. I shook Steve's hand and thanked him again.

*　　*　　*

When Steve talked about sobbing on the road, at the time, I really had no point of reference. My first road trip was a flight to Cincinnati, to open up for a *Star Search* winner, Mike Saccone, for a couple of nights. One of the bookers at the Comedy Scene set it up for me to season me. It didn't do much seasoning. A limo picked me up at the airport, I got put up at a nice condo, and I wound up sucking face with a chick at the bar after my first set. I felt like I'd won the lottery.

As I made out with the girl, Mike walked up. "Hear that?" he asked, smiling and pointing at the PA. "Rock'N Me" by the Steve Miller Band was pumping out of the speakers. Miller sang the lyrics, "I went from Phoenix, Arizona, all the way to Tacoma, Philadelphia, Atlanta, L.A.," and then Mike said, "That's your song, kid. Welcome to the road."

But as I went out on the road more and more, I often thought about what Steve (Harvey, not Miller) said and relied on his wisdom when things weren't pretty. I drove around in my van, the first vehicle I'd ever purchased (which I'd rigged with speakers from my home stereo), until it died, and then a Buick Skylark my mom sold me, and then a 1989 Ford Probe that got excellent gas mileage and had a CD player. Queensrÿche, Metallica, the Cult, and Judas Priest were my copilots. If I didn't want to spend money on a hotel, having those CDs along would buy me four to six hours of alert driving easily. If I was down in Miami, *Operation: Mindcrime* would get me up to Orlando, then Metallica's . . . *And Justice for All* would take me from there to Clearwater. That was how fellow comedian Lou Angelwolf and I would measure distance.

"How long's the trip?"

"Two Metallicas, a Queensrÿche, and maybe a live Eagles."

That was the fun part. Sometimes I'd go out on the road by myself and wind up in hotel rooms where other comedians were tripping on acid, taking ecstasy, smoking crack, or bringing in hookers. There were times when I'd check into another motel even though I had no money, just because I was scared to go back to the club-provided condo. Eighty percent of them were total flophouses, and I lived in constant fear of bedbug and rodent infestations. I relied on Steve Harvey's lessons to get through it.

Lou Angelwolf was a tremendous help and mentor. I was a young guy full of energy, and he was a crusty, long-haired, rock 'n' roller comedian who ruled the roost at the Comedy Scene. He was forever an optimist and always had something nice to say. He'd always throw work my way.

One Friday I got a call from him. "Hey, Breuski. Wanna come do this gig with me in Daytona?" I had the night off from my day job waiting tables at the Innisbrook golf resort, so I agreed.

We each drove across Florida, and when we arrived, we saw that the club was not really a club, but a nasty biker bar without much of a stage. None of its patrons gave a shit about a comedy night. You know a gig is never going to be good when the bartender has to stand on the bar and bang on a glass for five minutes to get everyone's attention.

"So who wants to see some comedy?" he yelled. There was no human response, just the sounds emanating from the pinball machine and video games.

"Can y'all stop playing pool and pinball?" the bartender said patiently. "I'll give you your quarters back. We're gonna turn the TVs off, too. We just need an hour of your time. And when the laughs are all done, you can do your thing."

No threats were issued, but I was pretty sure the bikers were going to murder the bartender. Thank God I was opening, so all I had to do was twenty minutes. It was painful. No one paid any attention. When I finished, I walked past Lou and was like, "Good luck!"

The only thing I remember after that is crashing at some flophouse in Daytona, waking up the next morning, grabbing some coffee, and feeling pretty good about getting home. I walked into Lou's room to see if he was ready to go. His mattress was on the floor and he was still fully clothed from the night before, half under the covers, sparking up a fat bowl of weed. "Breuski, you want some?" he rasped, precious smoke escaping from his mouth.

"Lou," I said. "God no. It's ten in the morning. How do you even enjoy that?"

He started laughing, not out of joy but just at what he perceived as my naïveté. "You're young, man!"

"What does that have to do with anything?" I asked.

He exhaled and said plainly, "Life sucks, Jimbo. You'll embrace this one day."

"Come on, Lou. Look at what we're doing, man!" I said. I'd never seen him so negative. To me this was way out of character. "Okay," I continued. "So we're not in the best place in the world, but at the same time, last night you earned in forty-five minutes what some people get paid over two or three days."

He packed another bowl and shrugged. He took a hit and then said, "I'm a little disappointed in God. In fact, I'm bummed about what God has to offer me."

"Don't say that, Lou," I said, chiding him. "Don't bring Him into this."

"God sucks," Lou said.

"What?" he continued, surprised that young Breuski had an opinion about God.

"You're just cranky, Lou. Today's a new day."

"You just don't get it, do ya?"

"Quit feeling sorry for yourself."

"You'll see," he said, starting to hack again. "By the time you're my age, you're gonna realize God's got nothing to offer. And life's got nothing to offer."

"Lou," I said, trying to be patient, "there's a lot to look forward to. Don't blame it on God. You gotta stop talking this way."

"*Ohh*-kay, buddy," Lou said, starting to laugh harder. "I guess that's where we disagree."

"Good-bye, Lou." I'd had enough. I was going to drive back home.

"Safe travels, kid," he said. "Be sure to pray for me!"

Lou had his own car, and more gigs, so he'd get back to Clearwater on his own. I couldn't figure out why he was so bitter. It was a side he'd kept hidden. A couple of months went by, and I was emceeing at the Comedy Scene. I had not seen Lou since Daytona, so I asked a comedian named Kevin, who was standing around with a couple of other comedians and waitresses, how everyone was doing.

"You didn't hear what happened?" Kevin said with a look of disbelief. Everyone's jaw dropped.

"No," I said. "What are you talking about? Why are you guys acting so weird?"

"Oh God, bro," Kevin groaned. "Lou got in a terrible car accident. He was supposed to be dead. He's born again now."

"You guys are *sick*!" I even threw in a courtesy laugh for their trouble, even though I thought the joke was in extremely poor taste.

"It's real," Kevin said. "A Mack truck hit his car head-on, and they had to pry him out with the jaws of life. The man now has bolts in his hips. No shit."

"For real?"

"Yep," Kevin said. "He says that when he was on his deathbed, Jesus came to him and asked if he wanted another shot at life. Now it's all he talks about."

"Well, we ought to have something to talk about on the drive to Naples," I said. Lou and I were on a bill in Naples that weekend.

"Don't get in the car with him!" Kevin warned. "I'm begging you. He's nonstop with Jesus."

"Don't worry about it," I said. "He's not gonna infiltrate me. I just hope Jesus doesn't mind Metallica, 'cause that's what's getting us to Naples."

The whole drive to Naples I jammed metal and teased Lou, who was trying to point out the music's shortcomings. "Lou," I said, cranking some AC/DC, "I don't have evil thoughts when I listen to this music, but is it truly evil?"

"Absolutely," he replied. "Absolutely. It is definitely evil. You know what, tomorrow you ought to go to a service with me."

"Church in Naples?" I asked. "No thanks, Lou."

"It's going to be way different than you ever experienced." He prodded me for forty-five minutes until I cried uncle.

"Okay, Lou," I said, conceding. "Why not?"

The next morning we walked into a place that looked like an overgrown lawn mower shed.

"How did you even know about this place?" I asked.

There were no stained glass windows. There was no image of Jesus. The "church" was filled with a wide array of worshippers, some in jeans, some all dressed up. The congregation looked like a gathering of ordinary people sharing something in common. The service was actually right in tune with what I'd believed my whole life. You didn't have to be ordained or a priest, or wear a fancy outfit, to share your message. You just had to speak from your heart.

* * *

It seemed like all of my Florida road gigs brought me closer to something—friends, faith, an unforgettable lesson. One late Thursday morning in the spring, I was waiting tables at Innisbrook, and I got a phone call. It was Brett, one of the head guys at the Comedy Scene.

"Dude," he said sternly. "Get out of work. There's a huge opportunity in Jacksonville at a new club called the Punch Line tonight. You gotta be there by seven thirty."

"You're crazy!" Jacksonville was a five-hour hoof. It was almost noon.

"Hear me out," he said. "They have a bunch of clubs. If you nail it, it's four weeks of work. I sold you hard to them; time to pretend you're sick and get someone to cover your shift."

"Well . . ."

"Are you in, Jimmy?"

"Yeah!" I said. "Thanks for thinking of me." Innisbrook was packed. I tried to bribe the bartender to cover my shift for the next two hours.

"Nah," he said. He wouldn't take it. "Just go knock 'em dead."

I hit the road with twenty dollars in my pocket (good thing he didn't take my bribe), which was about all the money I had to my name. There were no ATMs in those days, so I was hoping to earn enough money to be able to eat and drink, or that twenty was going to get stretched a long ways. The whole drive I was envisioning the four weeks of stage time. I was going to crush the room. Five hours later I arrived at the club, only to learn they hadn't sold *any* tickets, so there was no show. The owner did give me keys to a condo, though, and told all of the comedians we'd try again the next night. Well, their big Friday-night early show had eight people. The late show had twelve. The other comedians were nervous about getting paid, but the headliner said he'd asked the owner for a small advance and gotten one. I boldly went and asked the guy for a twenty.

He laughed in my face. "Bro, I just don't have it," he said. "Look around. If we draw a crowd tomorrow night, I can pay you twenty-five dollars. Until then, I have nothing. Sorry."

This little venture was turning into a real kick in the nads. At least they were feeding me wings, otherwise I'd have starved. By Saturday night I was down to eleven bucks.

The other comics weren't as broke as I was and decided to go dancing at the hotel across the street from the Punch Line.

"I have no money," I explained, pouting. "I can't join you."

The headliner, a thirtyish guy, said, "I'll spot you ten bucks. There's a band over there. Maybe you'll meet a chick."

I hated loud clubs, and that's what this was. Every silly jacked-up Jacksonville nut was in this Holiday Inn. I wanted out immediately, but the comedian who'd driven us from the condo to the club that night was intent on staying. But before we could even go inside, a bouncer relieved us of ten dollars each for the cover charge. Now I had no money for a drink. The headliner was intent on making sure I didn't sneak away. "C'mon, I'll buy the first round." We walked into a smoke-filled, loud cesspool of bad mall suits and cocktail dresses.

I finished my drink and figured it was my destiny to have to walk all the way back to wherever the condo was. My plan was to first stop back at the Punch Line and see if I could hitch a ride from a cook or waitress, if anyone was still there. I headed toward the door, but as I was about to exit, the singer in the band started wailing. His voice stopped me dead in my tracks. It was amazing. Faced with a long walk home or listening to this guy belt out precision Journey lyrics, I decided to turn around and hang out for a few songs.

The guy was wearing jeans three sizes too small, his hair was total metal curly frizz, and his shirt was popped open wide enough to let his carpet of chest hair breathe. Amused, I took a step farther and stopped dead once again. It was Jimmy Sciacca! My high school buddy.

Like in *The Matrix*, everything froze, and I pushed my way to the front of the stage and started yelling, "Jimmy! Jimmy!"

In the middle of their song, he finally recognized that it was me yelling his name, and without a second thought, he said, into the mic, "Holy shit! Are you kiddin' me?"

After a sucky weekend, this was a small miracle. It turned out Sciacca lived in Orlando, not far from me, and we kept in touch. Since then he's toured with me, been a part of my radio show, and performed on his own all over the place. I stand by my word when I say he has one of the most amazing voices God ever gave anyone.

* * *

Toward the end of my stay in Florida, I had a moment when the temptations of being on the road took me off my path. Temptations come for all of us, but especially those who have even the tiniest bit of fame and some free time. And when you hit those little roadblocks, you can lose your message and your way. By the end of this trip I had to look in the mirror and ask myself what I was doing it for.

I was on a bill with Gallagher's brother, Gallagher II (who looks exactly like his brother, squishes stuff, too, and, well, that's a long story), and afterward a bunch of folks (but not Gallagher II) went out for some drinks. Many drinks. By the time we wound up in what I thought was a dive bar, I was severely polluted. Now, I'm generally a happy drunk who can find the good in everyone. I didn't and don't usually drink a lot, but that night, for some reason I was raring to go.

So we were sitting in this dive bar, and all of a sudden this woman just hopped up on the bar and started taking her clothes off in time to the music. I could not believe my eyes. I became really concerned for her safety and told her to get down from the bar immediately.

Her response was to take her pants off. In my state, I thought she was on a bad acid trip or something. I started unbuttoning my shirt, then I tried to throw it to her, saying, "No! No! No! Put this on!"

Everyone in the club, except for me and the bouncers, started laughing. Could no one recognize what was going on? And the more I reached out to cover her with my shirt and then my jacket, well, the more upset the bouncers got. Finally they lifted me up and man-handled me out the door.

Drunk and angry, I fumed in front of the club. My friends came outside and pointed out that we had actually been inside a strip club. That was how out of it I was. Humiliated, angry, and yes, still intoxicated, they helped me get back to my hotel room, where I rode out the bed spins and passed out, only to be woken up by my own intense projectile vomiting a few hours later. I opened my eyes to see a geyser splattering the floors. When I stopped puking a half hour later, I was oddly lucid for a drunk guy. Then came the self-loathing. I looked around the room and thought of how careless I was. Had anything Steve Harvey said sunk in? I wept most of the next day, and when I wasn't weeping, I was praying. I didn't want to be another guy chewed up by the road.

It was now time to go to New York. I had to get out of Florida, pursue my dream, grow up, and be a man.

Chapter 5

Engaged

By January of 1992, I'd been back in New York for a while with one thing on my mind: my career. I didn't want to see any chicks, date any chicks, nothing. Five months later, I was engaged to be married.

The whole reason I went up to New York was that a year earlier, a fancy Big Apple manager—who shall henceforth be known as the Rat—saw that I was a rising star in the stand-up world and told me that if I came to New York City, he'd manage me and get me on TV. I'd just landed a couple of guest-starring spots on the Nickelodeon teen sitcom *Welcome Freshmen*, which filmed in Orlando, but I wanted more. The Rat, I was sure, could pave the way.

So for a solid year in Florida I saved every penny. I worked three shifts at restaurants, from five A.M. until one A.M. And when I wasn't doing that, I was getting $200 and $300 to do comedy road gigs on weekends or picking up dough emceeing at the Comedy Scene in Clearwater. I was building up my material and my cash reserves.

Before I moved, I periodically checked in with the Rat from Florida to make sure we were still on. When I'd met with him previously, in New York, he would spin his Rolodex, showing off all the famous names. I was going to be one of those names.

Every journey begins somewhere, and mine started in my old friend Phil's parents' basement on Long Island.

As I got out of the taxi and schlepped my suitcase to their door, Phil's mom was waiting to give me a hug. She squeezed me, and without so much as a hello, she said, "Do you know who the hell this Dee woman is? You're not even living here yet and she's leaving messages for you, Jimmy. Doesn't that strike you as a little forward?"

I had no idea which Dee she could be talking about. I was friends with a Dee in Florida. I'd met her through that girl Kelly, with whom Kristen had tried to set me up—Dee was Kelly's best friend, and from time to time I used to stop by Dee's house to make her and her parents laugh. I had fun with them. But why would Dee be calling me now? And here? It didn't make sense. "This Dee gal is a pain in my ass," Phil's mom continued ranting.

I apologized to her for all the phone calls, then went inside and called my mom to let her know I'd arrived safely.

"Did you call Eddie yet?" she asked. Mom knew Eddie was the considerate, thoughtful older brother who would help me out if I needed it, and I was sure that knowing we'd been in touch would give Mom no end of comfort.

"Ma," I said. "I just got here, I will get to it.

I blew off both Dee and Eddie for a couple weeks. I was in New York to become a big star, with leather pants and a pet kangaroo. I wasn't there to fill up my social calendar.

But when I landed a gig in Manhattan at the renowned comedy club Dangerfield's, I figured it was time to meet with Eddie. I'd told Eddie that I was going on at eleven P.M. and that he should meet me at the club beforehand, and I'd impress him even more by telling him about the TV developments my manager was working on. I got dressed in a shiny silver satin shirt and my fancy skinny black jeans, and I was rocking my Daryl Hall–esque mullet. I blew it dry, so it was extra fierce and spiky, then took the LIRR into the city, hopped in a cab to the Upper East Side, got to the club, tipped the driver, and went inside.

Near the entryway, there was an official-looking little old man wearing a navy blazer seated at a wooden podium. I walked up to him and proudly announced, "Jim Breuer for the eleven P.M. spot."

He dragged his index finger down the clipboard, then reached up and adjusted a little banker's light above the clipboard, looked down the clipboard again, and said, "Nope. Don't see ya."

"Hey," I said, my heart starting to pound faster. "I'm pretty sure that it's confirmed that I'm on at eleven tonight."

He pulled out a pair of glasses and went down the clipboard again. He kept flipping pages, putting them back in order, dragging his finger down each page, then flipping them back again. He finally he took a deep breath and let out a sigh.

"Says here you go on at twelve fifteen."

"Twelve fifteen?" The place was going to be dead by then. And I wasn't sure if Eddie would want to hang out that late, then drive all the way back to his house in Old Saybrook, Connecticut, in the middle of the night.

"Any chance I could go on earlier?"

"No," the little old man huffed.

I thanked him and started walking dejectedly into the club when he called out for me again.

"There's a gentleman waiting at the bar for you."

It was Eddie. I sat down next to him. We reconnected and checked out *a lot* of comedians. Eddie laughed hard at their stuff, but by the time I went on, there were only four people left in the room to whom I wasn't related. I am sorry to say that I did not crush at

Dangerfield's. The lack of laughs coming out of Eddie's mouth confirmed as much. After the set, I walked Eddie to his car. As he got in, he said, "Jim, I gotta level with you. Have you ever given anything like the National Guard a thought?"

For months afterward, whenever I'd see him, Eddie would laughingly recite jokes by the other comedians from that night at Dangerfield's and then remind me about signing up for the National Guard. He was certain that it was a worthwhile safety net for me. To add insult to injury, two days later, my manager called me into the city and dumped me. He said he was just too busy, and wasn't ready to manage me yet.

"I can still book shows for you, though," he said. "And by summertime, who knows what could happen? I might be able to take you on full-time."

I felt like I was totally screwed. My ego was kicked more than anything else. To me, this validated the opinion of family members like Eddie. Devastated, I took the train back to Phil's place on Long Island.

I woke up the next morning with Phil nudging me, phone in hand. "It's your mom," he said. "Wake up."

I grabbed the phone. I could tell by the way my mom sang, "Good morning," she was anxious and excited to learn how my meeting went with my manager.

"Hi, Mom," I said groggily.

"So how was last night?" she sang again. "How did it go with your *new manager*?" She didn't wait for an answer before continuing. And then she started getting choked up. "You said you were going to do it, and you are! I can feel it."

I had a choice. I could tell my parents I was going back to the drawing board—which would mean Dad would have to go to his friends at the Elks Club and tell them that his son wasn't going to be a TV star anytime soon—or I could lie to her and spare her feelings.

"Mom," I said, "it's going amazing. My manager is really psyched. He's putting a plan together." I thought this would buy me more time, but all it did was set off an avalanche of congratulatory follow-up phone calls from my sisters, brothers, and friends, and they all wanted specifics.

Telling more lies and not returning phone calls sank me lower and lower. Phil knew something was up, though, and eventually I confessed to him what had happened. After I came clean with him, he reminded me of all the offers for gigs I'd gotten from the tapes I'd made and sent out on my own. He was right. I'd gotten knocked down, but it was up to me to come back with a vengeance and control my own destiny.

I started booking my own clubs and soon had no problem getting gigs. I began to think that maybe a manager was a distraction more than anything else. I worked out in Phil's basement, did my shows, and now that my journey was taking a more circuitous path, I figured I finally had time to call Dee back. I told her I'd entered the Make Me Laugh Contest at a bar out in Bohemia, Long Island, and asked if she'd come along. To me, it was a win-win. I'd collect some cash at the contest and hopefully get her to stop calling so much.

She agreed and we decided to meet at a gas station, then ride to the contest together. (Classy, right?) Well, I got to the gas station, parked, and got a bag of corn nuts. And I waited. And waited. Here she was calling me all the time and now that I finally wanted to get together, Dee was MIA. When I'm meeting up with someone before a gig, I can't stand it when they're late. I have to work, and if you mess with my schedule it's disrespectful. You might as well pee on my doorstep. So I waited a couple more minutes before saying, "Screw it." I made it a hundred feet out of the parking lot before my driver's-side window malfunctioned and slid down into the door. When I stopped and tried to fix it, I realized that I was almost out of gas, so I went back to the gas station. As I filled my tank, this goofball in coveralls came out of the garage and started doing a dance across the parking lot.

"Jimmy Breuer!" He was shouting and smiling. "Jiiimmy Breuer!" As he got closer, I realized it was Charlie, a skinny, high-energy dude I'd met in the theater department at Nassau Community College. Back in school, our thing was impressions from the old *Batman* TV show, so right in the gas station lot he started yelling, "Do King Tut! Do King Tut!"—a villain from the show—then he pretended he was the Riddler.

"Come on in the garage and hang for a while," he said excitedly.

"Hey, thanks," I shouted. "But I'm running late, Riddler. I gotta gig to go to."

"That's cool, dude," he said. "Why don't you just come inside quick so I can write down your phone number?"

I realized there was no point trying to be on time, so I followed him into his office, then he sat down at his desk and wrote down my number.

And then he looked over my shoulder and asked, "Can I help you?"

I turned and just like in the movies everything went into slow motion, and there she was. This wasn't the Dee I remembered, the frazzled teenage girl in Florida who would ask me to buy her beer when she cut school. She had a presence. I lost my breath for a second as her eyes twinkled and smiled. It hit me like nothing before in my life. Still in slow motion, I heard a voice inside of me say, "This is my wife." Not girlfriend. Not someone to date for a while. My wife.

The ride to the club was really awkward. Dee had been calling for a reason, and the attraction was obviously mutual. I remember telling her, "Wow, you really grew up, Dee," in my astonishment and also in an attempt to strike up a conversation. That night I won the contest. Ripped the place to pieces. On the way home, it was just as awkward in the car. But *good* awkward. We reflected on old friends like Kristen and the whole evening that had just played out. She was blown away by my confidence in the room that night and that made me feel good, because back in Florida she'd always seemed confused by my pursuing comedy as a career choice.

Anyone reading this can say, "Wow, what a coincidence that you'd meet up with Dee in Long Island!" I don't see it that way. She calls my home out of the blue the day I leave to move to New York. My mom tells her where I am headed. Dee moves from Florida to live near friends in New Jersey. She meets a guy who lives on Long Island, starts dating him, then goes to live on his boat. That falls apart and somehow she calls me and wants to meet. I don't give it much thought one way or the other, but we set something up. And she's late. So I leave the gas station, but my car window breaks, so I have to go back there. And at that moment, my old friend Charlie shows up and delays me just long enough so that I actually meet Dee. Sorry, bro. To me this is way, way more than a coincidence.

When I got back to Phil's basement that night, I sat down on his couch and he said, "How'd it go tonight?"

"Great," I said. "I won."

Phil looked at me with a half scowl. "Are you kidding me? Who is she?"

"What are you talking about?" I said, laughing.

"You've got this look like cupid nailed you right in the ass, dude."

"Oh, you mean Dee?" I asked, trying my best to downplay my giddiness. "She's just a friend."

"You came up here to do stand-up and get on TV," Phil reminded me indignantly. "You're here two weeks and you're in love."

For the next month Dee and I were inseparable. We could talk for hours without repeating ourselves, boring each other, or running out of things to say. We'd sit in diners late at night, drinking pots of coffee and talking. I was convinced that Dee was the one, but I was reluctant to make a move for fear of ruining the great friendship we were developing.

Maybe my slowness to act caused Dee to reconsider her feelings or wonder why I hadn't made a move, because one night, after we'd gone to see *My Cousin Vinny*, we were sitting in my car, and I finally found the courage to kiss her. I leaned in, puckered my lips in anticipation of the big moment, and nothing happened. At the last second, Dee had backed away.

"What's the matter?" I asked.

"Nothing," she whispered, then repositioned herself in her seat, farther away from me.

"Oh man, I can't believe *that* just happened!" I said. I felt like a fool. I leaned back and looked out the window.

"It's not that I don't want to," Dee explained, touching my arm. "It's just that—"

"No," I said, cutting her off. "You don't understand. When one person goes in for a kiss, and the other backs away, it's over!"

"We can still hang out!"

"No way!" I said. "Now it's forever going to be out there that I'm into you, so it's not going to work, hanging out as friends."

We drove to her place in silence. I was confused. She tried calling me for a couple of weeks and I completely shut her down. No calls back. She started leaving pleading messages for me: "Please! I really wanna talk. I need you as a friend."

I finally agreed to meet her at Friendly's in Valley Stream, where we'd often get ice cream. In my mind, I'd give her one more chance, and if things got weird, I was out of there. Over a banana split, I laid it all out for her. "Dee," I said, "ever since we met at the gas station, I felt like we were on the same wavelength. And the signals I was getting were that you were into, you know, being with me, so hanging out as friends is going to be dicey."

"I know, I know," she said sheepishly. "I was just scared. Give me some time. I love being around you."

Deep down, I was sure Dee was into me, and even though it might sap my energy to get jerked around while she figured that out, I had to give it another shot. I was glad I did. After two weeks, she came to her senses and we kissed. We've been together ever since.

One night at a diner, we decided to let all of the skeletons out of our closets. My thinking was that if Dee and I were going to be together forever, I wanted her to know everything, to lay it all on the table, because I never wanted anything from my past to come back to haunt me or derail us in the future. Dee offered to go first, which was fine with me. I ordered some apple pie with whipped cream and another coffee and settled in. As Dee spilled the beans about different guys she fooled around with, I got to thinking, "Maybe I'm not gonna put *everything* out there." See, Dee's confessions were rated PG. Whereas my confessions were NC-17, involving stuff I decided I should probably sit on, like drugs and things like, well, use your imagination. I was on the road as a young hot comic at the age of twenty-two. I was cocky, with a New York attitude and accent, playing one-nighters in places like Kentucky. Tennessee. Ohio. Alabama. I felt like and acted like a rock star. That's all I'm gonna say. You figure out the rest.

In the end, I told her my PG stuff and tossed her one risqué confession—taking 'shrooms in the woods—and she didn't judge me for it.

"I think that's amazing that you did that," she said.

Despite not unloading all my baggage on her, the connection I felt with Dee was stronger than I'd ever had with any friend. This sounds corny, but about a month after we kissed, we were sitting on the sofa in her apartment and we both just started sobbing in each other's arms over the intensity of being in love. Maybe that's just drama that goes along with being two youngsters in our twenties, but we were both astonished and relieved that we'd found each other. And if that makes me gay, so be it.

At the same time, as Dee and I got closer, her parents were giving me the cold shoulder. They were living in New Jersey now, and when Dee would take me to see them they'd ignore me and ask about her old fiancé.

After getting the freeze-out from Dee's parents for what seemed like forever, I finally brought it up with them one night over dinner at their house.

"I feel like you guys don't like me," I said as casually as I could while ladling some gravy on my roast beef.

"No," her dad said, scoffing. "No. Come on, Jim."

But Dee's mom waved her hand, cutting off Dee's dad. She offered a different take on the situation. "Well, Jim," she said softly. "Dee went from being engaged to a man who had a good head for business to going out with a guy who spends most of his time in bars."

"What?" I said, letting the ladle crash into the bowl. "A lot of my gigs take place in *clubs*. But I'm not a big drinker, and it's not like I'm there just hanging out."

"We know, dear," she said. "It's just that—"

"We're happy together, Mom." It was now Dee's turn to interrupt. "Remember, not so long ago, you were the ones telling him to ask me out."

Her dad began to say, "We never suggested—"

"Save it, Dad," Dee said, then rubbed my arm.

Her parents eventually came to their senses, and after just a few solid months of dating, during the beginning of June 1992, I concocted my proposal plan: I'd pick the most awesome day of the summer—the Fourth of July—and make plans with Dee and all of our friends to go to Jones Beach in Long Island. After the sun went down, and as fireworks were exploding in the sky, I'd turn to Dee and ask her to marry me.

"I hate it when guys are lazy," Dee said a couple of weeks later while we were eating lunch with my sister Dorene, "and propose on a date they can't forget, like your birthday, or Valentine's Day, or the Fourth of July."

"Ugh," Dorene agreed. "That's so cheesy."

That sank my proposal idea. I still wanted it to happen soon, though. So, my brilliant solution was to move the date by one day: I'd ask Dee on July fifth at the beach. It was perfect, because nobody ever proposed the day *after* a major holiday. Dee wouldn't suspect a thing. In fact, it was one of the more depressing days on the calendar. For most people, it meant the holiday was over and it was time to go back to work. It was the kind of contrarian thing that Dee wouldn't expect, but would love.

When we got to the beach, Dee got out of the car, then I opened my door, stuck my hand in my pocket for the ring, grabbed it, and promptly dropped it into a pile of old leaves, shiny pebbles, and broken glass next to the car. It was gone. Poof. Panic instantly introduced itself to me. I believe I even started to hyperventilate. I jumped out and started rummaging through the leaves and underneath the car. I couldn't find it! The more I tried to look for it and the deeper into the leaves I dug, the further into Gonesville that ring went.

Dee was walking away and then she stopped and looked back in my direction. "What's going on?" she asked. "Are you on the *ground?*"

"I dropped some change when I got out."

"It's change—forget about it," she said, shrugging. "Let's get to the beach and we'll look for it when we come back."

"Nice going, Breuer," I thought instantly. "What are you going to do now?"

"They're some rare coins my dad gave to me," I improvised. "He had them during the war. It's a good luck charm."

"Oh," she said, sounding concerned now. "In that case, I'll help you look for them!" She began walking back toward the car.

"I'm okay," I said. "I found them!" I ran to catch up with Dee and send her back in the other direction. I still had major anxiety-induced swamp ass going on. I had to get that ring. In a last-ditch attempt, I slapped at all my pockets and said, "Oh, my God, I left my wallet in the car."

"You don't need—"

I cut her off and started running back to the car to take one last look for the ring. I opened the driver's-side door and pretended to dig around for the wallet, while also looking on the ground for the ring. As I kicked the leaves around, I finally decided it was no use. I was giving up.

"What's going on?" Dee shouted impatiently.

I figured that this could only happen to me. How does an engagement ring evaporate? Defeated, I closed the car door slowly, looked down, and there was the ring. Sitting perfectly atop a pile of leaves, lying right there at my feet. I snatched it up. I was so relieved, but my legs were so rubbery, I had a hard time wobbling back to Dee.

As Dee and I strolled on the beach, my heart was pounding. I had planned to look on the sand and say, "Hey, look what I found!" and when she came to check it out, I'd be down on one knee, then I'd produce the ring and pop the question. But after nearly losing the ring once already I was riddled with anxiety.

"I'd like to live on the beach someday," Dee said.

"Me, too," I agreed, shuffling through all the rubbish in my pants pocket—when I picked up the ring, I grabbed some pebbles and leaves, too—to make sure I had the ring in hand for when I was brave enough to make my move.

"Are you feeling okay?" she asked.

"Yeah," I answered. "I'm fine."

Then Dee began to pick up pebbles and shells. We had the entire beach to ourselves. She looked beautiful with her smiling eyes, picking up her little treasures, showing me what she'd found.

To this day, I still can't believe what happened next. Dee bent down to scoop up more of the shiny pebbles. They glistened sharply underneath the sun.

"Wouldn't it be great to find a diamond ring out here?" she asked. I couldn't believe what she just said. Had she seen the ring?

"What did you say?" I asked her.

"I said, imagine if we found a diamond ring out here. Wouldn't that be amazing?"

I reached out, grabbed her hand softly, and pulled her close. I took the ring from my pocket. "Yes, that would be amazing," I said. "But I already found one just for you." I slipped it on her finger and asked her to marry me.

After the engagement, Eddie was the first person I called. He was excited and couldn't wait to meet Dee. He'd recently seen me do a show in Connecticut and he couldn't believe how much I had improved since that depressing night he saw me at Dangerfield's. He was still trying to figure out a way to apply his business expertise to my comedy career—by teaming up to create a funny magazine or something—but I knew I still didn't have him convinced 100 percent of my talent.

A little while later, I flew to Florida to tell my parents about the engagement in person. My dad, for the first time that I can remember, jumped up off of the couch, shook my hand, and showed real pride in me. "Congratulations, son," he said. "I'm very happy for you. You're a man now." It was a simple gesture, but I'd never seen him do that before.

By the way, readers, know this: Engagements are moments that last literally that long . . . moments. Then everyone else gets involved. Pop the question, and before too long, a full-blown tsunami of distractions from concerned parties will come flying your way: "What's the actual date?" "You need a date!" "Where's the engagement party?" "Flowers!" "Dresses!" "Bridesmaids!" "Groomsmen!" "Who's the best man?" "Don't invite so-and-so!" "Who's paying for it?" "Don't think

I'm paying for it!" "How are you going to pay for it if you don't have a real career?" "So, how are you going to survive?" "Where are you going to live?" "Are you thinking of having children?" "Got any names picked out?" Ad infinitum. My advice to anyone getting engaged: Don't tell anyone for a month.

By this point, the Rat had started drifting back into my life. While he'd claimed he was too busy to manage me, he had been booking shows for me. But I'd been booking a lot myself, too. I was working a lot of gigs all over New York, New Jersey, and Connecticut, sharing the stage with great comedians like Adam Ferrara, Kevin James, Bobby Collins, Bob Nelson, and Ray Romano.

The Rat informed me that he was done booking shows for me unless I signed a deal with him. He said that he had cleared his schedule up and now had time to manage me. To continue getting shows from him, I had to sign a contract. A commitment of three years, and if he landed me a TV deal, I'd be stuck with him for another three years.

As far as I was concerned, his ship had sailed. He could send me a postcard. I met with the Rat at his office and told him I was getting married.

"Ugh," he said. "It's going to ruin your entire career. Get rid of her!"

I knew that he had a calculator going in his head, and he was figuring that maybe I wouldn't be willing to go the extra mile if I were married. And that could cost him money. My gut told me, as it had before, that I should just move on and not get tangled up with him again. But he held that carrot of TV out in front of me, and I couldn't resist grabbing for it. I've noticed that many times, just when you feel great about your soul and your life, that's when evil wants to get in and ruin it at all costs. Sometimes, in fact, we invite it.

I hadn't left his office for more than a few hours when I got a phone call from him.

"I got a TV audition for you, Jimbo."

"Finally," I said. I was only half joking. "Where is it?"

"In Harlem," he said. "That's about all I know. They're looking for a funny white guy. If you're interested, I'll be happy to give you a ride."

"Sure," I said. "Let's check it out."

During the car ride to Harlem, he produced a management contract. "I want you to have a look at this and think it over," he said. "I really think we should make it official." This contract stipulated that the Rat would now receive 20 percent of all of my comedy gigs, along with whatever else he could land for me, for three years with a three-year extension, if a TV gig materialized.

After looking it over, I said, "I'm not feeling this." Six years was an insanely long commitment. "No can do."

"Okay, but I'm just not going to be able to book gigs for you anymore if you don't sign," he said flatly.

"Let's say this TV thing works out," I said, countering. "Why don't you just take twenty percent of that and leave the bookings alone?"

"You'll become a star, in high demand, and I won't have any of your comedy bookings, movies, none of it," he whined. "I'll just have twenty percent of the thing that first made your career and enabled the rest of it."

"Relax," I said. "Let's just see how this audition goes."

The audition was for an unnamed show that would later become *Uptown Comedy Club*. I improvised with their cast and hit it off with Kevin and André Brown, the show's producers. It went as well as I could have expected. On the drive back downtown, the Rat again produced the contract.

"Why don't I take it home for a couple of days?" I asked.

"What?" he said dismissively. "Why?"

"I'd like to show it to my sister," I said meekly.

"Suit yourself," he said. "She's not going to know how to read it, but go ahead, show her anyway."

The contract, even to a naïve meathead like me, seemed like a really bad deal. Dollar signs and screaming fans called out to me, while my gut told me this whole situation was shady. Two days later, I had a callback audition for the show in Harlem. I nailed this one, too, and I could tell by the enthusiastic response of the producers that I had the gig. I clicked with the rest of the cast and I wanted it. But the Rat clammed up on me. I'd call him every day, asking, "What did you hear? Do they want me to go back up there? Why is the decision taking so long?"

Every time he'd respond with some variation of "I haven't heard anything," followed up by, "Are you ready to sign the contract?"

A week went by. I hadn't worked much in TV or done many auditions, but I knew I should have heard something one way or the other by then, especially with the vibe I'd gotten from the producers. I suspected that the Rat was holding the gig hostage until I signed the contract with him. I called Eddie for advice and he told me not to sign.

I'd stayed friendly with a girl named Carrie who'd booked me for some gigs in Florida, and she now lived in New York and worked for this manager guy I'll call Leon, who repped Jay Mohr and Dave Chappelle. So Dee and I went to visit Leon one afternoon, and he struck me as a totally different breed of manager from what I was used to. He wore jeans and had long hair and seemed like someone I could relate to. I explained what had been going on with the audition and the other manager.

"I see you on TV in less than a year," he said enthusiastically. Calmer and cooler than the other guy, he walked around the room, then took a seat on a windowsill that looked out onto the city.

"So what should I do?" I asked.

"Don't sign anything," he said. "I'm going to be gone for about a week. Sit tight and let me snoop around when I get back. There's got to be a simple explanation."

"Thanks," I said.

"Just promise me you won't sign that contract," he repeated as I left his office.

Now nearly two weeks had gone by and the Rat was still tight-lipped about whether or not he had heard anything from the Harlem audition. All he knew for certain was that I should sign his lame contract, and he made sure to tell me every time I reached out to him. Both Eddie and Dorene suggested I go back to him and tell him I'd like to take the contract to a lawyer. I didn't know what else to do. Not coincidentally, he contacted me at the same time.

"I'm tying up a lot of my resources," he started to explain in his smarmy tone. "I can't keep waiting for you. Sign the contract today, or else we'll have to part ways. It's up to you."

"What about the show?" I asked.

"I still haven't heard," he said impatiently. "But regardless, you and I need to have a deal in place."

So I reluctantly went to his basement office in Queens. He met me at the door with a pen and the contract. There were some seriously bad vibes in the air.

"I'd like to take this to a lawyer first," I told him. "If he's cool with it, I'll gladly sign it for you."

"What?" he asked exasperatedly, walking back to his desk and sitting down. "Lawyers don't know anything about comedians. All they do is take your money while they waste your time. They're going to make a bunch of little changes that will cost thousands of dollars. Do you have thousands of dollars?" He didn't wait for me to answer. "And not only that, but it will take months for them to make those changes.

"Do you want me to go on?" he asked, now standing up again and starting to pace. "If a really good last-minute gig comes in for you, vetting it through them will kill it. Lawyers just don't move fast enough. You'll miss out."

I was feeling seriously pressured. Everything inside of me was screaming that this was not worth it. Success shouldn't feel this crappy. But I also felt so close to that TV show that I didn't want to walk away now. Nobody would ever make a deal with a devil unless the terms were very tempting.

I began to wilt. Some of what he was saying seemed like it was making sense. We started bartering about the length of the contract itself. And against my better judgment, we struck a compromise. Two years, with a two-year extension. I couldn't believe it, but I was on the verge of signing. Before I did, though, I gave him a moment to be honest. "I'll sign right now," I said, "if you will look at me and tell me the truth. Have you heard anything about me and the Harlem TV audition?"

He couldn't make eye contact with me. He simply looked at the floor and shook his head no. "I'll try calling them again after you sign. I promise."

I still signed the thing. I don't think I've ever felt lower, more ashamed, and more stupid. I betrayed everyone in my family who had pleaded with me to be patient. I was going against what my gut was telling me. As soon as I made the last *r* in my last name, he became deliriously giddy.

"You're gonna make so much money," he exclaimed. "Trust me. This is gonna be great. Let's go have dinner! I'm buying."

We went out to a steak house, and in the middle of the meal he smiled and with a shrug said, "Well, why don't I try giving Harlem a call?" He excused himself and went to the pay phones in the lobby. Almost immediately, he came back and sat down giggling maniacally. "You got it!" He was ecstatic. "Finally we got some news! You got the show!" Surprise. Surprise.

Under normal circumstances, that would have called for a bottle of champagne. All my hard work, writing, self-promotion, persistence, saving money to move back to New York—it had all culminated in reaching my goal: to be on TV. But I felt like I'd cheated. I excused myself from the table, walked outside, and started sobbing. Just like De Niro playing Jake LaMotta in *Raging Bull*, I punched the brick walls. I was a sucker.

Later that night, I hopped on a train to pick up my car and drive to Dee's place. I desperately tried to think positively. And slowly, it sank in that no matter how crappy this deal was, I was still going to be on TV. I'd somehow make it work on my terms. I became re-energized, cranking metal from the car stereo and pumping my fists out the window.

Out of all the people in my family, something made me want to tell Eddie first. Not to show him up for suggesting I join the National Guard, but to make him proud. And, okay, maybe to tell him, "I told you so." I wanted him to know that he never had to worry about me now. In a year I'd be taking care of him and the rest of the family, no doubt about it.

I quietly went into Dee's apartment. It was around one fifteen in the morning, but I didn't care. I couldn't contain myself as I began to dial Eddie's number. My heart began to pound. I kept imagining Eddie's big hearty giggle, which was a lot like mine, only deeper. "Good for you!" he'd say. My fidgeting with the phone woke Dee up.

"Who are you calling?" she asked. "It's late."

"Eddie," I said, cradling the receiver on my shoulder. "I got the show!"

"You did?" She smiled. "Awesome!" Then she clicked the base of the phone and hung up the call. "Eddie's got three kids," she said.

"Dee," I said, "I'm going to be on TV! *Real* TV!"

"It can wait until morning; that's only five hours from now," Dee said. "Call him at six thirty A.M., he'll be up early."

"All right, all right, all right," I said disgustedly. "I just really wanted him to know tonight. I'm one less person he's gotta worry about, Dee."

"He'll be so happy to hear that," she said. "In the morning!"

We fell asleep, and Dee's phone started ringing at five thirty A.M. The answering machine picked it up. "Jimmy?" my niece Denise cried out. "It's Eddie! Eddie's dead! Pick up the phone!"

I groggily picked up the phone. "What's going on?" I asked, confused.

"Eddie died of a heart attack last night."

Kristen's passing was heavy. It was jarring to me to see a peer pass away, to be reminded that we can be taken at any time. But Eddie's dying was far more profound. It was gutting. I'd learned from Denise that he'd passed around one fifteen A.M., right around the time I would have been calling him. Just like that my jubilation over my great TV show and my complaining about my shitty contract didn't mean zilch. Reality was back open for business.

What sticks with me to this day is that I might have been trying to call while Eddie was dying. Do you call that a coincidence? I could have done any number of things after learning I got the TV show, but calling Eddie after one A.M. was at the top of the list. Why? I could have stayed up all night and celebrated. I could have driven out to Phil's place. But something compelled me to call at that particular time. Why? Don't ask me. I know I couldn't have prevented Eddie from dying, but something compelled me to reach out.

My entire family was devastated. I went up to his house and found my mom sobbing uncontrollably.

"When I see Lefty," she bawled, "I'm going to slap him right in the face. Right in the face."

"What are you talking about, Mom?" I asked. Lefty was Eddie's father, who'd been killed two months before his service in World War II ended, having never met his son.

"He told me in a dream he was coming to take him," Mom cried.

I was sure my mom was having a mental breakdown. "What do you mean he told you in a dream?"

"I had a dream two weeks ago," Mom explained through sobs. "It was raining and Lefty was in a tunnel. He said, 'I'm sorry, Doris. But it's time for me to be with my son.'"

The day Eddie was buried, I went to Dorene's house to take a nap. As I fell asleep, I felt like I entered a world that we might recognize only when our time is up. Some people may write this off as a dream, exhaustion, or whatever, but Eddie appeared to me, plain as day. He was standing on the lawn at my grandma's house—a place I hadn't seen since I was five years old. Calmness and contentment washed over me. Eddie was wearing his usual: khakis, a blue oxford shirt and tie, loafers. He was carrying his navy blue blazer over his shoulder, and he was constantly pushing up his glasses with his finger.

"Check on the boys for me," he said with a smile. "They'll be fine, but let them know you're there for them and don't worry about Mom. She's got you to lean on if she needs."

I assured him I would. He smiled and turned to leave, and I stopped him and said, "Wait, wait, don't leave! What about you?"

"I'm super," he replied convincingly and calmly. "I am just super." Then he giggled and poof, he was gone. I immediately woke up. All I could think was, "He came to me in a dream," just like you always hear about but never believe. Now I believed for sure. There was nothing to fear. You can call me a wacko or a freak, but you'll never be able to take this moment away from me or explain it. It's real. It happened.

Chapter 6

From Harlem, It's the *Uptown Comedy Club*

So I had my first TV gig. Eddie had just died and my family was looking for something positive. One of us had made it. Everyone wanted to know about the TV show, but I didn't feel very comfortable talking about it because the timing was horrible. It was like, "Hey, Eddie's dead, but I'm on TV. Let's party." No thanks. Beyond that, I hated my manager, the Rat, but I was now contractually obligated to him for four years; Dee and I were engaged, but my working twelve-to-fourteen-hour days, an hour and fifteen minutes from our New Jersey home, immediately strained our relationship; and the TV gig itself, while great, wasn't going to pay me for at least the first three months I worked on it.

If someone had told me when I was a kid that one day I would be going to work in Harlem, my thoughts would have revolved around dying in a shocking and painful way the second I arrived. By the time I was an adult and had seen a little bit of the world, I was nothing but excited to go to Harlem. In August of 1992 I headed there with an open mind to do a new sketch comedy show, *Uptown Comedy Club*. And any concerns I may have had were alleviated from the get-go by the two brothers producing the show, Kevin and André Brown. (André unfortunately passed away a few years ago, but you might know Kevin as Dot Com from *30 Rock*.) *Uptown Comedy Club* was their first time putting together a televised comedy show, and even though the Browns had help from the people who ran *Showtime at the Apollo*, it felt a little like they'd just lucked into this TV thing and were racing to produce it before it got taken away from them.

For starters, the place where we rehearsed and filmed the show wasn't a proper studio but their club, the Uptown Comedy Club (naturally), on 125th Street and 5th Avenue in Harlem. By day it doubled as their karate studio. The Browns were renaissance men; they performed, they produced, and they were totally ripped badasses obsessed with teaching the discipline and art of karate to Harlem kids. If any cast members got to the club early, we'd just have to wait for karate class to end. It was fascinating watching them spar—just a whirl of arms and legs under perfect control—but it also inevitably led to their trying to convince me to join in, which I wisely refused every time.

The show was raw as could be. There were no wardrobe people, nor any hair and makeup people. We had no dressing rooms, just clothing racks we'd change behind. The club had a small stage, and back behind it there were hallways where we'd sit on the floor and write sketches for twelve to fourteen hours a day, six days a week. We had no typewriters, just pens and notebooks. And when we taped in front of a live audience on Saturdays we had no cue cards; you just had to rely on your memory.

But I trusted the Browns with everything, because above all else, they stressed unity, and they were fiercely protective of their show. To this day, I wish I still had producers like that. What they lacked in experience they made up for in sheer humanity and effort. They were at the club every minute, and occasionally they'd sit us down for impromptu talks that went way beyond the work we were doing.

"There's no guarantee it's going to happen," André would say, pacing back and forth in front of the stage. "No one owes you anything. But how are you going to carry yourself if you get famous? What are you going to be like? Will your family still recognize you? Trust you? Depend on you? What are you doing this for?"

The Browns schooled us on life, character, ambition, and the ghetto, along with juicy show business stuff. I remember sitting in the club one afternoon with Tracy Morgan, who joined about seven episodes into the season, when the Browns walked in, having just returned from Los Angeles on business. We both got up to greet them.

"Stay sitting down, okay?" Kevin said. "'Cause this is gonna be heavy."

"Oh, man," André said, laughing. "Hang on to your hats."

"Hollywood was *crazy*," Kevin added.

André continued. "We were at a party, and people were talking about seeing [some very fam<u>ous</u> comedians and an equally famous basketball player, all of whom I'm still too freaked out to mention] all chicken-hawking."

Immediately, all the black guys on the cast started laughing.

"C'mon, man," a tall, skinny comic known only as Ye-Ye said. He and a guy named Macio were my writing partners most of the time. Ye-Ye was a couple of years younger than me and he always had a shit-eating grin on his face like he'd just done something bad and only he knew about it. "Now you're just making up stories!"

"Whoa, whoa, whoa," I said. I had no idea what the heck they were even talking about. "What's chicken-hawking?"

"You sayin' you don't know?" another comic said to me.

"No idea."

"Whew," he said, and ran his hand across his forehead, then burst out laughing. "That's a relief." Then the whole room erupted with laughter.

"Chicken-hawking is when you cruise around and pick up transvestites," André explained.

"What?" I said, befuddled. There was no way. One of the guys had been my hero forever. If he were into that stuff, surely I would have heard about it. "No way," I said. "I'm not that gullible."

Kevin liked to joke about the sexual predilections of these celebrities. He went on to say, "You guys have no clue what Hollywood is all about. It's phony. Smoke and mirrors. A charade. You've got guys picking up transvestites. Famous actors you could never in your wildest dreams imagine living in the closet, all 'cause they don't want to rock the boat. They're chasing that fame."

I guess I was lucky that I had no burning desire for transvestites competing with my desire for fame.

The show was hard to find, initially, on the cable dial, but with syndication it grew and grew. Early on, though, people I knew were skeptical. "What's up with your *show*?" they'd ask, not believing it was ever going to see the light of day.

In all, there were about a dozen of us on the cast. Me and a guy named Rob Magnotti were the only white people. We were all so eager to be a part of the experience—and were all spending so much time together—that racial issues were mainly something that happened on the street, outside the walls of the club. But there were of course some cultural clashes.

When Ye-Ye and I first sat down to work, it was like an armadillo and a cat meeting for the first time and studying one another. He'd never spent that much time with a white person before, and I'd never spent that much time with a black person before.

"Why is your hair like that?" he'd say, making a curious face. "Do you use a blow-dryer? It's so straight."

"Why do you use a pick in your hair?" I'd respond. "You pick it and pick it and it always looks the same to me."

After a while I was simply a member of the cast. So much so that no one had a problem listing their complaints about white people when I was around.

And most of the time I'd find myself agreeing with them, because the more time I spent in Harlem, the more I could see the experience that black people were living. Keep in mind that this is the Harlem of the early nineties, where there were no million-dollar condos and gentrifying white folks. I certainly saw some bad behavior up there, but a lot more good, and I was curious as to why the good had always been kept from me growing up.

I liked Harlem, and it didn't take long to feel a part of the neighborhood. Every day, when I would park my car around the corner from the club, I'd walk by two black women sitting on their porch right across the street from the chicken and waffles place where I liked to eat. Sometimes we'd talk, and if not, then they'd at least give me a shout-out, like, "Hey, what's up, white boy," or "Don't worry about your car, white boy, we'll keep an eye on it for you," then they'd laugh and laugh. When they found out I was on the show, they'd say, "You gonna make them laugh today, white boy?" I loved it.

Tracy would see this and say, "Everybody in the ghetto loves you! They love you like they love Jim Carrey."

I was walking out of the bodega around the corner one afternoon and from just outside the door, I heard, "Get him. Get him." I looked up to see people scattering out of the way of this short, skinny black guy who was running right at me, with a bunch of slow-footed cops trailing after him. For a split second I thought, "If I put my shoulder out I could take this guy down easy. I could be a hero." And then I thought to myself, "You're a guest in this community, on good footing; don't screw that up." Was it the right thing to let an alleged criminal run right past me? Probably not. But knowing the relationship between the police and the residents of Harlem, I was taking the side of the people who lived there.

The show got a lot of notoriety for its sketches and its musical acts—we had Wu-Tang Clan, Mary J. Blige, and Kriss Kross on—and a lot of attention right away for the snap contest, where cast members and comics would end the show going head-to-head onstage, trying to outdo one another with "yo mama" jokes. Monteria Ivey and Hugh Moore were the geniuses behind it. André Brown came by a rehearsal early on and announced, "We're gonna need a white guy to do some snaps, too."

I volunteered but ultimately could not bring it. Growing up, I was really good at insult humor. I could paint a mental picture that would just nuke someone, but by the time I got it out, it wasn't exactly a snap anymore.

So I got up onstage and said, "Your mama is so fat that they need a crane to get her out of bed, and once she's out of bed, the neighbors think there's an earthquake and—"

"Okay," Kevin said. "That's enough."

"What?" I said.

"We don't have all month," Kevin replied. "That means you're up, Rob."

"Nah," he said. "Snaps aren't really my forte. I don't think so."

"Well, I do think so," André said, admonishing him just a smidge. "So take a day to work on some. Hugh will help you out. Come back ready tomorrow."

Hugh Moore was a funny young guy from Minnesota who carried himself so slowly and deliberately that he reminded me of Grady from *Sanford and Son*, so I started calling him that (until he asked me to stop shortly thereafter). He was also the best snap writer ever.

Rob showed up the next day pretending he was sick. He had a scarf around his neck and a cup of tea, and as he dunked his tea bag, he explained that he was getting laryngitis and really needed to rest his voice because he had to do a show later that night. We all knew he was faking, but he was not budging on trying to worm his way out of it.

"No one's gonna be able to hear me," Rob said.

"That's okay," Kevin said. "Just do your snaps quietly."

So Rob gingerly took the stage, armed with Hugh's snaps, wearing a scarf around his neck and gently dunking a tea bag into his cup. He wore a total deadpan look on his face and as he slowly whispered, "Your mother is so fat, she can't wear an X jacket, because helicopters keep landing on her back," then took a sip of his tea, we all knew that we were witnessing something amazing. A character was born.

The first week he did snaps, Rob became a star. The crowd ate it right up, and a Harlem crowd is the toughest. If they don't like you, they'll just point right at the door and stare you offstage. If you crush in front of them, it's a huge accomplishment. With his droll delivery, Rob sounded like a menacing mobster who was not to be crossed, and for ten straight weeks, he blew the competition off the stage. It put him on a real high, and rightfully so, because it was such a genius execution. Hugh and Rob were as formidable a team as Mickey and Rocky. Until one day Rob showed up and broke the news that he now was writing all of his own snaps and didn't need Hugh anymore. Hugh had created a monster and Rob got cocky. Hugh sort of shrugged off the news, and when it came time for Rob to deliver his own snaps, he got annihilated instantly and lost the title.

*　　*　　*

Initially, being away from Dee so much was tough. We'd moved to an apartment way out in Hillsborough, New Jersey, a great distance from the city. Dee had friends out there she wanted to hang with (but never did) and for our money, the apartment was a heck of a lot bigger and nicer than anything we'd seen closer to the city. Here's the thing: The seventy-five-minute commute to New York City turned out to be a monster. My long hours and our poor communication led her to call it quits on our engagement several times when the show was just coming together. You gotta remember, this was a time when there were no cell phones. No texting. No e-mail. And I couldn't tie up the club's phone with my personal calls, and most of the pay phones in Harlem didn't work, and when one did, I'd have to use a little calling card that I'd bought at the bodega and hope she was home from her job as a car checker. (She worked at this place I thought was kinda scammy, where they hooked up computers to people's cars to diagnose what was wrong with them.) I could leave a message on our machine, but she had no real way of getting in touch with me.

Before we had figured out how to make it work, there was one time when Dee and I were feuding. I wasn't going to be funny with conflict eating away at me. So, about midway through rehearsals, I walked up to Kevin Brown and told him I was leaving for the day.

"Things aren't going the hottest at home right now," I said.

"What are you saying?" he asked.

"I don't know," I said. "I think I gotta split for today and clear some things up with my fiancée so I can come back tomorrow with better focus."

"You go do what you need to do, Jim."

Like I said before, the Browns appreciated and respected the value of family. So with his blessing, I drove home to New Jersey. But, naturally, when I got to the apartment, Dee wasn't there. And it looked like she hadn't been there since the morning. My worst fear was that she'd left for good. I was already envisioning telling my parents and friends that the wedding was off and I was now single. Then the phone rang. It was Dee.

"What the hell are you doing at home?" she screamed as soon as I picked up. I could hear car horns blaring and pedestrians in the background. City noise. She was furious.

"Where are *you?*" I said.

"I came to visit you!" she yelled.

"I took off work early to surprise you!" I said.

"Well, this was a great surprise!"

"Dee," I said, "just come home now, so we can be together before I have to be back there tomorrow. Sorry, honey. I thought you'd appreciate me trying to work on us."

"I do!" she said, finally warming up to me. "I have to figure out how to get back from Harlem."

It's at that point that I think I might have told her to go *east* on 125th Street and look for signs that would take her to the George Washington Bridge, and that would bring her safely back to New Jersey. I meant west. Regardless, I didn't hear anything from her for a while, and when I did, she was not in New Jersey.

"I went over a bridge," Dee said. She was calling from another pay phone. "And it wasn't the GWB. It was way smaller. Now I tried to turn around, and I have no idea where I am." There were more city noises in the background. It was getting dark out and I'm pretty sure I was more nervous than she was. She just sounded annoyed.

"Uh-oh," I said. "I think you might be in the Bronx."

"All the buildings look like they're going to fall down."

"Yep," I said. "You're in the Bronx."

She hung up and another two and a half hours went by. I had the phone next to me and the TV turned on, watching the news, waiting to see her overturned car in flames on-screen somewhere. Believe me, the visuals going on in my head were not pretty. Finally, I heard a key turn in the door, and Dee walked in, completely exhausted. With the help of a few gas station attendants, she'd gotten turned in the right direction, and despite the drama, the engagement was still on.

*　　*　　*

When Tracy Morgan joined the cast, he'd never been on TV before, but we all knew how hilarious his stand-up was. He would help with sketches, but he wouldn't write. He couldn't sit still long enough. So if you were anywhere near him, writing was your job. Not that I minded. Sometimes Tracy wasn't even part of a sketch originally— he'd just wander by, start casually riffing with you, and automatically take whatever you were working on to the stratosphere.

And he'd disappear into character for who knows how long. It was hilarious and annoying at the same time, because it was impossible to get him out of it. When he came onboard, he and I hit it off like two kids who found each other on a playground and liked to play the same games. He became my best friend on the show. No matter what was thrown out there, we could both imitate it and go nonstop. He was by far the most physically gifted comedian I'd encountered.

Tracy would take the train in from the Bronx, wearing this little beanie hat like the one Spanky from *The Little Rascals* wore, only Tracy's had a propeller. He was late every single day and he'd always set rehearsals back even further, because he'd come in with a story and then start doing all of the characters in it. He could adopt the tics and mannerisms of anyone he saw, even if only in passing—it could be some lady he saw dropping cantaloupes at a supermarket, a crotchety neighbor he'd gotten into an argument with, the conductor on the train, a bunch of people from the last three blocks of his commute, whoever.

He would freely riff on any topic and hold nothing back. When you see him on TV being interviewed and he starts acting crazy, just keep in mind that he's not acting. That's his real unfiltered personality. I liked how honest he was and that would lead to deep conversations between us.

"Where you from?" he asked one day when we first met.

"My family's from Long Island, near Queens," I said.

"I'm straight ghetto, if anyone asks," he said. "I don't mind saying it. That's where I'm from. I've been a ticket scalper. Sold some other things people might frown on. I do what I gotta do to provide for my family. Bottom line."

One day I was rehearsing when I heard fireworks right outside the front door.

Tracy emerged from another room and said very matter-of-factly, "Who got shot?"

I laughed, and he said, "No, really, someone got shot outside."

"Sounded like firecrackers to me."

"Nah," he said, "that was a drive-by." He peeked out the window and then said, "Come on, he's across the street."

Sure enough we saw a young black man, down on all fours, bleeding all over the place right in front of the deli I ate at every day. Tracy and I approached him as a crowd of about fifteen people gathered around and watched him struggle. He was bleeding so heavily that it was rolling off of the sidewalk, down into the gutter. He repeatedly tried to get up, only to fall powerlessly back to the ground. You could hear his flesh slapping the cement every time this happened.

"Look at you now!" a woman screamed at him. "Look at you now!"

There was still gun smoke in the air. The paramedics showed up quickly and did their jobs, but the dying man seemed almost like an interruption to their day. They were mostly white guys and never broke their conversation about baseball for too long as they strapped him to the gurney.

"Yeah, I don't know why they traded for O'Neill. I liked Roberto Kelly."

"Well," his partner said, "Kelly just wasn't—" Then he paused to address the dying man, who was still for some reason trying to get up under his own power. "*Listen, stay down, man. Quit moving!* . . . Kelly just wasn't living up to his potential."

They moved with the nonchalance of a train conductor collecting tickets on the LIRR. They hoisted him into the ambulance and drove off. Just another day at the office.

After the shooting, Tracy and I were sitting out in his car on 125th Street, discussing the situation. He was playing old R&B—

stuff like the Isley Brothers and Al Green—and despite what had happened earlier, it was nice to hang out and talk without it being a work situation. Later, when we were both on *Saturday Night Live*, he and I would share an office, write together, and get to hang out a lot more outside of the show, but on *Uptown*, no one really *wanted* to hang out. It was like we all lived together anyway. After spending fourteen hours a day with each other, when we were done working we all just wanted to go home. At the time, Tracy had four young kids waiting for him, and he took his parenting very seriously.

"Why can't the whole world do what we're doing, right here?" he said.

"What do you mean?"

"Just hanging out, talking," he said. "A lot more problems would get solved if people sat down together and got to know one another. Right now, down the block there's probably a white fireman in a firehouse who is pissed he has to work in Harlem, 'cause he thinks we're all animals."

"You think so?"

"I know so," Tracy said. "But he's not the only one who's prejudiced. There's black people around here that see the same guy as the devil. They're mad that he thinks he can come up here and protect the community. 'He doesn't live here, why's he trying to help us?' They're wondering why one of their own can't have that opportunity.

"Life is different up here," he said. "What you saw today happens all the time."

"Why wouldn't you just move?" I asked.

"Where?" he said, surprised. "You need a job. Who's gonna hire a black man from the Bronx or Harlem? Somebody in Iowa?"

"I don't know."

"What about your neighborhood? You think someone's gonna sell me a house in your neighborhood? Be real, man. This is the ghetto and it's going to stay the ghetto. And most of these people are stuck here. You think we get the same education here as they do in your neighborhood? No. But there's also a lot of love to go around here, only you're not allowed to see it. You see it now, but that's 'cause you've been around here for a while. All you'll see on the news tonight is a black guy shot and killed another black guy, and everyone else will breathe a sigh of relief."

I knew he was right when he said that, and it saddened me. It was so surreal for me to see another man, regardless of what his background was or whether he was involved in drugs or not, struggling for his last ounce of life out on a sidewalk in America in broad daylight. Seeing it play out, and hearing Tracy's perspective, taught me never to judge anyone based on the picture that's presented to me in the media.

A couple of other heavy racial moments happened while I did the show, and they told me a lot about where I was going and where I was from. A cast member named Flex and I went to grab a sandwich at the deli near where the man had been shot, right across from the club. Whenever I'd go in there, I'd get a chicken Parmesan and the old guy behind the counter would scold me.

"You gonna get fat eating that sandwich, white boy."

"Don't worry about me," I'd say with a laugh.

"You should be eating that ham if you wanna stay skinny."

"Ham, huh?"

And he'd just nod. I thought it was crazy that he thought ham was going to keep me fit. But it was his deli, so whatever. I was gonna stick with the chicken Parm. Anyway, one day, I was in line with Flex getting a sandwich and chips, and I felt someone bump into me from behind. It's New York, that stuff is bound to happen, so I wasn't too concerned. Still, it felt a little forceful, so I slowly craned my neck to take a look, and I saw a very well-dressed, buff guy in a suit. He didn't look like trouble, so I went back to minding my own business. Then he spoke up.

"What?" he said indignantly.

"I didn't say anything," I said. Then Flex looked back, too, and just rolled his eyes, as if to say, "Oh no."

"You don't belong in here, cracker ass," the guy in the suit said. "Why are you here, anyway?" He continued chastising me. The rest of the people in line took a step away from us but kept their eyes glued on the situation, like they were going to be seeing some free lunchtime theatrics. Then Flex piped up.

"You don't know him!" Flex yelled angrily to the guy. He later told me the guy was a member of the militant Nation of Islam and probably hated any white person he'd ever see.

"Shut up," the buff guy said, addressing Flex. "Uncle Tom."

"You don't *know* Uncle Tom," Flex said. "All you know is hate. You're going against everything your religion is supposed to be about right now, brother. In fact, I'd trust my kids with this guy more than I would with you."

The guy glowered at Flex and then fixed his gaze on the counter, trying to ignore him. The crowd of people went back to their own business.

As we walked out, Flex kept churning over the incident and mumbling. "They're bad for our people. I don't even understand them, to be honest. Bad for our people."

The other incident happened away from Harlem. About a year into the show, I decided to head out to Valley Stream and meet Phil and some other high school friends at a bar. To be honest, I was looking forward to fluffing my feathers around my old stomping grounds. It was totally vain of me, but I was hoping the locals would recognize me from being on television.

I got to the bar early, ordered a beer, and bumped into a guy I went to high school with. He'd gotten beefy, a little pudgy even, but he'd been a buff athlete. Someone more popular than me. I'd even looked up to him.

"Breuer," he said, smiling. "Mr. Television."

Bingo. I was feeling validated almost instantly. We shook hands and I said, "How ya doing?"

"Great," he said, taking a sip of his beer. "Looks like you're doing great, too. I've seen you a couple times and the show is funny, man." He paused for a second and smiled. "I gotta ask you though, what's it like working with all those niggers?"

My mind was blown. This was the early nineties, but not the 1890s.

"They're good people," I said, smiling and shaking my head.

He considered what I said for a minute and then said smugly, "Oh, I get it. They're paying you, so I guess you gotta say that."

"No," I said emphatically. "I really—" Then I caught myself, realizing that I was never going to change this guy's mind. I didn't bother waiting for my friends to show up. I left. My feathers hadn't been fluffed, but they had been ruffled.

After two years and twenty-five episodes, *Uptown Comedy Club* went off the air. It was by far the hardest I'd worked in comedy, and it was an education unto itself. I consider everyone who was a part of it a really close friend, and I love them all.

Chapter 7

It's a Breuer Family Wedding

As Dee and I were about to get married in Union, New Jersey, in 1993, we pooled all of our money together and it came out to a grand total of $248. I dug *Uptown Comedy Club*, but I definitely wasn't getting rich doing it.

The night before the wedding, I drove to the hotel where the whole wedding party was staying, with my '89 Ford Probe packed with all the stuff Dee and I were going to take on our honeymoon: tennis rackets, a boom box, all of our clothes, a huge video camera. That night, Phil and some other friends, Gene and Joe, and my dad and I all went out to a bar, and I had way too much to drink. Phil drove us back to the hotel, pulled up next to the Probe, and said, "Let's bring everything up to the room."

I was tired, wasted, and didn't want to hear it. "I'm not bringing all that stuff up *now*," I groaned. "Let's wait until the morning."

"God forbid anything happens," Phil said, shrugging.

"Listen," I said. "It's two in the morning. Nothing's gonna happen. If you feel compelled to haul stuff up to the room, knock yourself out, but I'm not bringing anything up."

Phil, being the great guy that he is, said, "I'll just grab the tuxedos, then." So he got them out and hauled them up to the room. In the morning, we went down to get the rest of the stuff out of the car, and it was gone. The parking space was empty.

"Maybe it rolled away?" I said, scanning the parking lot. "Did we put it in park?"

It hadn't rolled away.

Phil, Gene, and I took a lap around the parking lot like a bunch of jackasses, just to double-check that we even were looking in the right place. Defeated, I went in to the front desk.

"My car," I said quizzically, nodding toward the parking lot. "Is missing?"

The balding manager at the desk smacked his forehead and grumbled. "You, too? That makes six cars last night."

Thank God Phil saved the tuxedos at least. And thank God I had car insurance. I did my best to not let the theft ruin the mood of the actual ceremony. I saw it as just another obstacle trying to get in the way of my marriage, and I wasn't going to let that happen. Besides, it wasn't easy to think about anything in a church that was 110 degrees. The AC was broken and there were no fans. After the wedding, everyone lined up to throw rice at us on the steps of the church, but a flash monsoon sent them running, so by the time Dee and I got outside, there was no one waiting for us. Later, people had so much fun dancing at the reception that no one ate any food, and the band came back to the hotel to party into the night.

In the end, Dee's mom was generous enough to loan us her car for the honeymoon. Obviously, at the time we couldn't afford a really nice getaway, but I got an idea doing stand-up once in the Hudson River Valley in upstate New York. I played at a dude ranch called the

Rocking Horse. I knew Dee liked horses, so I thought that would make her happy. When we got to the dude ranch we were the only honeymooners there. It was all families, decked out in rodeo-style clothes, and we had to eat dinner at these communal picnic tables with them. None of them could believe we were honeymooning there. But it was our trip.

When we got home, the police had found the Probe. They told us our car had been used as the smack-up car. When these crooks were out stealing cars, they always used one as a decoy—if there was to be a chase, the smack-up car would be the one the crooks wanted the cops to go after, while their partners in crime drove the other way with the more valuable cars. The smack-up car tended to, well, get smacked up. Mine was no exception. It was beat to shit.

Dee started sobbing when she saw it. It was a sad reality to see something I'd worked so hard for completely trashed. But it was oddly thrilling to see where they'd been. The backseat was filled with night-club flyers and White Castle wrappers. They'd stolen everything out of the trunk except the tennis rackets. Car thieves don't play a lot of tennis, apparently.

Chapter 8

Babysitting Billy

Now that *Uptown Comedy Club* had ended, one of the perks of not being bound to any one gig was that I could make my own schedule, and the nice thing about that was that there was actually a schedule *to* make. I was well past dreaming about being a comedian. Booking shows in and around New York was way easier, and I was getting more and more college and out-of-town gigs, too.

For convenience and sanity's sake, Dee and I moved from New Jersey closer to the city and were living in an upstairs duplex in Franklin Square, Long Island, above this elderly couple who were also our landlords. This brought us a little closer to Eddie's three sons, too, who were just north of the city in Connecticut. I couldn't get them off my mind, and I felt a great responsibility to be there for them. And they were slipping. Big-time. They were all teenagers now—a tough enough time for any young guy, father or no father.

A couple years earlier, right after Eddie had passed away, one

Sunday afternoon Dee and I took a drive up to visit the boys, and the youngest one, Billy, who was about eleven at the time, met us at the door.

"Uncle Jim," he said proudly, "you're going to love this. You've got to see what I made for Dad." He led us to his bedroom and showed me this little shrine he'd made out of family pictures, a necktie of Eddie's, and a LEGO set they'd once built together. "This oughta help me keep Dad's memory alive, right?"

He said it so earnestly, and the way he'd put it together and showed it off to us was so innocent, that my knees nearly buckled. It gave me a lump in my throat for a week afterward. Well, that shrine was sweet, but it ultimately couldn't keep Billy from getting into serious trouble shortly thereafter. I couldn't imagine having to go through the death of a parent like that, so I was in no position to judge the kid.

By age twelve or thirteen, Billy was boozing it up and had his stomach pumped in the ER several times. He was just lost, trying to make sense of it all. The middle brother, Eddie, who was a couple years older, also just totally fell off the cliff. He had a real anger built up inside of him, and he was wild as could be. The oldest son, Christian, was at first glance the most like his father and did not rebel at all. If anything, Eddie's death made him more responsible, studious, and committed to being a success like his dad was. In a weird way, that made it even harder on his younger brothers. The younger two had been straight-A students, too, but that soon went out the window.

I watched it all unfolding and realized I should step in. So one year, as New Year's Eve was approaching, when Billy was thirteen, I called Eddie's wife with a half baked but well-intentioned plan.

"Do you think it would be helpful if Dee and I took Billy in for a few nights over New Year's?"

"Of course," she said immediately.

"I'm doing a bunch of sets in the city on New Year's Eve, and he can tag along and be me and Dee's special guest."

"Come and pick him up anytime. I know he's going to love it."

The plan was for me to do a set around midnight at this club in the Village and for Billy to come along and watch it. Dee was nearby with some of her girlfriends, and we were all going to meet at a diner afterward. And then I'd do even more sets late into the night.

On the way into the club, I asked the bouncer, who seemed like a nice guy, to keep an eye on Billy and to keep him away from the drunks. There was a little foyer behind the bouncer, where Billy would be able to take a seat on a stool, stay out of the cold, and watch me do my set. In my mind, this was a great solution.

So I did my twenty-minute set and grabbed Billy, and we started walking down Bleecker Street.

"Uncle Jim," he said, "I'm hungry. Can we just grab a slice of pizza quick before we meet Dee?"

"Of course," I said. It was New Year's Eve. As far as I was concerned, Billy could have whatever he wanted. So we walked into this little narrow pizza place, and there were a few revelers seated in there, eating slices off paper plates at round tables. We walked up to the register to order, and all along the walls there were mirrors to make the place feel bigger, I suppose.

Anyway, I started to eyeball the slices, but out of the corner of my eye, in the mirror, I could see two college-age dudes laughing at us from their table. They spotted me looking at them and kept laughing and gave me a thumbs-up.

"Amateur night," I said to myself, writing them off as moronic drunks. But on the other side of me, there was an older guy who was shooting me disapproving looks, like I was a total child molester.

Then one of the two college dudes piped up. "That's cool that you've got the little guy out and you're getting him messed up for New Year's! We salute you!"

I turned to ask them what the hell they were talking about, but they were finished eating and throwing away their garbage and walking out. I looked down at Billy for the first time since we'd gotten in there. He'd seemed totally fine on the walk, but his eyes were now all screwy and he was weaving and hanging on to the counter like it was a waterskiing towrope.

"What the hell happened to you?" I said.

He didn't answer me. Out the front window of the pizza place, two cops on horses trotted past and caught his eye, and he slurred, "I wanna go pet the horses." And he started staggering toward the door. I freaked out. If he got out there, I was sure I was going to get arrested for something, and I didn't even know what was the matter with Billy.

"Oh, Uncle Jim," he slurred. His face lit up, he had a plan. "Look at the cops. We gotta talk to 'em and find out the horses' names. We gotta let them know how much we like the horses. Wouldn't it be awesome to ride one? Think they'd give me a ride on one?"

"Come on," I said, grabbing ahold of his arm. "Let's slow down, champ."

"No!" he said, walking out the door. I was reaching for his jacket collar, trying to delicately—but forcefully—steer him away from the cops without looking like a crazed child abuser, but it was close to impossible. "I don't think you understand me! I *need* to ride one of those horses! It's New Year's Eve!"

And then in the middle of Bleecker Street he slurred, "Happy New Year's, New York City!" at the top of his lungs.

I was beside myself. We had two blocks to walk to the diner to meet Dee, and I felt like this was an unbelievable task I had in front of me. Like tiptoeing past sleeping Nazis or climbing Mt. Everest or whatever. The only thing that worked on Billy was his voice box. His legs had turned to pure jelly, and I didn't look forward to explaining a wobbling thirteen-year-old to the authorities, or worse, having him die on me. I had no idea what he was on. This was turning into the worst after-school special you could imagine. And I was in the middle of it.

As we edged farther from the cops, I asked him again, "Billy, what did you have tonight? Can you please tell me?"

"Ah, jeez, Jim," he said. "Just a coupla beers."

"Where did you get beers from?" I said. I was livid.

"I love what ya do, Jim," he said. "This has got to be the greatest New Year's Eve of my life."

"Where did you get the beers?"

"The bouncer got me a sixer of bottles."

"A freakin' six-pack?"

"Relax," he slurred. "I could only finish five of 'em."

We made it safely to the diner. Dee and all of her friends were sitting in a booth wearing the tiaras and New Year's Eve trinket-y stuff and laughing it up. They scooted over to make room for us, and so now, as the clock struck twelve and everybody was whooping it up, I was across the table from a drunken thirteen-year-old.

If you've ever been in a diner while drunk, it can go one of two ways. You eat something greasy and blissfully relax, or you get the spins and the fluorescent lights really start to irritate you and everyone's food grosses you out, and you can feel your temperature rising and you just need to bail and get fresh air before you puke all over everything. Which way do you think it would go for a thirteen-year-old kid who's had sixty ounces of beer in twenty minutes?

Billy kept bobbing and weaving in the diner, just as he had in the pizza place. And sure enough, pretty soon everyone in there was looking at us, and I'm sure it looked bad. Really bad. It's a real buzz kill to see a young teenager wasted when you are tipsy yourself. And that's what we had on our hands, on display for all the partiers to see. And soon Billy was starting to heave, like doing the worm, from the stomach up to his head. Within three seconds, I leapt up from my seat, grabbed him by the collar again, and pushed him out the doors of the diner. We made it a foot before he started puking down a staircase to a basement-level apartment.

He was geysering up buckets of vomit just off of Sixth Avenue in the Village on probably the most crowded night of the year in the city. And sure enough, in between all of the bouts of retching, I began to hear another familiar sound. The *clip-clop, clip-clop* of police horses. I was near a lot of restaurants, so I already began to formulate a defense in case the cops stopped: "The kid just overindulged tonight. Cheese fries. Doritos. Giant soda. He overdid it. New Year's Eve. What are ya gonna do?"

Luckily, they didn't stop. But now puke was coming out of his nose, and it just wouldn't quit. I started panicking, thinking he had more than just beer. Who could puke that much after just forty-five minutes? I was really nervous that I was going to have to take him to get his stomach pumped, and that's when the shit would really hit the fan.

"Did you do *any* shots?" I said. "Tell me the truth."

"No! Swear to God!"

"'Cause if you did, I'm going to have to take you to the hospital."

"No! No! I promise."

"I don't want to have to call your mom!"

"No," he groaned. "Don't call her! Don't call her!"

We sat there for at least another half an hour. He probably weighed 85 pounds and puked 145 pounds. Then Dee came outside to check on us.

"Dee," I said calmly, "this kid won't stop puking. We've gotta just get out of here. Can you get some plastic bags from the restaurant that he can barf into on the drive home?"

"Yeah," she said. And that was pretty much the end of her New Year's Eve fun.

Billy puked all over the car, everywhere except into the plastic bags we'd grabbed. It was about 30 degrees out, but with the smell in the car we braved the cold with the windows rolled down for the whole forty-five-minute drive.

We got home to Franklin Square, and naturally he was even less mobile than he had been when he was puking down the stairwell in Manhattan. Dee unlocked the door, and I carried Billy up the steps and into the foyer. I had this great plan to throw him over my shoulder and fireman-carry him up the creaky wooden stairs, but he was a dead weight. It felt like trying to lug a giant deflated life raft up a flight of stairs. The sound of me readjusting Billy woke up the elderly neighbor couple, who were also our landlords and had a door adjoining the stairway.

All the husband saw were his tenants attempting to lug a drunken teenager up the stairs.

"Holy Jesus," the old man whined. "What did you do? Is that the thing now? Get the kids inebriated?"

Soon his wife was standing behind him in her housecoat with her hand over her mouth. "Proud of yourselves?" she muttered.

"I'm sorry," I said, doing my best to hoist Billy up the stairs. "I gotta explain this to you later."

"Don't bother," the old man shouted. I was sure we were going to be evicted. Once inside, I stripped Billy down to his underwear, put him in the shower, and just hosed him down. During the process, he eventually passed out. I dried him off and put him to bed.

He slept until noon the next day. He woke up and wandered into the kitchen, and I poured him an orange juice and sat down with him.

"No one was prepared for what happened last night," I told him. "You weren't. I wasn't. And that's really dangerous."

He just nodded.

"You can't escape from what happened by getting wasted."

He nodded again.

"And you can't behave like this to the people that care about you."

He didn't answer right away. He took another sip of his orange juice and then looked up and said, "Do you think it would be cool if I moved in with you guys?"

"Uh, no," Dee said immediately.

"Yeah," I said. It would have been like housing the Tasmanian Devil. "I don't think any of us are ready for that. But here's the thing: Call me as much as you want. Come visit as much as you want. I'll call you. I'll come visit you. And if you tell your mom what happened, I will find you and beat you up."

"I get it," he said quietly.

"I'm sorry, Billy," I said. "I don't have any answers for you. I'd be lying if I did. You got a raw deal. But alcohol and drugs aren't going to help."

I didn't want to tell his mom about what had happened because I feared she'd *never* let me watch him or try to help again. Not surprisingly, the partying continued. His brother Eddie Jr. was worse. He began collecting guns and broke into some houses. It took a long time before they got on the right track. Later, when I think I was more capable of helping and the boys were more receptive to growing and figuring things out, I'd bring Eddie Jr. out on tour with me.

By the way, I went back and got that bouncer fired.

* * *

Around this same time, I found myself touring some far-flung places I'd never been to before, including Fairbanks, Alaska. I wasn't going to make a lot of money after expenses, but it represented a good escape from everything. I don't remember anything about the gig, but afterward, a bunch of people took me over to a bar that was built into a giant barn. The ceiling was spacious, they had well over a hundred different beers on tap, and the open areas were filled with pool tables and jukeboxes.

The best part about it was outside there was a giant fire pit. It was bitterly cold that night, and if you faced the fire, you could feel the heat rippling up your face, while the backside of your body turned numbingly cold within two minutes. As I stood there rotating like a rotisserie chicken, one side of the sky started turning a bunch of colors, green, orange, red, blue, yellow. Someone told me it was the Northern Lights. I'd never seen them before.

* * *

The next morning, before my flight out, I went into an empty little hippie café. I sat down and listened to Tom Petty come on the radio right after the Rolling Stones. I began to reflect on my trip, the Northern Lights, and how lucky I was to be doing this for a living. I started to talk to Eddie in my head. "You would have loved the Northern Lights, Eddie. You'd really like this lifestyle. I miss you so much. I miss your guidance, too. I wish I knew more about business, and I wish you were here with me right now." As I was thinking, and saying all of this stuff in my head, I really felt like Eddie could hear it. As soon as I said, "I wish you were here with me right now," sure enough, "Sailing" by Christopher Cross came on the radio. I had tons of great memories of Eddie taking me sailing out in the Long Island Sound, and that song had always made me think of him. I couldn't hold back the tears. What were the odds? It was so unreal. I felt it was a message directly from Eddie himself, purposely toying with me.

Chapter 9

God Fired Me from *Buddies* So I Wouldn't Cheat on Dee

The *Uptown Comedy Club* show was a grassroots operation right in the middle of a gritty neighborhood, and it kept me humble. *Buddies*, the prime-time sitcom on ABC I landed a couple of years later, was the complete opposite. Before I even filmed one episode, I began to view the show as my one-way, first-class ticket straight to the VIP world of celebs. My head swelled, and I forgot all the valuable lessons I'd soaked up in Valley Stream, Florida, and Harlem.

The premise of the show was really unique. You could call it groundbreaking. Dave Chappelle and I were going to play buddies. And here's the twist: He's black and I'm white. Okay, so maybe it wasn't so original. But it was an opportunity to work with Dave, and that was something I couldn't turn down.

I'd been friends with Dave for a couple of years. One night Phil, my old buddy from the Jefferson Avenue gang, came into the city from Valley Stream to check out some comedy clubs. As luck would have it, we wandered into the Boston Comedy Club, near NYU in the West Village, took our seats in the back, and waited for the next comedian to take the stage. It was Dave—and before he even opened his mouth, Phil and I were sold on him. He had quick, funny gestures and a way of exaggerating his body language without forcing it.

"Who's he?" Phil whispered.

"No idea," I said, "but he's going to be a star."

"No kidding," Phil replied.

And we just sat for the next twenty minutes with our mouths hanging open. Dave just improvised the whole time, asking the crowd questions, then going into riffs about apartments, cops, getting high. As soon as he came offstage, I went out of my way to introduce myself, and that was something I usually didn't do. It didn't always seem genuine, but in this case, I was really approaching the guy with praise.

After that Dave and I would see each other on the circuit all the time, and we'd goof around trying to make each other crack up. Pretty soon, we shared the same manager, Leon. He'd helped me wrangle free from the Rat, with whom I'd be tied up in litigation well into the midnineties. Leon worked hard at finding projects for us, and before too long Dave and I each had these wonderful *almost-completed* development deals—where a network pays you not to do anything else while they try to develop a show for you. I was on the verge of a huge one at NBC, with the guy who produced *The Fresh Prince of Bel-Air*. They'd work on a sitcom for me, while I would collect $250,000 and sit still for one year.

Dave had an even bigger deal in the works at HBO. A completely unheard-of, pants-crappingly huge amount of cash for a stand-up special *and* his own talk show. To top it off, he was only nineteen or twenty. He was on fire. I remember my wife and I went to see him in *Robin Hood: Men in Tights*, the Mel Brooks movie, and both of us thinking, "Wow, this is the coolest thing in the world. Look at Dave! He's in a movie! He has it totally made!"

While this stuff was going on, unbeknownst to Dave and me, Leon scored himself a producing deal at Disney/ABC. He then went to them and said, "I have two of the hottest young comedians working now. They're about to do separate deals, but *I* can deliver them to you together. Let's develop a sitcom around both of them." If ABC bought it, Leon would be making money on both ends of the equation. My gut told me not to leave the *Fresh Prince* guy and NBC dangling. My agent Ruth was really against Leon's plan, too. She and I were introduced by Leon, and I knew from the get-go that she had my back. She helped my career tremendously.

"There's a lot of passion for Jim at NBC," she'd tell Leon during these long, drawn-out conference calls.

"Well," Leon would grumble, "we'll go and get an on-air guarantee from ABC." And we went around in circles for a few days until one day that's what he did. The money Disney/ABC offered Dave and me was drastically lower than what else was on the table, but they promised Dave and me three guest appearances on *Home Improvement* and a minimum of six episodes of *Buddies*. No matter what, I was going to get the money. But I wasn't thinking of the money. I was thinking, "I am going to be on TV very soon."

Still, my feeling on this was awful. But just like when I signed with the Rat, I had a way of letting my greedy brain overrule my gut. I called up Dave to see what he thought.

"I gotta be honest with you," I told him. "I don't know if I would walk away from an HBO deal. That's every young comic's dream—to have their own HBO special."

"Jim," Dave said, "it's not one special. It's two."

"Then you're really crazy."

"And don't forget the talk show."

"So, why are we even on the phone?" I said. "I really have to advise you against this ABC thing."

Still, ABC was going to put us on the air. The other things were *likely* to happen, but not 100 percent, and Dave and I found ourselves sucked in by the immediacy the *Buddies* deal offered. We made a pact with each other.

"I'm not going to do *Buddies* if you don't do it," he said.

"Well, I'm not going to do it if you don't do it," I said. "But again, I've got to stress, I don't know if I would do it if I was you. I'm not too worried about me, but you're a little farther ahead in the game than I am."

We went back and forth on this for a while, until in a stroke of pure genius we decided to do *Buddies*. By the time Dave and I landed in L.A. to make the pilot episode, every celebrity-chasing woman in Hollywood knew why we were there, and every aspiring actor envied us. At night, we would go out to the Improv and I would strut around with an attitude like "Get used to it, you're gonna be seeing me everywhere."

One night Drew Carey was standing next to me—this was long before his show even aired—and he said, "No offense, but I hope your show tanks, because I'm next in line after you guys."

I said, "No offense taken, but I'm pretty sure we've got a hit. And we're guaranteed six episodes, either way, so enjoy the wait."

"Okay," he said. "No problem. I'll just be hanging around. You know, waiting for you to fail."

I liked Drew and his deadpan humor, and knew he was half-joking, but that conversation underscored a truth I'd soon discover about Hollywood—envy, pettiness, and competition fueled every part of the machine. That attitude permeated every conversation and seemed to serve as people's main motivation for doing what they did—trying to be a star at any cost. I began to fit right in.

Our home for the next few months was the Sheraton Universal Hotel. Even though we were newlyweds, Dee stayed behind in New York, working her job as a nanny. She wanted to make sure this sitcom was going to fly before she quit her job. I felt single again. Single in a city full of young women, with skies that were sunny and blue, and where I was cruising around in a free Ford Mustang convertible.

Dave, on the other hand, was given a Lincoln Town Car. It was too nice to be a taxi and too small to be a limo. But still, it had *chauffeur-driven vehicle* written all over it. The studio used a special car leasing company for long-term rentals, and since Dave didn't drive much, when it came time to pick out a car, he told the lady, "Just bring me whatever. I'm cool with anything." Well, Dave definitely wasn't cool with the Town Car.

The car leasing company had a guy drive it up to the hotel, and I think when Dave saw him pull up, he just thought the guy was picking someone up to take to the airport. But then, the guy parked the car, jumped out, tossed Dave the keys, and handed him the paperwork.

Dave turned and looked at me and whispered, "It's because I'm black."

"You think the woman on the phone knew you were black," I asked him, "and decided to give you a Town Car?"

"Oh, she *knew* all right," he said with a sneer. "Always givin' the black guy a pimp mobile," he muttered. "And not even a good pimp mobile at that. Stupid Town Car."

But it didn't take long for Dave to get the itch to start driving that pimp mobile around. Our first stop was an acting lesson at Gordon Hunt's house in Beverly Hills. The directors had been all over us about developing our craft. To me, this was exciting because Gordon was *Mad About You* star Helen Hunt's dad. Dave and I both wanted to drive our new cars, so we did just that. I'd follow closely behind Dave because, well, he sucked at driving.

Dave had grown up in D.C. but spent a lot of time in New York City, obviously, and had never really gotten a handle on driving. And that was no biggie. But the thing was, this was L.A., a whole new sprawling territory where you used a car to get around, not the smelly Q train. So he couldn't wait to get behind the wheel.

"Dave," I said, trying to warn him one day as he was about to leave our hotel, "traffic here is nothing like anyone has ever seen. Even people that are from here can't take it. That's why they have freeway shooters in California. People get so aggravated that they just shoot random drivers. It's practically legal."

"I hear you, man," he said.

"Just be careful," I said.

"Yes. I hear you, man."

"Check your mirrors and your blind spot before you change lanes," I told him. "And don't give anyone the finger. Never, ever do that."

Dave just nodded, tossing the keys from one hand to the other impatiently.

"Better yet, don't even make eye contact with any other driver," I said. "And keep your driver's license in your shirt pocket. That way they'll be able to identify you quicker, in case something happens."

Dave pulled cautiously out of the hotel parking lot and I followed behind him in my Mustang as we made our way to the freeway. I could see him getting more comfortable behind the wheel, bobbing his head to his car stereo. Then came the moment of truth—the on-ramp. Dave coasted down it flawlessly, put his turn signal on, changed lanes, and drove perfectly for about three hundred yards before he got into a fender bender. It looked almost calculated, like bumper cars. He tapped the back bumper of a Chevy economy car, driven by a little Asian guy.

Both Dave and the little Asian guy pulled over to the side of the road as cars whizzed past. As I pulled up behind them, I could see the Asian guy looking kind of cautious as he got out of his car, because it was such a weird accident, like maybe the collision was done on purpose, a setup in order to rob him. Dave hopped out of the Town Car, shaking his head, hands up in the air, saying, "My bad. My bad."

Then, as Dave started to reach into his pocket, probably to show the guy proof he was actually allowed to be driving, I jumped out of my Mustang laughing my ass off. This totally spooked the little Asian guy. He freaked out and looked at us like we were going to carjack him. He started running backward, glasses falling off, yelling, "This is a setup! I know it." And he jumped into his car and got the hell out of there.

There wasn't, in the end, just the one accident. When we got to Gordon Hunt's, I saw that his driveway had an elaborate rock wall and as I pulled in I stared at it and drifted too close to it, completely scraping and mangling the side of my Mustang. I never reported that. I felt like it was one of the hazards of lending out a Mustang to a comedian. You shouldn't expect to get it back perfect. I didn't even tell Gordon, because I didn't want to have to pay to repair my acting coach's driveway wall.

We hadn't been in California too long before Dave went through three more cars. He just kept calling the car leasing company and trading them in. He didn't like any of them. It was like the princess and the pea with that guy. I started to think that maybe Dave and driving didn't mix.

Finally, late one night, just as I was ready to go to bed before a big day of rehearsing, there was a knock on my hotel room door. I opened it reluctantly and there was Dave, just standing there, smiling.

"Let's go cruising!" he said.

"What?" I asked. "Come on. Do you realize what time we have to be on set?"

"I got a new Toyota."

"We've been through this before," I said, rubbing my eyes. "You're gonna hate it in twenty-four hours."

"No," he insisted, "this time it's real. I went out and got a new leather jacket. A *driving* jacket. And a bunch of new CDs. This car is changing my life."

"All right," I said. "But I'm driving, too. I'll follow you."

So we pulled out of the hotel parking lot and drove through Laurel Canyon down into Hollywood. I saw Dave's head bobbing up and down, Dave getting into his music. I had my top down. We were living the dream.

We got to Melrose, parked our cars, and went into a coffee shop. We were eating some dessert, drinking coffee, talking about how great everything was, and then Dave looked out the window and said, "Man, I think I just saw my car go by."

"What?" I asked. I thought maybe he was hallucinating.

"I think I just saw my car go by," he repeated. "Out the window. I'm sure of it."

"Dave," I said, trying to reassure him. "There's a lot of Toyotas in the city. Relax."

"I gotta get out of here and find out."

We paid the check and walked down the street. We passed by my Mustang. Top down. CDs were scattered all over the seats and the floor. I think I even had a gym bag sitting on the backseat. All of it was untouched. We strolled by a couple more cars, nothing unusual, and then we turned the corner and saw an empty space where Dave's car had been.

"Maybe the cops took it," Dave said, scrambling for an answer. "Maybe it got towed."

"I think the first stage of loss is denial, Dave." While he stood there in shock, I looked around at the parking signs to see if maybe it had been towed.

He folded his arms together and gritted his teeth. "This is some foul, foul shit."

"Who cares?" I asked him. "They'll just bring you a new car."

"It's the principle," he said, boiling over. "I just put gas in that car. And my leather jacket was in there. Some brother," he said, "is driving my car, wearing my leather jacket, blasting my Mary J. Blige CD, with a full tank of my gas. Damn, that burns my ass up!"

Maybe Dave's car hex was an apt metaphor for my whole time in California, because professionally, things were just as screwy. For starters, we were going to do the three episodes of *Home Improvement*, and when we got on set, Tim Allen was *such* a dick. Froze us out. Could not have ignored us any more if he tried. And whenever he did address us, he purposely called us by each other's names. We were taping one day, in front of a live audience, including some ABC executives who were involved with *Buddies*, and after about the eighteenth take, the director became frustrated.

"Tim," he said, clearly unhappy. "Could you please get these guys' names right?"

"Why?" Tim said sarcastically. "Is it upsetting the suits?" Chilly.

Looking back, I don't blame him. I think he didn't like the whole setup. You take a super-successful television guy and use his show to spin off two new guys' show and he gets no credit? That's ballsy.

But at the time, I just thought Tim Allen was a jerk. I'd hoped we would bond, but instead I walked around wondering why he didn't know how awesome I was. Soon ABC shortened our "guaranteed" *Home Improvement* run from three episodes to one episode. No biggie. Except for the next bit of news. Leon called my hotel room one night.

"They want to let go of Dave," he said.

"Let *go?*" I said.

"Fire him," he responded. "ABC doesn't like him. He didn't test well."

"They can't get rid of Dave," I said.

"Don't worry," Leon said, "we'll work it out."

Also, at that time, HBO was trying to sue Dave for walking away from his deal. Even though nothing had been signed, there was trouble. So from what I understood Disney/ABC was going to have to pony up to make things good with HBO. Maybe they just wanted to get rid of Dave to end the drama. And to top it off, all of Leon's clients were now banned from HBO. There was no way any of us were ever getting on HBO. Eventually we moved forward with taping *Buddies*, and just as strangely as they surfaced, the rumors of Dave being let go drifted away.

Despite the on-set chilliness of *Home Improvement*, my gut telling me I'd made the wrong decision (while my ego told me I'd made the right one), and Dave's constant car issues, the thing that troubled me the most in L.A. was the ever-present feeling I had that I was going to cheat on Dee. I'd parachuted into a town of hot, superficial women who were interested in me only because I was going to be a TV star. I never had so many females wanting to hang out and be with me, inviting me to parties and hot tubs and parties in hot tubs. I had never dealt with that, and now I was confronted with it several times a day, and I didn't know if I was strong enough to handle it.

As always, when I got in a jam, I started to talk to God. Actually, I was praying my balls off to Him that he'd help me avoid ruining my marriage. In my heart, I was fully into Dee—but my ego was trying to overrule my heart just like it had overruled my gut.

I made rationalizations based on what I saw all around me. There was no way I couldn't have a girl on the West Coast *and* my wife, just like everyone else. Why not? That was just what you did in L.A., especially if you were a TV star.

I begged God, constantly, to step in and save me somehow.

What made the situation worse was that Dee said she wasn't going to quit her nannying job, even though she'd complain about it every time we talked.

"Why can't you quit and come out here with me?" I'd ask her. "Isn't this what our dream is?" To me, the solution was simple, but Dee wouldn't do it. And that was pissing me off.

"Listen," she'd say, "it's not that easy. This family needs me. It's a regular job, and we don't know yet how the show's going to pan out for you."

All that told me was that she didn't respect what I was doing. She didn't understand. And all of the frivolous attention I was receiving only fueled my anger toward Dee even more. Did she not realize that everyone out here knew that I was a star with a bright future? Why couldn't she? As far as I was concerned, I already had a hit show. I didn't want to sit and listen to her complain about laundry.

And she also knew my eye was wandering. All of her instincts were spot-on. "Are you cheating on me?" she'd ask.

"No," I would say, which was the physical truth, if not emotionally honest.

And the thing was, all of these arguments, discussions, and tough questions took place via telephone, at my hotel. This was the pre–cell phone era. So once I hung up, I could just disappear and stay out of touch, with no calls or texts to help remind me what I had back East. The temptation was intense.

There was a sea of resentment brewing inside of me, and it took me further away from the guy I thought I was—the one who not so long ago had cleverly plotted his seaside proposal, then cried tears of joy when his girlfriend said she'd marry him. Where the hell was *that* guy?

Instead, I'd gotten to the point where I was more committed to cheating than I was to upholding my marital vows. I'd even set a date in my mind when I'd act upon my selfish desires. Dee hadn't planned a single visit yet, so to me her absence and preoccupation with taking care of someone else's kids was as good as a green light. If she didn't care, neither did I. I was doing a set at the Laugh Factory one night— I was doing two sets a week while I was in L.A. to keep my stand-up skills fresh—and after it was over, I was going to go for it with whoever was around.

Still, I'd been praying like crazy for a sign that my marriage wasn't over. Sure enough, just as the host was about to introduce me, Dee surprised me by walking into the club. I couldn't talk to her or hug her because I was going onstage, but I was elated and relieved. But despite this obvious sign that my future was with Dee, my ego still kept screwing with me. When I saw her walk into the club, a part of me was also angry that her showing up had ruined my chance at cheating. I was so messed up that I looked past the fact that my prayers had literally been answered when Dee walked into the Laugh Factory.

Dee and I had fun during her visit. Dave and I were on the front section of USA Today, and as she and I drove around apartment hunting—she was warming up to the idea of moving—we looked at it together and cried. For that moment, we felt like we'd won the lottery. But after Dee went back to New York, my feelings about cheating and my disillusionment about the fact that I still wanted to go through with it only grew more urgent. I came to the conclusion that this town was going to beat the snot out of our marriage, and I was going to cheat. Heck, maybe Dee was going to cheat. I prayed and prayed for yet another sign.

And soon one came. A big one. The commercials were already airing for the first episode of Buddies. We were on the cover of TV Guide. My friends from Valley Stream Phil and Gene flew out to see us film an episode.

One day the three of us rented a limo and went to Disneyland. When we got back to my hotel room, there were messages from Leon. He was staying a couple floors down from me. I picked up the phone and called him back.

"Hey," I said. In the background, the guys were raiding my mini-bar and plotting out elaborate room service orders, and I didn't care. I was psyched to be showing off for them.

"Hi, Jim," Leon said. "Can you come down here for a second?"

"Yeah," I said. "Mind if I bring the guys down to meet you?"

"You should come alone," he said solemnly.

"Okay, no problem."

I took the elevator down to his room and he told me to take a seat on the couch. He was lying on his bed and he didn't look well. He was pale. My first thought was, "Oh my God, they actually fired Dave

Chappelle." But we were too far along. There was no way they were going to fire him now. The ABC machine was up and running.

"Jim," he said, "I don't know how to tell you this, but you and the show are not going to go."

"What do you mean?" I asked incredulously. "The show's not going?"

"No," he said, propping himself up on his arm. "The show is going. You're not. They fired you."

I didn't see any of this coming. Not a rumbling. No rumors. Nothing.

"What about Dave?"

"We can't find him to tell him," Leon said. "He's not answering the phone."

When I walked back into my room my friends could tell immediately that something terrible had just gone down.

"What happened?" Phil asked.

"They fired me from the show."

They started laughing. I didn't. "You're kidding, right?" Gene said.

"No," I said. "I'm not kidding."

"Can they do that?" Gene asked.

"They just did," I said.

"Well," Gene said, "we're still taking the limo out all night, 'cause it ain't like you got a job to go to in the morning."

And we started to laugh. He brought it all right back to being a teenager. There was nothing to wake up for in the morning, so we might as well party. It was pure Valley Stream logic, and it was exactly what I needed to help me process what had happened.

So we went out in the limo. Once we were driving around I told the guys, "I've got to do a spot at the Improv just to get this out of my system." We pulled up at the club and I was immediately set upon by a random comedian who shook my hand.

"Hey, lemme ask you something," he said.

"Shoot."

"Let me get your perspective on your character." Before I could even ask what he was talking about, he added, "Sorry you got fired. But I'm going in to read for your part tomorrow, and I just want to know how I should play the guy."

And the same thing kept happening the rest of the night. That's how fast the powers that be were casting for my part. It made me think ABC must have known for a while that they were going to get rid of me. Why didn't they clue me in earlier and salvage a little bit of my dignity? Back at the hotel, the phone rang with calls from different people on the cast. I walked into the bathroom, away from my friends, to talk to the woman who played my character's wife.

"I feel so terrible," she said. "I'm so sorry. Did they tell you why? Did they tell you anything?"

"No. I don't really know why," I told her. "All I heard today is that they might cast Brendan Fraser for my part."

Her mood changed immediately.

"I love Brendan Fraser!" She squealed. "That would be so awesome."

That's really when it sank in that L.A. was nuts. It was a cold town.

I caught up with Dave a couple of days later and we went out for lunch.

"I gotta stay on, man," he said, half frowning, referring to the show. It was true. What other choice did he have?

A twentysomething waitress/actress came up to our table, and as she was taking our order, she looked us up and down. "You guys look familiar," she said. "Are you in town for pilot season?"

"Um, yeah," I mumbled. Dave started laughing.

"That's so cool," she said. "So"—she leaned into the table, lowering her voice to a whisper—"did you hear about the guy who was *fired* from his sitcom after just one show? All the commercials were already airing with him in them. It's crazy."

Dave laughed even harder.

"Yeah," I replied. "I heard that he doesn't even know why he was fired. They gave him no answers. Nothing."

"Gosh, that's terrible," she said, putting a hand over her mouth. "I can only imagine how he feels."

"I know!" I said. I thought Dave was going to fall out of his chair. "I can only imagine how he feels, too."

The first of several final insults was set in motion the next day. In *Variety*, there was a story about my getting fired. "He's a great talent," the suits at ABC/Disney said. "We just had to go with more of a veteran for that role." Reading that, Fox called immediately and had me audition for a show called *Herman's Head*. I went over, auditioned, and got the part, right there on the spot.

That night my phone rang. It was my agent Ruth.

"Jim," she huffed, "you're not going to believe this." She sounded like she was dying to throw something.

"Now what?"

"Disney won't let you out of your contract. So you can't do *Herman's Head*," she said with a sigh. Sometimes she got the bad news before Leon, and this was one of those times. "They said to just sit tight, and they'll find a pilot for you to jump onto."

Now I just wanted to get the hell out of L.A. God had already answered my prayers. I wasn't going to cheat on Dee. Getting fired made me put the truly important things in perspective real quick. I just wanted to be back in New York with my wife. I called Dee.

"Why can't you just tell them you're going home?" she asked.

I didn't have an answer. What could they do to me if I left? I didn't want to find out. Dee's whole point of view was based on simple common sense. But there was no common sense in Hollywood, so I couldn't ask those kinds of questions because I was worried I'd piss the wrong person off. I wish I had the strength to listen to her back then, instead of trying to stick it out. When you've got stars in your eyes, you're a dog chasing the stick.

Soon Ruth got a call about *Clerks,* a series based on the Kevin Smith movie of the same name. I loved Kevin and I was glad to hear he was writing the show. I was given the part of Randall without an audition. On my first day on set, one of the producers approached me.

"It's been kind of a dramatic time around here," he said. "We hope you'll bear with us."

"What do you mean?" I asked.

"We parted ways with Kevin," he explained. Super. Kevin was the whole reason *Clerks* existed in the first place. That would be like doing *Star Wars* without George Lucas's involvement. He was why I was excited to do the show, and I never even got to meet him before they got rid of him. That meant another call to Dee.

"Is that all they ever do is fire people out there?" she asked.

"Yes," I said. "That's why I am getting out of *out there.*"

We filmed the pilot and I got released. I could go home for a month. If *Clerks* was picked up, the show would be a midseason replacement on the WB. Back in New York, I got another phone call. They'd fired my *Clerks* costar because he didn't test well. So they needed to reshoot the whole pilot, which meant I had to go back to L.A. for a couple more weeks, only this time I didn't ask for a Mustang convertible.

In the end, the aborted, maligned version of *Clerks* never did become a midseason replacement and *Buddies* lasted on ABC for five episodes. Looking back on this whole period fifteen years later, I can see that it wasn't a waste. I learned that I wasn't a Hollywood kind of guy, and it was good that I found that out in my twenties instead of my forties. And of course I'm *waaayyy* glad that I never cheated on Dee. That would have been chasing short-term gratification at the cost of a long-term journey, and also the worst mistake of my life.

Chapter 10

Joining *Saturday Night Live* . . . and Becoming Joe Pesci

As the *Buddies* debacle came to a close and the *Clerks* pilot stalled, wouldn't you know, execs from NBC came sniffing around again, basically telling me, "When you're done with your ABC/Disney deal, let's talk. No hard feelings about breaking the earlier deal." I was unbelievably appreciative. Their plan, apparently, was to try to develop something for me for their late-night lineup. By mid-June, they had a new suggestion: *Saturday Night Live* was revamping for a new season. Did I want to audition?

My first thought was, "Dear God, no." I knew Jay Mohr, whose status as a cast member was in limbo going into the summer of '95, and he was not happy. A disgruntled Janeane Garofalo had bailed partway through the last season, and I'd heard plenty of horror stories from other people associated with the show. Without fail, they all hated their experience on *SNL*. Everyone coming out of that factory was miserable, and I didn't want to be angry and ugly, because you know what? I was already there. I needed to get back to doing something uplifting.

After the Fourth of July weekend, NBC came back and said, "It's gonna be different this year. Please, just audition." In the end, I decided I'd give it a go. Why not? How could it go worse than my stint in L.A.? If I made the cast, *Saturday Night Live* would at least allow me to stay in New York. And after thinking a bit about the show's legacy, I had to admit I was honored they were reaching out to me. At the time the show was at its nadir, but it was still *SNL*.

One afternoon in July I went to Studio 8H at Rockefeller Center in midtown Manhattan for my first audition. I walked in the room and it seemed like not a single person was there. A female page wielding a clipboard told me to get on that famous Studio 8H stage and go right into my act. It was like walking into a warehouse. My footsteps echoed loudly in the deadly quiet room. Once I was onstage, I spotted Lorne Michaels, pacing and scratching his chin, with a few other executives buried in the shadows behind him.

I'd been warned in advance that no one watching was going to laugh and that the cameras pointed at me were set up so execs at NBC in Los Angeles could tune in. I launched into the Shut-up Guy, a character I'd developed to make my friends laugh. He had a heavy New York accent and would ask questions, not wait for an answer, then tell the person he was asking to shut up as they tried to respond. He was your basic irate New York City jerk. As I'd been told to expect, I heard nothing from the small crowd, although at the end a short giggle escaped from a woman in the back of the room. That gave me enough juice to keep going. And I really needed it, because this was not my normal shtick. I do stand-up, and I feed off the crowd's response. I did a few other bits, then capped it off with a fake news report on body piercing from a heavy metal show at Madison Square Garden, complete with pratfalls. It was pretty tough throwing myself to the ground without an audience to play off of. I left thinking my performance was somewhere between a 6 and a 7 on a scale of 1 to 10.

The next morning I was sound asleep when I was awoken by a call from Phil.

"Whatever you do today," he said, "don't read the *New York Post*."

"Gotcha," I said sarcastically. "Sure thing." I was groggy and had no idea what the heck he could be talking about.

I hung up and bolted to the newsstand. Inside the paper there was a huge picture of Lorne and a story about the hunt for new cast members. The story quoted Lorne as saying, "Well, you can write off Jim Breuer." Then it went on to say something like "Breuer has in a matter of a few months already had two sitcoms go bust." Really uplifting stuff. I was *soooo* glad NBC pushed me to audition. I was really confused as to why Lorne would say that to a reporter.

Saturday Night Live was in trouble. A writer from *New York* magazine had embedded himself with the cast and the article he wrote described the show as "Saturday Night Dead." The 1994–95 season was the worst they'd ever had and the show was on life support. To ratchet up the pressure even more, in '95–'96, they'd be going up against the first season of Fox's sketch comedy show *MADtv*. My agent later explained to me that people at NBC—the ones who called me to audition—stepped in and told Lorne that for the first time ever they were going to be part of the audition process and were going to have a say in who got hired.

Obviously, Lorne's response was, "Screw you. It's my show."

The NBC suits said, "Sorry, it's our network, and you're gonna take a good look at Jim Breuer."

So that explained the chilliness. It was a political pissing match, and I was caught right in the middle of it. At the time I had no clue; I knew only that I'd been insulted. Over the next couple of days, I got asked to go back in to talk to Lorne. He'd told my agent he thought I might have been "on something" at the audition.

When I went to Lorne's office, he just sat there eating from a big bowl of popcorn. It was the strangest and most awkward business meeting I'd ever attended. He didn't say much at all as I rambled on uncomfortably about my accomplishments. Eventually he came out with: "I should tell you that some people want you here, and some don't." Not exactly a vote of confidence for me.

I had one more audition at Studio 8H and then had to do stand-up for them one night at the Comic Strip on the Upper East Side. In between, I went back into NBC to meet Lorne again, along with one of the show's writers, Steve Higgins. On my way in, I ran into another writer, Fred Wolf. I knew him from doing stand-up and he was firmly in my corner.

"Do your thing, Jimmy B," he said, shaking my hand. "Don't let them rattle you."

I went into the meeting and sat down with Lorne and Steve. I immediately felt like this was a clique that was going to be tough to penetrate.

"Is that your real hair?" Steve asked.

"My hair?" I had no idea what he was talking about. "Yeah."

"Okay," he said. "You cool with it?"

"Yeah?" I said. I was sure he was screwing with me, and it upset me. I felt like asking if he was okay with his weight and glasses.

He continued. "It's really important that we know if you're bald or not. You'll be doing a lot of different characters, and we need to know if you have implants. You know, like David Spade."

"Oh yeah?" I asked. I thought it was ballsy of him to dish out the gossip to a potential newcomer.

"No," he said. "Just kidding. He doesn't." It felt like a surreal scene from a Coen brothers movie. The rest of the meeting didn't go any better.

After I did the stand-up gig at the Comic Strip, it still took a couple of weeks for NBC to let me know my fate. Lorne told me he had to go to L.A. to make his final decision, and then he'd let me know. "If you get the job," Lorne explained, "we've got a huge cast, so it'll be tough to get on. And if you do get on, then you'll grow and leave the show eventually and you'll resent me like all the others."

I figured that Lorne was upset about losing big cast members like Adam Sandler and Chris Farley (though I'd later learn their parting from the show was a mutual decision), and that the show's struggles were stressing him out. When they told me I got the part, I decided that winning over Lorne would be my number one goal.

NBC held a press conference with Lorne, showing off all of the new and returning cast members. Even Warren Littlefield, the network president, was there fielding questions. Before the festivities started, one of the NBC PR guys made his way through the studio giving out instructions. When he saw me, he stopped and gave me his spiel: "Hustle into makeup, and think about what you're going to say today. Really focus. Have fun, and you'll be fine."

As we all walked down to Studio 8H, it was the first time I realized I was part of something pretty heavy. The hallway was lined with pictures of John Belushi and Dan Aykroyd in their bumblebee suits and Eddie Murphy in his Gumby costume; there were photos of sketches with Steve Martin, Bill Murray, and tons of famous past hosts. The magnitude of the institution began to sink in. A bunch of newspaper and television reporters fanned out in front of a giant table waiting to meet us all. Photographers were snapping pictures, cameramen were shooting video. On the table there was a podium, and behind it stood Lorne and Warren, and behind them, there were bleachers for the cast to stand on. I remember being next to Norm MacDonald—he'd just been admonished for smoking inside the studio—with David Spade positioned one row in front of us. I couldn't believe I'd made the show.

Lorne and Warren addressed the reporters, saying, "We're confident the show is going to rebound. . . . Here's the new cast; if you have any questions, fire away. . . ." So the reporters lobbed some softballs at the cast, nothing too difficult to tackle. Everyone was providing typical sound bites. And then came my turn. Having done stand-up for years by that point, I was pretty confident in my ability as a public speaker.

The first reporter said, "Being from New York, this must be tremendous for you. What was it like watching the show as a kid, and now you're here?"

"I never watched the show as a kid." I instantly had no idea why I admitted that. Norm and David snorted and started chuckling.

The rest of the room grew very quiet, and the look on Lorne's face told me I'd put my foot in my mouth, so I quickly scrambled to make a joke of it: "Yeah, my parents were real sticklers about putting me to bed early." Then Warren tried to help me out even more.

"Okay, Jim," he said, smiling. "But what about when you got older? Surely you watched the show on Saturday nights?" I nearly kicked my teeth out scrambling to stuff my foot back in my mouth.

"When I was older, I was out having fun on Saturday nights," I explained. "I wasn't a *loser*."

Warren was slightly staggered by my incompetence, and Norm started laughing even harder. My face grew very warm. I knew Lorne already didn't like me, and I figured this gaffe was the final nail in my coffin. How could I be so nuts as to sit there and insult this man's franchise?

Then the questioning pivoted to Norm, and my idiocy was soon forgotten.

"Everyone knows that *SNL* is full of partying and wicked practical jokes," one mustached, older reporter said to Norm. "So as a senior cast member, Norm, what kind of practical jokes do you have lined up for the new cast?"

"What?" Norm spat. He hated lame questions like this.

The reporter continued. "Sure. Pranks. Have you got any pranks for the new cast?"

"Oh, oh, I see," Norm said, pretending he now understood the question. "Well," he said with a completely deadpan expression, "the first thing we're going to do is anally rape them. Just take their pants off and stuff 'em. They'll be like, 'Oh my God, I'm being anally raped.'"

Content with his answer, Norm smiled innocently and looked around the room. Crickets. No one said a word. The reporter who asked the question shot Norm an expectant look, like he was waiting for Norm to stop clowning around and elaborate on what real pranks he had concocted.

"So," Norm asked, still totally deadpan, "does that sound like a good prank?"

We'd barely met, and Norm stepped up and took the heat off of me by saying something so offensive and preposterous no one would ever remember what I said. A few of the reporters laughed uncomfortably, others groaned. David Spade did his little machine-gun cackle. Will Ferrell and Molly Shannon snickered, and I muffled my laughter as best I could because I was already on thin ice. Lorne and Warren just smiled gingerly and went to the next reporter with a raised hand.

After the press conference had sufficiently crashed and burned, I stopped by Norm's office and asked him how he got away with saying something like that.

He started laughing and wheeled his chair around to face me and explain. "Listen, Breuer," he said, "the press doesn't give a shit about you! They don't care what you say. It doesn't matter what they put in the papers. All anyone cares about is if you're funny on television."

That was the moment I realized that Norm's the guy who, when you show up for your first day at work and you've endured a big formal orientation, walks up and says, "You don't need to know any of that shit. The best place to hang out is the stockroom, on Thursday mornings you can come in late, and always disregard whatever the assistant manager says."

Norm was a great guy to know because *SNL* was a much more complicated place than *Uptown Comedy Club*. On *Uptown*, we needed all hands on deck, so if you were alive and remotely funny, you were on the air. It was that simple. We flew by the seat of our pants and had fun doing so. *Saturday Night Live* was fun, obviously, but it was more of a machine. A big, political machine. As those first weeks went by, I discovered that just because you were the funniest, or just because you had come up with the best character, it didn't necessarily mean you were getting on the air. Nothing was a lock. Making it all the way through dress rehearsal and to the main show meant you had weathered a perfect storm of timing, humor, luck, and the powers that be—Lorne and the head writers—digging it. And as we prepped for the first show, I thought I'd nailed it.

I went through the first week with a Shut-up Guy sketch looking like it was going to make the lineup. I flew my mom and dad up from Florida. It was monumental and I wanted them to be a part of it. I was psyched that I already potentially had an original character in play. Before the "real" live show that airs, as you might already know, there's a dress show, where the whole program is rehearsed to make sure the timings are right and that every sketch is coming together. In the end, there are always a couple of bits from the dress rehearsal that don't make the final cut, for many different reasons, and that's just the way it goes. My parents came to the studio for both the dress rehearsal and the live show, and Shut-up Guy got cut between the shows. With that sketch dead, I wasn't on the show at all. I did warm up the crowd beforehand though, and that was something I'd end up doing a lot, just coming out and doing five minutes of stand-up before anything was televised.

At the end of the show, I met my parents and Dee on the studio floor and we were all going to go to the wrap party. I could see that Dad was especially cantankerous about me getting cut.

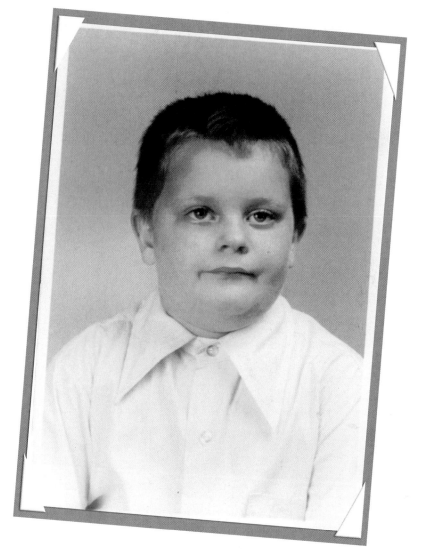

I was a fat kid.

With Mom.

With Dad.

Leaving for my senior prom.

My "Class Clown" high school yearbook photo, complete with typo.

Jim Bruer

With Kristen at Busch Gardens.

My early headshots are a
horror show of hairstyles.

Jim Breuer

JIM BREUER

Jim Breuer

Sitcom builds off 'Home Improvement'

By Jefferson Graham
USA TODAY

Will Dave Chappelle and Jim Breuer be the next Tim Allen or Roseanne?

They will, if Matt Williams and partners Carmen Finestra and David McFadzean have anything to say about it.

The trio that created *Home Improvement* — Williams gets solo credit for creating *Roseanne* — will deliver a *Home Improvement* spinoff for ABC starring the stand-up comedians.

The sitcom, tentatively titled *Buddies*, is expected to air in the post-*Improvement* time slot (9:30 p.m. ET/PT) for four Tuesdays in April. (*Grace Under Fire* takes a break until the May sweeps.)

Chappelle and Breuer appear as lifelong pals who start a video production business in Detroit. The show proposes to tackle issues ranging from the impact on friendship when one pal suddenly gets married to black/white relations in the late '90s.

Racial tension "is still a big problem in our culture," says McFadzean. "We think we can talk about it and still have a 'unny show."

Chappelle and Breuer will e introduced in an episode of ?me *Improvement* in late irch.

When Tim Taylor (Allen) is ng his latest edition of *Tool* *hannelle* and Breuer

'Buddies' duo: A Disney match made in Montreal

DAVE CHAPPELLE: His comedy is derived from social commentary; it's 'whatever's on my mind.'
New York Entertainment

Dave Chappelle and Jim Breuer were discovered last summer at the Montreal Comedy Festival, which is for new comedians what the Sundance Film Festival is for young directors and actors.

"I thought I was just going there to make some money up in Canada," Chappelle says. "I didn't realize the entire industry would be there."

Chappelle, 21, and Breuer, 27, did separate stand-up sets, but they were deluged with offers afterward and ended up at Disney. The studio sent their tapes to Matt Williams, "and he just hit it on the button," says Breuer.

"I wanted to do a show about my lifestyle, that's what my humor is all about," Breuer says. He's a newlywed, and his routine describes the difficulties his friends have in dealing with that.

Chappelle, who has had small roles in *Robin Hood: Men in Tights* and *Undercover Blues*, doesn't have such a well-defined comedy persona.

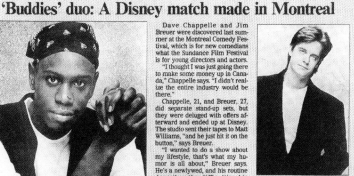

BREUER: The newlywed wants to do a show about his lifestyle.
New York Entertainment

"I just do social commentary," he says. "Whatever's on my mind."

audience to talk about problems with wives and girlfriends.

Naturally, Tim offers his advice and makes things even worse. The episode was videotaped last weekend.

The video business Chappelle and Breuer run starts out with weddings and living wills, but Finestra says the show's

producers might figure out a way for them to do a little work for *Tool Time*, which would enable them to cross over from show to show.

The producers have been asked many times to create a spinoff for the 4-year-old *Home Improvement*. So why now?

Former Disney studios chief Jeffrey Katzenberg, in one of

his last acts before stepping down last summer, asked Williams and company to consider doing a show with these two comics. (*Home Improvement*, produced in association with Touchstone Television, tapes at Walt Disney Studios.)

"We always figured we'd do a spinoff when the right subject came along," says Williams.

"Once we saw these guys, the whole series jelled for us. They're raw and untested, but there's a freshness there."

The producers, partners in Wind Dancer Productions, which also produces ABC's *Thunder Alley*, will be scrambling to get the new series on the air. Filming begins at the end of March.

The *USA Today* piece about what a big star I was about to be.

With Dave Chapelle on the set of *Half Baked*.

The 1997 cast of *Saturday Night Live*.

The first "Goat Boy" sketch with Tom Hanks.

I had a blast working with Mayor Giuliani on the show.

Meeting my idols, De Niro and Pesci.

My family is everything these days.

"The show sucked!" he said. He was irritated, cranky, and being dramatic. I'm sure he thought by some twist of logic, I'd see his negativity as being supportive.

"Dad," I said calmly, "there's going to be so many other shows, I'm not worried about it. I'm happy to be here. It'll work out."

"Yeah, but it sucked!" he said insistently.

"No," my mom said, smiling. "It was great. Don't listen to him."

"It was terrible!" my dad said, raising his voice, just in case we weren't clear on his position.

I hustled them out the door, into our limo—it was shocking to me that I got a free limo for the night—and we went to the cast party, at some fancy restaurant downtown. Dee, my sister Dorene, my friends, Mom and Dad—you name it, they were all there, and when we walked in, the bouncer took a look at the camera Dee was carrying and said, "No pictures."

"That's okay," I told the guy. "I'm on the cast."

"Okay," he said. "But we still don't allow pictures. So can I hang on to your camera until you're ready to go?"

"What?" I said. "*Really?* Whatever. Sure. Here ya go."

That's one of the rules of the *Saturday Night Live* after-party. And as much as you may read about them, or see pictures of cast and stars arriving, you'll never see pictures from inside the after-party. At least you didn't for many, many years. I don't know if they've relaxed the rule now or not. At the time, I may have been mad about the bouncer hassling Dee over her camera, but I came to view both the party and the rule as a nice break from the rest of the whole machine.

So we went inside and celebrated. I told my guests they could get whatever they wanted, as I was certain, after learning of the free limo, that NBC was covering the tab. As the night wore on, I introduced my dad to different cast members, like Norm and Molly Shannon, and the host, Mariel Hemingway. The cast and their friends and families all mingled, the vibe was light, and I felt like I was getting off on the right foot. *Saturday Night Live* seemed like a great fit for me. I saw Lorne putting on his coat and wanted to make sure my dad met him before he left.

"Dad," I said, "come with me, let's say good-bye to Lorne."

"What?" he asked. "Who?"

"Lorne, Dad," I said. I was pretty sure I'd explained to him a couple hundred times in the process of landing the show who Lorne was and what he did.

"Lorne?" Dad said incredulously, pausing to consider it. "*Lorne?* Is that really a name? How would ya spell that?"

"Dad," I said impatiently. Lorne nearly had one foot out the door. "Let's just go meet him."

"Well who the hell is he?"

I quickly reminded Dad that Lorne had created the whole show, then grabbed him by the arm and hustled him over to the doorway.

"Lorne," I said, smiling. "Before you take off, I wanna introduce you to my dad."

"Oh," Lorne turned and smiled warmly. "Pleasure to meet you, Mr. Breuer. Your son is very talented."

Dad just screwed up his face, looked at Lorne disgustedly, and said, "Yeah. So, I flew up here all the way from Florida to see the show. What happened to him?" He jabbed his thumb into my chest. "He wasn't on."

I immediately started sweating.

"That happens sometimes," Lorne said calmly and politely. "I can tell you that our host next week, Chevy Chase, inquired about Jim and is excited to work with him."

"Next week?" my dad said, grinning. "Who gives a shit about next week? I'm back in Florida then. Why wasn't he on this week? The show sucked."

"Nice meeting you," Lorne said drolly, then just walked out the door.

"Thanks, Dad," I said, certain I'd be given my walking papers on Monday.

Not too long after Dad and I rejoined our group, the waitress came over to the table with a bill for $800. I looked at the bill, and then I looked up at the waitress and said, "I'm sorry, I'm a cast member."

"Oh, cool," she said. "Can I take your credit card for this?"

"I don't think you get it," I explained. "I'm on the show."

"I know that," she said. "And I'm telling you that your bill is eight hundred dollars."

"But I'm part of the cast. NBC is paying for it."

"No, no, no, no," she laughed. I was the one who had something wrong apparently. "The cast pays for their own stuff. You ordered the drinks and the shots, *and* you get to pay for them."

My guest list got considerably smaller after that night.

*   *   *

I'd done stand-up by myself for so long that being part of a team again—and a dysfunctional one at that—was difficult. *SNL* had the most unusual system I'd ever had to navigate. You worked so hard that it was truly satisfying when you made it to air and killed, but getting there was such an effort.

For starters, there just wasn't enough airtime for the amount of talent on the cast that year. It was discouraging to sit at the pitch table and watch my fellow cast members continually bring in hilarious ideas. At the same time, I admired them, too. These folks were able to knock out everything. Week after week Cheri Oteri would walk in with slam-dunk characters. She had the cheerleaders with Will Ferrell, a little kid, a crazy woman on a porch, Barbara Walters, Debbie Reynolds, you name it. She was a monster. Molly Shannon was the same way, with her awkward Catholic schoolgirl, Mary Katherine Gallagher, blowing up. Mark McKinney had the Chicken Lady. And Will was basically in every single sketch; he was unstoppable. I quickly sized up the competition and concluded there was no way for me to get on the show. These guys were monsters.

Over time, the Shut-up Guy became one of the most popular characters never to appear in a sketch. Lorne liked him, and I worked for three years to get him onto the show, but the closest he ever got was the fifteen- and thirty-second show promos that aired during the week on NBC. In those first couple months, it was a self-perpetuating cycle. The more I worried about not getting on, the less funny I was. I had no confidence. And without confidence, it was impossible to make sketches go. I had a nine-episode contract and was certain I'd be shown the door if I didn't come up with at least one hit character by then. Later that season, in fact, two of my fellow brand-new cast members, Nancy Walls and David Koechner, were let go, so the pressure I felt was real.

By early November, I'd routinely pace the halls, looking for clues that I was getting fired. One night, I ran into Will Ferrell in the hallway and asked him point-blank if he thought any of us—namely me—were going to get canned.

"I'm just not getting my stuff on," I said, looking around suspiciously. "I don't think I'll be long for the show."

"No," Will said innocuously. "I haven't heard anything. Don't worry about it." Then he smartly kept walking. No one wanted to get tangled up in my bad vibe. The cast got along pretty well, but at the end of the day, everyone was fiercely protective of their own material and concerned mainly with their own job security. Being vulnerable or appearing vulnerable was something you wanted to stay as far away from as possible.

Since the show started, I'd gotten on where I could—I had a nanosecond in a fake commercial for A.M. Ale; I fell down the stairs in a Chevy Chase sketch; and I had a couple of beat-myself-up characters—pulled from my stand-up act—in sketches. But the week after Thanksgiving, I was running on empty. Anthony Edwards from

ER was hosting, and nothing I'd thrown out in Monday's pitch meeting stuck.

Pitch meetings kicked the week off. It was our first real chance to meet with that week's host and find out what they were into. We'd all go into a giant room and sit around a table with Lorne and the guest host, and toss out ideas for that week's show. It was a fun, loose process, but tough, too, because you were just recovering from the last week's show and you didn't always know what this week's host was going to respond to. Anything could happen.

Norm was known for fake pitches in those Monday meetings. He'd purposely pitch the worst stuff. Tom Hanks hosted one year, right around the time he'd won two straight Oscars. We were doing the pitch meeting and it was Norm's turn. He very energetically stammered to Tom, "I got this great idea where you're the, ah, 'shit my pants guy,' like you just, you know, shit your pants. But you don't know why! You're just like, 'Yeah, I shit my pants.'"

Tom, being superpolite, gave an anticipatory half smile, waiting for Norm to elaborate. Norm continued, completely earnestly, "And everywhere you go, you shit your pants. People stop and say, 'There's the guy who shits his pants.' It's gonna be funny."

Total silence. After a beat, Lorne just wrinkled his lips, raised his eyebrows, and said, "Next." Norm would never bring anything real into a pitch meeting. He had a steady gig—"Weekend Update"—and was the brightest star on the show at that time. He'd do these awkward, uncomfortable joke pitches only with really big guests, which made it even funnier.

Rather than get uptight about not having anything coming out of the pitch meeting, I decided to change my attitude. Good things always happened to me when things looked the worst. My folks moved to Florida—I overcame it and turned it into a positive. As a waiter, I never learned the elaborate drink glass system at TGI Friday's—I quit and wound up with a bunch of free ice cream. My manager inked me to a bad contract—I still got on a TV show, met Tracy Morgan, and learned a lot of life lessons. My first network sitcom fell apart—but I got to work with and drive around L.A. with Dave Chappelle.

So I came into work on Tuesday and just started winging it, trying to stay loose. Instead of walking around with fear, my goal was just to make people around 30 Rock laugh in their day-to-day existence. Never mind getting on air; I wanted to get back to just being funny for being funny's sake.

There was this hippie kid interning with the writing staff who was legitimately terrible at easy stuff like taking messages and remembering to give them to you. But he was funny, and I liked to stop and gab with him once in a while. So that Tuesday, with nothing much going on for me work-wise, I bumped into him in the writers' room and started doing Joe Pesci.

"What are ya, eatin' lunch?" I said. "You call dat a roast beef sandwich? Whatsamatta? Whaddaya bustin' my bawls for, kid? You got some noive." I went on like this for a few minutes, just riffing and trying to make him laugh.

He loved it. "How come you've never tried this on the show?"

"I don't know," I said.

"Pesci's gold," he said. "You've got him down perfect." I could see the wheels start to turn in his head, thinking about where this could fit into the lineup. He snapped his fingers and said, "You know, you really should take this onto the 'Update' with Norm."

"Really?" I said. "How would that work?"

"Well," he explained, "Pesci has a movie coming out. *Eight Heads in a Duffel Bag.* So you'd go on the 'Update,' as Pesci, to promote the movie, and ask Norm if he's seen it yet, and Norm, of course, hasn't, and that makes you mad and you just go off in a rage."

"That's great," I said, laughing, and started pretending I was Pesci berating Norm. One of the head writers, Steve Koren, walked by, then he stopped and came back.

"What the heck is so funny?" he asked, and looked at me quizzically as a grin spread across his face. "Wait, are you doing Joe Pesci?"

Out of all the writers on staff, Steve would end up being my biggest champion. He was a Queens guy, from near where I grew up. He had long hair and looked like the kind of guy who'd be happier in the woods than in an office. He'd helped Molly with her Mary Katherine Gallagher character, later went on to write for *Seinfeld,* and also wrote a bunch of movies.

"Yeah," the intern said enthusiastically. "Breuer does the most unbelievable Joe Pesci."

I kept talking like Pesci, and the intern told him his "Weekend Update" idea. Steve smiled.

"You guys got a few minutes?" he asked.

"Of course," I said. I had nothing but time.

"Come to my room," he said. "I've actually had an idea for a Pesci sketch for a long time."

So we went to Steve's office and sat down. I hadn't planned on any of this.

"I've always wanted to do Pesci as a talk show," Steve confessed.

"Yeah," I agreed. "He could even have De Niro as a sidekick."

Steve agreed. "Sure. And other people he worked with would be guests. My idea is that in making a movie with them, Pesci got mad or felt wronged by them, built up a grudge, and he's going to handle it like Tommy from *Goodfellas* would."

"Yeah," I said. The whole thing was building organically. "He could have a baseball bat at his desk."

"And one by one," Steve said, nodding, "he's going to have them on his show and settle the score by beating the crap out of them. Every single time."

"Totally," I said. "He could do that with any big-name star. Whoever our host is that week, he'd have them on, get really impatient with them for trivial crap, and then beat 'em down."

We worked Tuesday night and Wednesday morning, banging out the shell of a script. Steve had the idea stewing around in his head for a while, and I was fluent in all things Pesci, so it came together pretty fast. My stress disappeared and I felt like I had a renewed purpose. At the same time, I was impressed with Steve's command over how his words and jokes would come to life onstage. No detail escaped him. He knew what it took to sell a character, even the most comically absurd ones.

"Lock into Pesci completely and lose yourself," Steve said, bringing up specific scenes from *Raging Bull* and *Goodfellas.* "Remember how Tommy moves when he stuffs Billy Batts in the trunk?" he asked. "Get the body language down, and stay in character, no matter how over-the-top it seems, and Lorne will eat it up."

We ran the basic concept of the sketch by Anthony Edwards.

"I love it," he said.

"Do you do any impressions?" I asked. "Who do you think Pesci should beat down?"

"Ugh," Anthony groaned. "I really suck at impressions."

Steve pondered this news for a second before a mischievous grin spread across his face. "Macaulay Culkin?"

"Yeah!" I said. "Why not? Joe Pesci got his ass kicked in *Home Alone.*"

"You up for it?" Steve asked Anthony. "Don't worry about getting Culkin down, all you have to do is act like a little kid. In fact, let's make you an overgrown Culkin with too-short pants."

The key to the Pesci sketches was the impressions. The night Jim Carrey played Jimmy Stewart while Mark McKinney played Jim Carrey was surreal. The more twists the better. We wrote Anthony as Macaulay Culkin into the sketch and brought it to the Wednesday read-through, just to see what would happen. Often, some of the funniest stuff on the show wouldn't come together until late in the week. If there were any holes in the lineup, and you had something funny, you always had a shot. Everyone gathered around a big table, a couple of sketches were read, and then Lorne looked at us and asked, "Whaddaya got?"

"Hey," I said, looking around the room, going right into my Pesci voice. "I'm Joe Pesci and this is *The Joe Pesci Show!*"

Lorne started laughing immediately, rocking back and forth in his chair. People around the table were howling. We read through the script and Anthony loved it. It made the lineup. I'll never forget that feeling, knowing I had something locked, loaded, and going onto the show.

The biggest killing I'd seen on the show was Molly doing the hapless, crazy Catholic schoolgirl Mary Katherine Gallagher. I couldn't believe the roar of the live crowd while she was doing that sketch. After hearing that, I didn't want laughs. I wanted that sound—a huge, all-encompassing white noise. In the dress rehearsal that Saturday, the minute the sketch started and I said, "I'm Joe Pesci!" I heard that noise, and I knew that my contract was saved, at least for the rest of the season.

Shortly after the New Year, Alec Baldwin hosted the show. He had a big, serious movie—*The Juror*, with Demi Moore—coming out in a couple of weeks. Even back then, I marveled at the guy's versatility. He can take on any role, usually with a heavy display of bravado and masculinity, and knock it out of the park. I also knew, as he consistently proves nowadays with *30 Rock*, that he could be funny, too—darkly funny—and poke fun at himself in the process.

Because the first "Joe Pesci Show" crushed, Steve and I were feeling a little cocky. Walking around the studio, I was way looser. If I ever got canned and all people remembered of me was "The Joe Pesci Show"? I was cool with that. I'd killed on one of the legendary stages in American comedy, and no one could take that away from me.

Steve and I knew that to do the sketch again, and do it right, we had to have someone do a unique and great impression. Sketches get tired fast for many reasons, and doing them repeatedly just because they crushed once is a sure way to bore the hell out of people. Even most of the cast recognized that about their own sketches and would grumble to one another if Lorne or a guest host asked that a dead horse be trotted out to get beaten yet again.

But having Alec Baldwin as a host brought a prime opportunity to put our best stuff on the table and let him go to town on it. "The Joe Pesci Show," Steve and I figured, was no exception. Not only is he a superb actor, but Alec was one of the only *SNL* hosts besides Tom Hanks who was super approachable 100 percent of the time. Most were nice, undoubtedly, but those two guys just really got it. They dropped their ego and fame at the door and were game for whatever was going to be funny. From the minute he got there, Alec ingratiated himself to everyone, hanging out in the hallways, talking to both producers and custodians or having a sandwich in the writers' room with whomever was around. He was happy to learn about *you*—your wife, your family, where you grew up. And when he said, "We should all go to dinner Thursday night . . . ," he actually meant it, and he'd include everybody.

Early in the week, in the writers' room, Steve and I were BS-ing over lunch and studying Alec, who was sitting nearby, gabbing with a couple producers.

"Look at that mug," Steve said, nodding in Alec's direction. "You know what? He's De Niro."

"You're right," I said, smiling. "Think he'll do it?"

"Let's find out."

We waited until there was a lull in Alec's conversation and then slid our chairs closer to him.

"Hey," Steve said. "So we did this 'Joe Pesci Show' thing back in December. . . ."

"Yeah," Alec answered, breaking into a grin. "That was funny."

"We want to try it again this week," I added.

"Excellent," Alec said.

"And we were hoping that you would play Robert De Niro," Steve said. The warmth left Alec's face quickly as he clammed up and gave us a terse answer.

"Nah," he said with a shrug and a shake of his head. "I don't do impressions."

Both Steve and I started laughing because what Alec had just done, whether he knew it or not, was a spot-on impression of De Niro. It was classic De Niro, tight-lipped, not very forthcoming—he favors using short, compact facial expressions more than words to communicate.

"That's all you gotta do," Steve said, smiling. "You don't even have to speak, you're already hilarious."

Once again, Alec said, "Nah, really. That's not my thing," in a very De Niro way. "I couldn't play Bobby."

I backhanded Steve on the arm. "Did you hear him say 'Bobby'?" I turned to Alec. "You must know him," I said. "Only people who know him call him that."

"Oh, sure," he said. "I see Bobby from time to time, you know, at parties and events."

"Well," I explained, "all you'd have to say is two lines." In the sketch, a guest would come out and say the most harmless thing, and it would get misinterpreted by Pesci. The guest would be clueless, but then De Niro would remind the guest à la *Raging Bull* that he, too, had "heard some things" or that what the guest said was a "li'l bit" offensive to Pesci—in the same way De Niro's character Jimmy said it in *Goodfellas*. Naturally, it would all lead to an epic beat-down by Pesci.

"Two lines?" Alec asked with a glint in his eye. "That's all?" I nodded yes. That got him encouraged enough to start making the famous De Niro mug, where he tucks his chin in, doesn't say much, and almost looks like he's smiling. He started looking around the room, mugging, in character, twisting his neck and trying it out.

"See?" Steve said, reassuring him. "That's perfect."

"That's all you gotta do," I said. "You come sit next to me out there, and when the guest gets going, and Pesci gets offended, you just say, 'I heard some things,' and that will set Pesci off even more."

"Okay," Alec said, getting into it. "But I gotta have a glass of scotch in my hand and a cigarette." He remained in De Niro mode the rest of the day.

The sketch started off with Pesci introducing his old friend De Niro/Alec, who took a seat on the sofa. Then we brought out David Spade, who was playing Brad Pitt. There was a whole exchange where De Niro/Alec stood up from the couch to greet Brad/David and then he didn't know whether to sit or remain standing out of courtesy, and Brad/David didn't really know what was going on, which infuriated De Niro/Alec even more.

"What am I doin'?" De Niro/Alec said impatiently, addressing Brad/David. "Am I up? Am I down? What's the deal here? Sit down already. Just sit down." The crowd was howling. Then shortly after Brad/David sat down, Pesci/me got all paranoid and freaked out that Brad/David said something about him. Brad/David said, "No, I didn't say anything." And then De Niro/Alec said smugly, "I heard some things," and the whole place erupted, and the beat-down ensued. Alec was brilliant.

Over the next year, my standing on *SNL* solidified. Sure, there was turbulence, but I launched a second character—Goat Boy—that was just as popular as my Pesci. I was reunited with Tracy Morgan when he joined the cast, and we even shared an office. We teamed up to do Wong and Owens, cheesy retired eighties porn stars who were desperately trying to work straight jobs, but every situation would always drag them back to their more hard-core side. They came out of the typical conversations Tracy and I would have every day.

"Can anybody actually retire from porn?" Tracy asked me one afternoon, kicking his feet up on the desk in the office we shared. "'Cause you can't do it forever. That's not a physical possibility."

We pondered the idea, and pretty soon it became hilarious to us and Wong and Owens were born. I thought it would make for a great movie, even though it was probably the most embarrassing sketch I ever did. I was never required to strip down to a thong for any other job.

Anyway, with Pesci as a regular part of the rotation, I got to work with stars like John Goodman, Jim Carrey, and Kevin Spacey. They came to the show wanting to be in a Joe Pesci sketch. I felt pretty good, like I'd cracked the code. Lorne had private dinners on Tuesday nights, where only certain cast members got invited. And if you got an invite, that's how you knew you were doing well. And eventually I would get those invites, usually when a guest host was feeling a bit uncomfortable and the producers wanted someone to lighten the mood at dinner. I was happy to oblige.

In the late winter or early spring of 1997, an intern told me that both De Niro's camp and Scorsese's camp wanted tapes of "The Joe Pesci Show." That immediately ballooned my head. I was certain I was going to be in *Goodfellas II* or *Taxi Driver II*. My dreams from when I was a kid were all coming true. I was now going to be in movies with Pesci and De Niro, just like I promised Phil all those years ago when we were kids. I'd be the one calling De Niro "Bobby."

The tapes went out, and no one ever called. No one sent me any scripts. No letters on Scorsese's stationery ever arrived. But in early April, the head producer, Marci Klein, came into my office. If anyone made sure *SNL* happened, it was her. Marci was short, brunette, and tough, the daughter of Calvin. She'd been around the show for years, running things with a no-nonsense approach. She came in and shut the door quickly behind her, then stood in front of it. "Trouble," I thought.

"Joe Pesci is coming in next Thursday," she said, getting right to the point.

I was flabbergasted and asked, "What are you talking about?"

"You're going to meet with him. He and Robert De Niro want to make a cameo on 'The Joe Pesci Show' next week. That's it. And if this leaks, you get fired. End of story."

She walked out of my office, closed the door, and then poked her head back in and smiled. "Pretty amazing, huh?"

I had over a week to agonize, freak out, and, most important, keep it to myself. Dee was the only person I told. I was happy to show her that the long struggle was paying off. Now I was back to thinking I was going to be buddies with De Niro and Pesci. I couldn't wait to just connect on a regular-guy basis with my two heroes. Steve Koren had left the show by then; he was writing for *Seinfeld*, but he was the master behind the Pesci show, so we called him and he came back for a week to help write the script. He was more surprised than I was. De Niro didn't do television. Lorne told the rest of the cast and made it clear that this was not to be announced.

So Thursday afternoon came. I was anxious that Pesci would be a no-show and the whole plan would come unglued. Then an intern rapped on my office door and told me that the man had arrived with two beautiful female assistants (his and De Niro's) and wanted to sit down with me before rehearsing. I walked nervously to the greenroom and peeked in to see Pesci decked out in a full-on sharkskin suit. He was wearing a gold pinkie ring, and he had an expensive pair of Italian sunglasses pushed up on his forehead. He was squinting underneath them, looking at pictures and posters from the show that were hanging on the wall.

As I walked in, he pushed the sunglasses back down onto his face, turned to me, and smiled.

"So *you're* Joe Pesci," he said with a laugh.

I was so freaked out I couldn't even say more than "Hi."

"Why don't you sit down over here with me?" He motioned nonchalantly toward two sofas positioned next to each other. I walked over and sat down with him, and he started murmuring stuff about going to dinner last week at restaurants I'd never been to, with people like Jack Nicholson and "Bobby" De Niro. He was dropping names like crazy, I think, to indicate how he'd usually be spending his time if he weren't so graciously hanging out with me. Then he stopped abruptly, looked me directly in the eyes, and with all seriousness said, "Well—you gonna thank me for giving you a career?"

Before I could answer, he continued with a stern tone. "Listen, I like comedy. I really do. You like those cartoon guys Beavis and Butthead?"

"Yeah," I said. I was wondering when the punch line was coming.

"Yeah, me, too," he said, chuckling. "Freakin' idiots! *That's* comedy." Then he paused before continuing on, his smile disappearing. "But whatever it is you're doing as me—that *ain't* comedy."

I was stunned.

He continued. "Lemme ask you something."

"Go ahead," I said, nodding.

"Are you Italian?" he asked. By the look on his face and the tone of his voice, he already knew the answer was no.

"No, sir."

"Yeah," he said. "I figured as much. So tell me this: Where do you get balls big enough to use terms like *guinea, wop,* and *dago*?"

"What . . . what do you mean?"

"I always hear you, *as me*, using slurs like *guinea, wop,* and *dago*," he said. "And I never hear you disparaging other races. It's always derogatory about Italians and you're not even Italian. That bothers me."

"Well," I explained, "I always consult with an Italian writer."

"Frank Sebastiano?" he asked. Frank wrote for *SNL* for many years before he joined David Letterman. "Yeah, I know that guy. I talked to him. But here's the thing. You and I are performers, and you and I know that when we're on the screen, we're the ones liable for the racial slurs that come out of our mouths. So you are the one who uses these racial slurs. Am I right or wrong?"

"Y-yeah, um," I stammered. I felt like Spider from *Goodfellas.* He was attacking me perfectly and I had no comeback. The two assistant girls were across the room from us, both looking down at their shoes so intently you'd think they were made of gold. "No . . . yeah." I was sweating.

"Where did you grow up, anyway?"

"On Long Island." I thought knowing we were from common grounds might calm him down. "I actually have a lot of friends that say they know you. . . ."

"Oh yeah," he said cynically. "*Where* on Long Island?"

"Valley Stream."

"*Valley Stream?*" He said it shaking his head. "I don't know no one from Valley Stream."

He wasn't breaking character. So I just assumed he was a real-deal mafioso there to shake me down. And now I was going to have to pay him a percentage for the rest of my career. I was sure he was going to say, "For the rest of your life you owe me ten percent." He was that serious.

"You know, my grandfather came here and built lower Manhattan," he said. "I'm a just a simple family man. A nonviolent guy, and now I gotta deal with someone like you? Someone who portrays me as a vicious animal that walks around places *beating* people? My family turns on the TV and sees *you* doing *me* as a violent person, because of a character that I played in a film? That ain't Joe Pesci! You are doing a caricature of a character."

I wanted to ask him something: If I was responsible for the slurs I was supposedly using on TV, wasn't he responsible for the violence during his movies? But I knew that would just make things worse. He knew I was spoofing, right? I loved the guy. This was all wrong.

"I never meant to offend you," I said meekly.

"You never meant to offend me?" he asked in a tone that suggested he thought I was lying. He took his sunglasses off and placed them on his thigh. "Then why would you use these ethnic slurs? And here's another thing: Don't thank me for showing up here. Thank *Bobby*. This is his idea. He's the one who watches the tapes of your show, laughing his ass off, telling me, 'We should go on that show and bust this guy's balls. That would be a laugh.' A *laugh*. So that's why I'm here. I didn't want to do this. I'm offended by it.

"And for the record, I don't think you sound *anything* like me," he spat. "You make me sound like Mickey Mouse."

I stood up, convinced the sketch was toast. Pesci just came to clear the air, freak me out so bad I'd never embarrass him or demean his name again.

"I know you got upset when I said I didn't mean to offend you, Mr. Pesci," I said slowly and earnestly. "To be honest, I *really* didn't mean to offend you. Ever since I was a little kid and I saw *Raging Bull*, I looked for you in anything I could find. *Easy Money*—I loved it! I followed your career. I wanted to be you. I imitate you out of admiration. Not to be malicious."

I was pacing the floor now, like a lawyer making his closing statement.

"I will never do the sketch again," I said. "The last thing I want to do is hurt your feelings. But I do need to defend myself on one point. It might be splitting hairs, but if you really listen to the sketch, I never insulted Italians. I always do you getting mad at someone, and perhaps *their* prejudice, saying, 'What do you think, I'm some kind of crazy rigatoni? A spazzed-out scungilli?' But I never called an Italian that. I always accused a person of those thoughts as I beat them with a baseball bat."

And as I was saying that, Pesci's expression went from annoyed to annoyed with a little bit of sincere understanding in it. Then back to quietly annoyed.

"Yeah, yeah, yeah," he said, looking at me like I was a misguided chump. "I know that."

"This has been a learning experience," I said proudly. The armpits of my shirt were now oceans. "It's not worth it. I apologize. I think you're a phenomenal actor. We'll never do the sketch again."

"Wha? What?" he said, spitting out the words, scooting forward in his chair, the volatile, impatient guy returning. "Whaddaya mean we're not gonna do it?!" he said. "I already told Bobby we're gonna do it. Of course we're gonna do it."

He wagged his finger back and forth between me and him. "Jeez, I thought a guy from Long Island could take a little ball busting. I'm just playing games with you, Jimmy. Busting your balls. Sheesh."

"Okay," I said. I heaved a sigh of relief and, still, more than a little bewilderment. He'd toyed with me for fifteen minutes.

"You're a funny guy," Pesci said, breaking into a smile and nodding his head. Now I was feeling better. "I don't understand the goat thing, though. What's that all about? It weirds me out." Goat Boy had come to life that season, and it evoked strong reactions in people. It didn't bug me that he didn't get it; I was more than happy he didn't blow up the whole sketch and count me as an enemy. Still, I thought I'd at least explain.

"Well, he's supposed to be a—"

"Okay, never mind that," Pesci said, standing up and putting his sunglasses back on. "I've gotta car waiting for me downstairs. Here's what we're gonna do. I'm coming back tomorrow to block this scene. So you'll tell me where to stand, where Bobby's gotta stand, and I'll let him know, 'cause Bobby don't do no rehearsing. And we ain't showing up for this whole dress rehearsal thing on Saturday. We show up for the real deal and that's it. You got a problem with that?"

"No, sir."

He came back Friday and took over the set, entertaining everyone with stories from the movies he'd been in. And he was telling corny and dirty jokes trying to make me laugh, saying, "Jimbo, ever hear this one?" It was great. He was calling me "Jimbo"!

But then on Saturday night, a half hour before dress rehearsal, the wheels flew off completely.

"De Niro's not gonna make it," Steve said. I was in hair and makeup getting my Pesci nose put on.

"Ha ha!" I said. "Good one, Steve."

"No," he said. "I'm not kidding you. Apparently, he didn't know that *Saturday Night Live* is live."

"What?"

"He doesn't do live television."

That's how cool De Niro was. For the twenty years the show had been on the air, he had no idea it was live. So now we had to ask ourselves: Do we still do it? We'd heard nothing about Pesci bailing, so the producers asked Darrell Hammond to play a fake De Niro alongside the real Pesci. It was going to be me, Colin Quinn as a fake De Niro, the real Pesci as himself, and Darrell as a fake-real-fake De Niro. It made no sense. Steve Koren wasn't into it. I certainly wasn't into it. No one was into it. Steve and I argued with the producers that we should go with just the real Pesci and be insanely grateful for our good fortune. The dilemma lasted all the way up until the eight P.M. dress rehearsal show. I took the stage, got behind my desk, and when "fifteen seconds" was shouted and the studio quieted to a hush, I could see Darrell in a De Niro getup waiting in the wings, but both the real Pesci and De Niro were no-shows.

I knew the sketch was going to be a debacle. Defeated, I went into it halfheartedly, not giving my all to my lines or to my character. And Pesci and De Niro, real or fake, weren't due to come onstage until the very end, so I had to slug my way through the whole thing, with Rob Lowe impersonating Eric Roberts and Chris Kattan adeptly playing David Spade.

The sketch ground its way out, and right at the end, I heard the loudest roar from a crowd I've ever heard in my whole life. It was as if the Beatles were all alive and had decided to show up that night. I looked over to where Darrell was standing to see that the real Pesci and De Niro had emerged from the wings and come onstage. De Niro had a little hat on, and he was looking over at me with a sparkle in his eye, grinning his famous grin. I could not have been more surprised. They'd been nowhere near the stage, or maybe even the whole studio, until the very second they were supposed to walk onstage. And every time De Niro opened his mouth, the crowd went wild.

The big joke of the sketch was that after Pesci lectured me—much in the same way he lectured me in the greenroom—De Niro busted Colin Quinn, wagging his finger, eyeballing his horrible orange suit, and asking bluntly, "Who are you supposed to be?"

And Colin very matter-of-factly answered, "Colin Quinn. *Remote Control?*" name-checking his old MTV game show.

And once the dress sketch was over, they split and didn't return until they were due to appear on the broadcast show. By then, masses and masses of people had shown up, because word got out that Pesci and De Niro were on the show. Everyone's managers and agents, and all the friends they could sneak in, were milling around the hallway, hoping for a chance to see the goodfellas, even if only on the monitors. And just like that, the hallway noise died down, and the crowd parted like the Red Sea as Pesci and De Niro returned and made their way toward the studio. De Niro nodded politely every few feet, asking, "How ya doing?" to assorted hangers-on.

Pesci spotted me and winked. "This is the big night, Jimmy," he said, squeezing my arm. "You ready? We're gonna have fun. See you in a couple minutes." Then he and De Niro went into their dressing room. The next time I saw them was during the live sketch. I got into makeup and wardrobe and Lorne approached me much in the manner that Pesci did. "Big night," he said in his typical understated way. "You ready for it?"

"Yes," I said. "Thanks a lot, Lorne. Thank you so much."

"People are going to see this for a long time, Jim," he said matter-of-factly. Through all of our disagreements and misunderstandings, this was what I loved about Lorne. He always seemed to have a sense of how everything would play out. In one calm sentence, he'd subtly motivated me to focus. And he said it so simply and so assuredly that I really just paid attention to his words. He helped me make the moment. And it's one of the greatest moments, I'd wager, in the history of *SNL*. Over thirteen years later, it still makes me immensely proud, and I still hear about it from fans.

After the sketch, Pesci found me on my way to remove my prosthetic nose.

"You never met Bobby yet, did ya?"

"No."

"Well, he's *dying* to meet you."

We went into his dressing room, and I said, "Mr. De Niro, thank you so much. I swear to God. That was unbelievable."

"No, no, no," he said, closing his eyes and nodding his head quickly. "You're good. You're very funny. *Very* funny."

"Nah . . ."

"No," he said, and slapped me on the shoulder. "You're very funny."

"Thanks," I said, and without any hesitation, I added, "Can you sign my *Raging Bull* tape?"

"Absolutely."

So I went and grabbed the tape, De Niro signed it, and the inscription read: "To Jimmy Breuer, a real Goodfella, Robert De Niro."

Chapter 11

Birth of Goat Boy

As a kid, I always did impressions and characters, and when I got older I used my talent for mimicry to drive my coworkers at Sears crazy. And when I reached legal drinking age, I came up with the most messed-up personae I could imagine in order to get free drinks at bars.

I'd go into bars with friends on Long Island or in Florida and order drinks while they hung out warily behind me. It was important to go to a bar that was crowded, but not too crowded, and also to go fairly early in the night before too many patrons were smashed. Then in the middle of my order, I'd start rapid-fire bleating and rutting like a goat. "I'll take two beers and a sha-ah-ah-ah-ah-ah-aht."

When the bartender asked me to repeat the order, things would only get worse, with more bleating and rutting. From a few feet behind me one of my friends would look at the bartender and shake his head sympathetically. "Poor bastard has Tourette's," he'd say. If the bartender was remotely busy, or working by himself, he'd either give us the drinks for free, give us a discount on them, or tell us to get the hell out of there.

He wasn't the only character I'd do in bars. A lot of times I'd order drinks with an Australian accent. "G'day," I'd say. "Me fatha is a whala. He capchas whales and they convert the blubba to oil." I'd pretend I was a roadie for AC/DC ("a noice buncha blokes") just passing through, with a few days off.

"I do a lot of the rigging of the lights," I'd say. "It's loyk bay-in a stuntman. A real hi-wi-ah act up there. I've seen a lot—men falling to their death, glimpses down the shahts of beautiful lassies."

In the late winter of my first season, with things going well coming off of the Pesci sketch, I decided to pitch Goat Boy to some different writers on staff as a character. Steve Koren didn't bite. So then I cornered Tom Gianas, Fred Wolf, and Tim Herlihy together in the writers' room.

"I've got this character who has a Tourette's syndrome–like affliction," I said enthusiastically. "But instead of cursing, when he gets anxious, he starts making goat noises. Like bleating."

They all just stared at me blankly.

I decided that making the goat noise loudly a couple of times might help, so I did it and added, "And if he starts drinking at a party? Forget it. He'll start butting people with his head and eating the curtains."

That didn't help. Their lack of confidence made me think that maybe this Goat Boy idea was too out-there for anywhere but a Long Island bar. I shelved it and focused on other sketches. But a couple months later, Tom approached me.

"I was thinking about that goat idea," he said, smiling. "What do you think about this? He's a singer and pitchman for a CD of hit songs from the eighties."

It was pretty cool to have a writer so into one of my characters that he came up with such a far-out backstory. You never knew when you might get your next opportunity, and I trusted Tom, so we went for it. Having Goat Boy star in an infomercial, he thought, would be a simple way to introduce a surreal character and establish him for the next season. People loved it. I was psyched to have two characters—Pesci and Goat Boy—in the rotation after just one year.

Fresh off a string of Oscars, Tom Hanks was the first host of the opener of my second season. He hadn't seen the episode with Goat Boy from the previous season, so in the Monday pitch meeting, when I said, "He's just a guy who's part goat and sort of has Tourette's syndrome and really loves eighties music," Tom gave me a curious look.

"Okay?" he said.

"Don't worry," I said reassuringly. "It will be funny."

For the Wednesday read-through, Tom Gianas had created another insane masterpiece. I thought it was too many layers again—Goat Boy was an experiment gone awry who was sold by the military to MTV, where he hosted a talk show and interviewed the "other guy" from Wham!, Andrew Ridgeley (played by Tom Hanks). But it went over like Pesci did. Lorne and Tom were both chortling and my cast members ate it up.

"I don't understand Goat Boy," Tom said, "and I don't think I want to, but I just know it's funny."

During the dress rehearsal, Tom couldn't make it through without cracking up. That would set the crowd off and then he wouldn't be able to get his lines out.

Later, Mark McKinney even came to me with a great Goat Boy movie premise, once we saw how popular the character was.

"Picture this," he said one afternoon in the fall of 1996, pulling up a chair in my office. "It's a little bit *Teen Wolf* meets *The Elephant Man*." It was one of the weirdest ideas ever. The finale had a heart-rending scene of Goat Boy forced to climb a mountain like a real goat in order to take out a terrorist, after he'd spent the whole movie trying to move away from his goat past. Too bad it didn't get made.

Hey, dumber movies have been made from *SNL* sketches.

Chapter 12

Finding Farley

Chris Farley was returning to *SNL* in the fall of 1997 as a guest host. In the weeks leading up to his arrival, I started to piece together just how much the guy meant to *everyone* in the building. Producers like Marci, cast members like Norm, even the camera guys, grips, and all the other regular working guys were constantly telling stories about Chris. I hadn't heard such uniform excitement about a host in my time on the show. Even the hairdressers were gushing, "Oh, we miss him so much. He was our favorite. He had the biggest heart, he would always make us laugh. He'd come in and he could tell if we were tired. So he'd just put on a wig and do a character." That was the biggest audience he needed. A mention of Chris's name alone put genuine smiles on people's faces. And not fake smiles, either. These were hundred-thousand-watt, Christmas-morning smiles.

With cast members like me who didn't know him very well or hadn't met him yet, there was more of a curiosity. Whenever a big-time former cast member was coming back, you wanted to be taken in by them and learn from them. For me, Chris Farley and Adam Sandler were the two biggies. They'd kept getting more and more successful and it all originated at *SNL*. Chris was on the show, left, and now he was out in the world making movies and getting ten million a pop.

About a week before he was supposed to host, Chris stopped in to catch up with us all. It was a gesture that showed he was going to be in the trenches with us, helping us make the show as funny as possible. As I saw him interacting with the cast members and staff, within about five seconds, I understood why everyone was raving. He popped his head in the office I shared with Tracy Morgan and smiled. "This is a great cast, Jimmy," he said enthusiastically. "You're so funny." He didn't have to do that, and it made me feel great.

Everyone else in New York was excited, too. Cast members got two tickets per show, and that week I got more phone calls from people I knew asking if they could come to the show than at any other time I remember. Anyone could come by and hang out and sit around outside of the studio, but you got only two seats to give away. And on Saturday night I had at least ten people come to the show when Chris hosted, hanging out in my dressing room hoping to see or meet him. But that was later, after a long week. So let's backtrack.

Monday was upon us, and Tracy and I hadn't had a whole lot of time yet to spend thinking about getting Chris into one of our sketches. We did have one thing that we thought he'd think was funny. We'd goofed around and come up with a skit called "Break Time." Picture three low-key, mild-mannered executives toiling away in a nice office with oak-paneled desks—the works—and one would glance up nonchalantly at the clock, notice it was eleven fifteen A.M., and then quietly say, "It's break time, guys." Then the three guys (myself, Tracy, and hopefully Chris) would all mosh their brains out for thirty seconds—very physical, very funny—then we'd sit down again like nothing ever happened.

There'd be a chance to run "Break Time" by Chris later that afternoon in Lorne's office, but Tracy and I had a scheme to pitch it to Chris *before* the meeting to build some momentum going into it. When Chris wandered past our office, I jumped out and grabbed him, and we ran through it with him and he laughed.

"That's gonna be great," he said. "It's gonna be awesome." Then he immediately started digging around in our desk drawers looking for pot and whatever else we had. I'm sure he had a pretty good radar for finding illicit substances. I'd met him a few months previous in the men's room at the Aspen Comedy Festival. As I was peeing, he barged in and shouted, "All right, who's got the weed?!" I, of course, said, "I do," hoping to ingratiate myself with him. We never got to smoke together that night, but maybe somewhere deep in the recesses of his brain, he knew I'd be holding.

So, Chris found my weed in a drawer, then rummaged some more and pulled out an old fruit punch bottle Tracy had filled with booze.

"What's this?" he asked, then, not waiting for an answer, he opened it and took a swig.

Chris and I walked to the window, took a few hits of weed, and blew the smoke outside. Tracy sat at his desk and finished what was left of his booze after Chris manhandled it.

Before he left our office, Chris handed me back the one-hitter, looked at me, and said, "We're gonna have a great time this week, Jimmy."

"Jimmy"! Not "Jimbo," "Breu," or "Breuer," but "Jimmy." It was like being a little kid again and hearing a pal tell his mom, "I'm going over to Jimmy's house."

Tracy and I were psyched that Chris was into "Break Time." And after Chris wandered out of our office, we started jabbering about it.

His liking the skit meant we were going to be on the air that week. Then we'd probably start doing movies with him. We were his new best friends! This was definitely going to be a huge week.

But a little while later at the pitch meeting, Chris was in there, twitching and sweating. It was very awkward. He was losing it, grabbing at his face. Everyone knew something weird was going on.

I looked over at Tracy in disbelief and whispered, "That can't be from what happened in our room just now, can it?" It was not good. He was a wreck. A hit or two of weed could not have caused that.

After the meeting, Tracy and I went back to our room and Tracy was freaking out.

"Oh, he was on something, for sure!" he said. "More than just pot. What was up with him twisting and squirming around?"

I was stunned. It wasn't long before Marci Klein paid us a visit. "What the hell did you guys do?" she demanded.

"Nothing," I said.

(Up to that point Tracy and I had been really well behaved. Except for the time we raped Will Ferrell. I should explain.

Will had a habit of walking around the set in character and never breaking it. He had an early version of his *Anchorman* character Ron Burgundy, and another one who was a flamboyant painter. One night Tracy, Colin Quinn, and I told Will the Painter we'd like to buy a painting, but the money was in Colin's office. "Would you like to come and get it?" we asked. "Why, yes!" he exclaimed. "Yes, of course." He knew something was up, but to his credit he still stayed in character. In front of many cast members, most of whom were either laughing or freaked out, we dragged Will, howling, down the hallway and behind some garbage cans. He never broke character.

Then we began to fake punch him right in the hallway as he screamed, "Oh God, please help me." We pulled his pants off and everything.

Tracy stood lookout with a cigarette dangling from his mouth. "Hurry up," he'd say. "Someone's coming." Then he'd look over his shoulder at us and say, "Save me some of that."

Cheri Oteri was down the hallway from us, shouting, "I will call the police!"

When it was over, for the rest of the week, Will went around, still in character, asking if anyone had seen his assailants. And everyone would play dumb. And he'd say, "Well, I am going to get them and they are wanted by the law.")

"Don't give me that," Marci said. "Did you see Chris?"

We nodded slowly, still trying to figure out what she was driving at.

"Well," she said, "Chris was all excited earlier; he told me, 'Jimmy and Tracy are my boys, we're gonna hang . . . ,' so I know he stopped in here. What the hell happened?" She was getting very impatient. And that set Tracy off.

"Oh, no, no, no, no," Tracy said, getting angry. "I'm a grown man, Marci," he said, shaking his head and puffing out his chest. "I am a father of *children*, so you don't come in here and talk to me like that. You don't talk down to me. When we say we didn't—"

"Save it, Tracy," she said disgustedly. "This is what is going to happen this week. If Chris calls, you don't answer. If he asks you to go out with him, you don't go. If he wants to talk to you in private, you come tell me. Chris is in serious, serious trouble. Did you two know we have a nurse hired to watch over him twenty-four hours a day?"

We shook our heads.

"Did you know Chris Rock is here, hanging out to sub for him if it comes to that?"

Again, we shook our heads.

"Chris is in a bad place right now. He has a real addiction. And you guys are to stay as far away as possible."

"I had no clue," I said. "I'm really sorry." And we really didn't have a clue that things were that bad. I wanted to clear the air. "I'm not gonna lie to you. He came in here and had a one-hitter and a swig."

"But he was on some *other* shit in the pitch!" Tracy said.

"Tracy, I'm warning you," Marci said, then she stormed out of our office.

*   *   *

This great week we were going to have had soured a bit. But despite Marci's warnings, we still didn't think the situation with Chris was *that* heavy. So we worked on writing "Break Time" and kept our heads down. Coming up with skits with Tracy was pretty fluid. We bounced off each other really well. But, just like in the *Uptown Comedy Club* days the actual writing down of sketches fell on me. Tracy couldn't type for shit; a lot of time was spent just with him saying, "Yo, Jim, where's the *g* button?" Or "You need to type this, 'cause I don't even know where the *l* button is." We were great premise and scene guys, but we were terrible at sitting down and writing the whole thing out.

But by late Tuesday night, things with Chris got shady again. The office that we shared had a fogged glass door. You couldn't exactly see through it, but you could see shadows. During show week we practically lived there, and it was extremely late at night when we heard a slight yet persistent knock on the door.

Now I began to sense an evil feeling, way darker than the vibe I felt when Chris was sweating in the pitch meeting. A woman's silhouette took shape in the glass. I opened the door and there stood a tall, young, upscale (somewhat) brunette hooker. And next to her stood a slightly stockier hooker. Both looked to be in their late twenties, in cocktail dresses, and they looked *messed up*, definitely not caring about who I was or what the show was.

They had gruesome, vacant, hell-beast looks in their eyes, and they marched right past me to our couch. Chris teetered behind them, disheveled and sweaty in a button-down shirt and blazer, and he followed them directly in.

"Meet my friends," he slavered. His manic, happy charisma had given way to something completely deranged. He sat down in my chair and motioned to the door. "Shut it," he whispered. From his suit coat pocket he pulled a big plastic bag and from it, onto my desk, he dumped a mountain of white powder. I looked at the hookers. They were all business. This was routine for them but not my thing at all.

I bailed. I walked down to the writer Tim Herlihy's office. I was freaking out. The whole exchange was weird and disgusting. I popped my head in Tim's door.

"I just wanted to let you know," I said, "because I already got in trouble once this week, that Chris is in our office now, with two hookers and a big pile of powder."

And Tim just chuckled to himself and said, "Yeah it's bad." He knew it couldn't be stopped. "Don't worry about it. It's nothing you can control. You're not going to get in trouble for this. Go home."

So I went and walked around the city, wondering if this was really what success was all about.

*　*　*

The next day there was a dry read of all the sketches that were being considered for that week's show. Even as you got further into the week, you were never sure what skits were going to make it or what might be introduced late in the game. Sometimes Thursday would roll around and Lorne would say, "We could really use a Goat Boy this week."

And I'd be like, "Really? It's *Thursday*. Are you sure? It's gonna be awful."

The bizarreness with Chris continued. He was sitting between Lorne and Molly Shannon and he leapt up to do the moshing part of

"Break Time." He jumped around and shook his head violently. So far so good. But while Chris was shaking his head, a giant, bloody booger came flying out of his nose and landed right in front of Molly.

"Ewwww!" she gasped loudly.

Without missing a beat though, Chris, still violently shaking his head, swiped a hand down across the bloody chunk and put it in his pocket, like it was a quarter or something. Colin Quinn had been laughing his ass off, and when he saw that he froze like a cartoon. Chris finished the sketch and acted as if nothing out of the ordinary had happened.

To this day, to me, it was all very confusing. Here we have an extremely talented, funny, beloved guy surrounded by hookers and drugs, who has giant bloody boogers rumbling out of his nose and is sweaty and twitching 24/7. Where are his people? Who is watching him? Who is supposed to be helping him? Nobody apparently. Though there was no shortage of enablers and hangers-on making sure they partied with Chris.

Throughout it all, my wife kept telling me to pray for him. And I did, over and over. I was confused and bummed out. I'd started out thinking, "Wow. Chris Farley. It would be awesome to do movies together one day," but ended up thinking, "Keep this guy away from me! He's possessed!" On Thursday night I went home for a little bit to be with my wife and a friend. The phone rang. It was very late. No call that late is ever good. It's always a stomach sinker.

My wife answered. My friend and I looked at one another like, "Who's it gonna be?" And pretty soon, we heard my wife say, "Sure, hold on a sec, Chris. He's right here." She looked at me and mouthed, "Chris Farley," and pointed the receiver at me. I remember wondering, "Me? Why does he want to talk to me? How did he get my number?"

I took the phone, and Chris asked if I could meet him. I said, "Well, it's late and I'm visiting with my wife and a friend—we'll see each other tomorrow, you know?"

"C'mon!" he said, trying to convince me to join him at the hotel room he was staying in.

"Who are you with?" I asked. I didn't really need to know. I had a pretty good idea it was no one too helpful to his cause. Then an overwhelming feeling hit me. Instead of freaking out about him, I just thought, "Okay, I should try to talk to the guy for a minute. He's just a person. He's reaching out to me for some reason."

"You doing okay?" I asked.

"I'm great!" he shouted a bit too overzealously. "Come hang out, man!"

"Hey," I said, "the show is almost here! It's late. We should both get some rest. You sure you feel okay?"

He took a second to respond. And when he spoke, it wasn't the crazy party guy nor the movie star—it was just Chris, the kid who grew up in Wisconsin. I'll never forget what I heard in his voice. It wasn't quite desperation but real uncertainty.

"Jimmy," he asked, "am I *funny*?"

This set in motion a longer conversation and a whole cavalcade of questions. And I responded with only the truth—that everyone around the set pretty much laughed their asses off whenever he did anything. He liked to hear that. And then he said, "Like who?"

And I named cast members and people on staff whom he'd had laughing out loud all week. But then the heavier questions started again.

"Am I just the fat, dumb guy?" he asked.

"No!"

"But, you know, you saw me, I could only get hookers, right, Jimmy?"

"C'mon, Chris," I said. "You know that's not the truth."

My wife kept gesturing for me to go find him and hang out, but I knew that on this night, with who he was likely hanging with, it wouldn't be productive. It wasn't going to be a big catalyst for change for the guy. He only wanted to know, in this moment, that he was funny and not just a fat buffoon. It was so sad. Ten million a movie! And he was more insecure than a lot of us nobodies were.

I could hear voices in the background saying, "Tell him to come and hang out!" Girls laughing and partying. The conversation ended with his asking yet again if I wanted to hang out.

"Dude," I said. "I've got to get some sleep. You should, too."

Two nights later, he was hilarious, of course, on the show. For as truly screwed up and dark as the week had been, he absolutely destroyed us all on Saturday night. And this is when he really taught me a few things. He did "El Niño," where he played the hurricane, and then he did the final Matt Foley, the motivational speaker who lives "in a van down by the river."

For this Matt Foley sketch he played a health instructor. So Chris came in and Cheri, Will, and I were riding stationary bikes, just peddling away. I remember rehearsing the skit and he would fart, and Cheri and the girls would be like *Ewww! That's disgusting!*" And each time we rehearsed it, he would change it up, but it was always something little and gross and not a big deal.

But during the live show, he had a prop that wasn't there before, a pot of coffee—obviously not hot—and he just slammed the whole thing. And instead of swallowing the coffee he spit and sprayed it all over everyone. It was dripping off Cheri's face. The crowd lost it. I lost it. I am glad the camera was not on me then.

He waited until we were live before he pulled out the crazy stuff. Because during the dress show, I had thought I held my own. But once we were on the air he smoked me, and smoked me hard. He smoked everyone, just with those little nuances like that. And I wasn't like, "Oh, that bastard outdid me!" It was more an aha moment. As much of a mess as he was, he knew how to steal a scene. He knew how to blow the place up.

After the show, I didn't see much of him. Before the traditional

SNL after-party even got started, I could see the vultures circling him, and man, I didn't want any part of it. He was surrounded by filthy people. Drug dealers. Leeches. Satan's ring, I called them. My wife and I were puzzled by how these people could get access and control Chris. I headed home.

"Jimmy," he called out with a laugh. "You comin'?"

"Hey," I said. "I don't feel the greatest. I'll catch you later."

I paused for a second. That was BS. This guy was a legend to me now, and I couldn't and wouldn't hang. I didn't like the contradictions and the conflict that were piling up. He had just blown me away onstage, and now . . . ugh.

"Thanks, man," I said, genuinely. "Thanks for being part of my sketch. And thanks for flooring me."

He laughed, and that was that.

*　　*　　*

A few weeks passed, maybe more than a month. I started getting an overwhelming urge to call Chris. My rational side kept telling me he'd call if he wanted to. Spiritually, on some level I knew it was up to me, though, and the feeling would not go away. I couldn't get him out of my mind. Still, I'd ultimately talk myself out of it. "Jimmy," I'd tell myself. "He's Chris Farley. Someone close to him will take care of him. Don't worry about it. We only talked that one night. He'll be fine."

But the feeling would return. He, in some way, trusted me. I thought I shouldn't ignore that. I asked my wife what to do.

"God's telling you something," she said. "Listen."

And it was true. God talks to us a lot of the time. It's up to us to listen to His voice.

"Oh yeah? So what should I say when I call him?" I asked, then I didn't wait for her response. I quickly called my manager and said, "I've gotta talk to Chris Farley." He said he would get me his number.

The next week rolled around, and of course, I became immersed in the show and talked myself out of the urge to call him. This feeling came and went several more times. And as time passed, I knew that the urges I felt were God telling me what to do. I called my manager and he apologized for not getting me the number. The weekend was coming, and he promised to have it to me by Monday. He never got me the number. He's not to blame.

Chris died the next day. I don't want you to think that I feel like I am personally to blame or that I'm narcissistic enough to think what happened to Chris directly relates to me. I believe only that I had a chance. I had an opportunity to reach out to help. Would it have done any good? Who knows? I know only that God was telling me to reach out to another human being. I felt it, and I truly heard it loud and clear, and I ignored it. I will never turn my back on Him again. I felt like God wanted Chris to stay here with all of us, and in the end, his death was a terrible loss to pure evil. I dropped to my knees and apologized for turning my back and not acting on the messages that were sent to me.

I know it feels weird and kooky and surreal. And we are conditioned to tune out or fear that kind of stuff. I'm here to say, "Don't." You can make a difference. And when the big man gives you that urge, do yourself a favor and at least just give it a shot.

Chapter 13

Meeting the Mayor

A couple weeks after Chris Farley's appearance, our host was New York City mayor Rudy Giuliani. Unlike a lot of stars, the man kept to a schedule, moved with precision, and when the Monday meeting came, he and his security detail made their way politely through the building. He pulled up a chair next to Lorne, and you could tell he was completely tickled to be there. At the same time, he regarded it as a serious meeting, as he was eager to hear everyone's ideas and get down to the business of making a great show. He wanted it to be as memorable as we did.

We knew Giuliani's presence would give us great ratings, so the cast came armed with their A-list characters. Will had prepped a "Janet Reno Dance Party," Molly had a Mary Katherine Gallagher idea, Cheri had one for her old-lady character Rita Delvecchio. I was hoping to finally break in the Shut-up Guy. My idea was to have him serve as Giuliani's new press secretary, silencing any member of the media who dared question the mayor. The Shut-up Guy hadn't made a show yet, so I didn't have a ton of hope for him, but whatever happened, I knew it would be a historic show, so I was content to just fit in somewhere. "I'm very excited to be here," were the first words out of the mayor's mouth. He looked around the room and continued. "I'm excited to work with each and every one of you, and I don't mean to disrespect anyone, but where is Jimmy Breuer?"

"Am I in some kind of trouble?" I answered, raising my hand. Everyone laughed, including Giuliani.

"No, no," he said, smiling. "I really, really would like to do a Joe Pesci sketch. That's my favorite sketch. Could we do one?"

I was over the freakin' moon. It really made me feel validated in front of my peers.

"Sure," I said, smiling. "We can do that!"

"That's great, great news," he said.

Then we went around the room sharing ideas. When it was Cheri's turn, she said bluntly, "Mayor Giuliani, how would you feel about dressing up as a woman?"

"I could do that," he said, smiling. I'm pretty sure that was the first any of us knew about the ease with which the mayor would dress in drag, which is now, of course, old hat. And in the end, I have to say that sketch, with the mayor playing Cheri's mom as they prep Thanksgiving dinner while her kids steal beers and the neighborhood kids trash her lawn, was the funniest one of the night.

When it was my turn, the mayor said, "Oh, Jimmy, I already know what you've got in store for me," and laughed.

And I said, "Actually, I have another sketch in mind, too."

"Oh, yeah?" he said. "What's it about?"

"Well, I have this character that basically just goes around telling everyone to shut up," I explained. "He has no patience, and whenever anyone tries to talk to him he blows a fuse. I figured he'd be good as your new press secretary."

"Ha!" he said. "I like it. That sounds really funny."

The meeting came to an end, and Mayor Giuliani looked around the room. "This is tremendously exciting," he said, breaking into a wide smile. "This is going to be a really fun week."

I walked back to the office I shared with Tracy Morgan with two starring sketches in the works for the first time ever. I couldn't believe it.

The next night, the mayor took us all to the back room of this old Italian restaurant for dinner. We sat down at a long table, surrounded by security guards. Somehow, I was seated in front of both Lorne and Mayor Giuliani. Everyone was trying to talk politics with him the whole night, and I felt like it was probably the last thing he wanted to discuss. Interleague play had just resumed in Major League Baseball that year, and I knew that the mayor was a huge Yankees fan. What he did not know was that I was a huge Mets fan. When there was a lull in the conversation, I took the opportunity to change the subject.

"So what do you think of the Yankees and Mets being able to play each other again in the regular season?"

The mayor put down his fork, wiped his mouth with his napkin, and said, "I think it's phenomenal for baseball and for the city." And then he launched into a long spiel about his favorite Yankee teams and asked me which team I liked.

"My dad's a garbage man," I said. "So that makes me a Mets fan." I had his full attention just talking baseball for a half hour, and he became so animated, it was like he was a little kid on the street again, growing up in Brooklyn. Then the conversation turned to the mob and about how much he loved mob movies, like *Goodfellas*, and that's why he wanted to do the Joe Pesci sketch.

"In fact, my biggest Mafia bust when I was district attorney came from a transvestite snitch in the Meatpacking District," he said. "After mob hits, it was *her* job to chop up the bodies and dispose of them." He proceeded to tell us the most lurid mob tales just as matter-of-factly as if we were standing around a backyard barbecue. It felt like I'd made a new friend, and at the end of the night, the mayor said, "Jimmy, you ever do any stand-up around the city?"

"Yeah," I said. "Not while the show is on, but next summer I'll be doing Caroline's."

"Let me know the date," he said, "and I'll be there." He really did show up that summer.

Mayor Giuliani also came to Shea Stadium the following year for the Mets home opener. Dee and I had great season tickets for a while, and before the game started, as fans were filing in, we spotted him. So I got up and talked to one of his security guards. "Can I give a quick hello to the mayor?"

The guy recognized me and said, "Oh, yeah, he'd love to see you."

So I walked right up to him and I said really loudly, "We all know you're really a Yankee fan! We know you don't really wanna be here!" He blushed and smiled as I continued to razz him. "You don't have to play politics! You can go on home! You don't have to appease us." By now most of the fans in the lower boxes knew he was there and everyone was listening to the exchange.

"I'm going to get you back, Breuer," he whispered intently. "You just wait."

A couple of months later, I was scheduled to do a celebrity softball game at Yankee Stadium. To me that place was the enemy's nest. But it was for charity, and I knew it would be fun to run around the bases. Tom Arnold, Bob Saget, Matthew Broderick, and a bunch of other people I liked were in the lineup.

Sadly, we all were informed that the charity game was canceled. It had rained heavily the night before and the owner, George Steinbrenner, didn't want us tearing up his field before the Yankees took on the Red Sox.

"As our way of saying sorry," one of the Yankees' PR guys said, "why don't you all come up to Mr. Steinbrenner's personal box?"

"Why not?" I said. As a Mets fan, again, to me this was not a big deal. I can appreciate how special it would be for someone who loves the Yankees, but I'm not that guy. We all filed in, and Steinbrenner had a bartender in a little suit serving drinks. There was a leather sofa shaped like a baseball glove. The windows looked right out onto his box seats. The coolest thing I observed was that Steinbrenner was really not businesslike at all about the team. He was just a huge baseball fan who loved his team and wasn't shy about diving in and talking about the disagreements he had with Billy Martin when he was manager. He seemed like the ultimate Yankee fan, and this box was his chapel.

"You're great on *Saturday Night Live,*" he said. "I've known Lorne forever. He's great, too. You're lucky he likes you."

"I know," I said, nodding.

"So what do you think?" He looked around the room proudly at all his Yankee baubles. "Are you a Yankee fan?

As a die-hard Mets fan, all I could honestly say was, "Oh, I *follow* the Yankees." Technically, that was not a lie. And I followed it up with a first-class non sequitur evasion: "What a great establishment you have here, sir." Not a lie, either.

"Call us anytime you want to come to a game," Steinbrenner said. Then he started talking about great Yankee teams. "From the '78 club, who was your favorite, Jim? Reggie? Thurman? Catfish? Bucky Dent? Whose contribution meant the most?"

"Oh, my," I said. "They all did great!"

As I stuttered and stammered, Steinbrenner looked over my shoulder and shouted, "Rudy, I knew you'd show up!" I turned around to see Mayor Giuliani and his entourage.

"I'm not going to miss the Yankees–Red Sox game, George," the mayor said, shaking Steinbrenner's hand. "This is huge."

I gave the mayor a huge hello, and almost immediately he started smirking.

"You two know each other?" Steinbrenner said, observing our greeting.

"Oh yeah," the mayor said. "I was on *Saturday Night Live* last season. I did 'The Joe Pesci Show' with Jimmy. He's very funny."

"Wow," Steinbrenner replied. "That's great! That's one less introduction I have to make."

"My question," Giuliani asked Steinbrenner, "is what is he doing here?"

"He was going to play in a celebrity softball game, but the field's too wet," Steinbrenner said. "I don't want anyone getting hurt out there."

"But you know he's the enemy, don't you, George?" Mayor Giuliani said, the smirk returning to his face. Steinbrenner looked really perplexed. He didn't say a word. "It's true," the mayor added. "Jimmy Breuer is just about the biggest die-hard New York Mets fan in all five boroughs."

All the color left Steinbrenner's face. He looked like he'd eaten some bad scrambled eggs, and that look was soon replaced with disgust.

"I have nothing against the Yankees," I said insistently.

"Oh, that's a ringing endorsement," the mayor said cockily, his grin widening. "But it's not what you were telling me last time we met. You said you hated the Yankees and that you were a die-hard Mets fan. Matter of fact, weren't you gloating that the Mets beat the Yankees last summer?"

Steinbrenner looked almost remorseful, like his own personal baseball-fan radar had let him down. He didn't know what to think. Beads of sweat ran down my back to my ass. Before I could spit out another half truth, the mayor laughed and said, "Oh, I'm just busting Jimmy's chops. He's a comedian. He can take it!"

Steinbrenner didn't laugh. He looked me up and down and I could tell he knew I was full of crap. Mayor Giuliani just kept grinning. He leaned toward me and whispered, "I told you I'd get you back."

Back at *SNL*, after our big Italian meal, we motored through the rest of the week with both Pesci and the Shut-up Guy in the lineup. Tracy had a part in the Pesci sketch as D.C. mayor Marion Barry, trying to sell Mayor Giuliani old garbage trucks for cash. In the dress rehearsal, both sketches killed. And after that response, I was pretty sure it would be the first time I had two characters in one episode. That didn't last.

Shortly before the main show started, one of the writers came up to me and said, "Hey, Jim, sorry to do this to you, man, but you've gotta pick one of the two sketches. It's such a big week here, we gotta be fair to everyone."

"That sucks," I said. To me, it was bullshit. Plenty of people were in multiple sketches every single week. With Steve Koren and Fred Wolf gone, I had no real backers on the writing staff who could swing their weight around. I felt like I was being frozen out. If I could hit a home run, let me hit a home run, don't put me on the bench just so everyone can bat.

"I know," he said. "Can you just decide quickly between Pesci and the Shut-up Guy?"

So of course I picked the Pesci sketch, because that was the one the mayor wanted to do. I was very happy with it, and most important, so was the mayor. Well, our mayor. The next week Marion Barry from D.C. was in *The New York Times* demanding an apology from the show for our portrayal of him.

Chapter 14

Chris Kattan, Heavy Metal Man, and the End of *SNL* Days

Life on *SNL* gradually became miserable for me. Don't get me wrong; my overall experience on *SNL* is irreplaceable. It's just that political tiffs and ego blows had accumulated over the years and by the summer of 1998, things had come to a boil. I had enemies on the writing staff who wanted me fired, and I didn't really care to stick around.

The only way I found out things were that bad for me was that this high-level NBC exec, who was the grand pooh-bah of all of the channel's late-night programming, called me during the summer of 1998. He was a huge fan of mine and I was a huge fan of his.

"What *happened* last season?" he said.

"What do you mean?" I asked. He made it sound like I'd walked through the studio with a running chain saw and no pants on.

"We just had our end-of-the-year meeting for *SNL* and I learned that some people are trying to get you off the show. Did something happen between you and any of the writers?"

"Something happened, but I thought we worked it out," I said. I went on to explain a *situation* with a couple of the show's top writers that transpired earlier in the spring when Matthew Broderick was the host. I explained to the exec that we patched it up but that there might still have been some hard feelings there.

"Maybe you should talk to Lorne," he said. "Or go have dinner with these guys."

"I offered," I said. "But no one's taken me up on it."

The *situation* that got me in trouble occurred when the *Godzilla* remake starring Matthew Broderick was coming out, and he was scheduled to host the show. Tracy and I sat down and started talking about *Godzilla*, wondering if it was going to be like the old versions, and we started riffing on old monster movies. Pretty soon we were like two little kids, just going off making all these airplane, air raid, and machine gun noises. We were like, "Why don't we do *this* for the monologue?"

Our plan was when the show opened, we were going to come out and bombard Matthew with a spastic barrage of questions about the movie, like: "Is it gonna be like the old *Godzilla?*" And he'd say, "How do you mean?" And we'd start doing loud sound effects with our mouths, like the old prop airplanes shooting at Godzilla, and muffled voices from loudspeakers saying stuff like, "People of Tokyo, run for your lives!" Then Tracy would say, "Are the twins from the movie *Mothra* gonna be in there? Remember the twins, they be singing that song? 'Oooh-wah, do-do-wah!'?"

We wrote it up and it really came to life as a performance piece in the read-through. Matthew loved it. He was cracking up. And the way it was written made it really easy for him. He wouldn't have to do a lot of work—he could just come on stage, do his shtick, and we'd take the ball and run with it. However, one of the head writers had his own monologue sketch. It was a spoof on all the *Godzilla* advertisements, like, "His tail is four blocks long. His teeth are two stories high. His testicles are like two overstuffed bags of leaves. . . ." And after a few of them, it was like, "I get it!" It was funny . . . for about thirty seconds.

*　　*　　*

Tracy and I learned on Thursday that our monologue wasn't going. We weren't happy, but that's life. I still had a sketch involving my character the Shut-up Guy in the mix, so to me that was a decent consolation. Matthew and I rehearsed that later on Thursday, and during a break he asked, "Are we going to do your monologue, too?" He seemed pretty excited about it.

"It didn't get picked," I said, and shrugged. I let him know that this stuff always happens and didn't bother me anymore. Later that night in the hallway, two of the show's producers stopped me and wanted to get some answers about why the monologue wasn't happening.

"Are we *really* not doing it?" one of them asked. "I know for a fact Matthew loved it. Does Lorne know about this?"

That was the first time I'd ever heard that question. I had always just assumed Lorne was present during the decision-making process, and offered his opinion one way or another. So I said to them, "Jeez, I really don't know. I'm just a cast member. *You* guys are the producers! Don't *you* know?"

They wandered off, presumably in search of the truth. I figured nothing would come of it. Friday night I was at home when my phone rang with a call from one of the producers.

"We need you to come in as fast as you can," he said excitedly. The rehearsals for the monologue usually happened on Friday nights. "We're now going to camera block your monologue. We called Tracy and he's already on his way in."

When I arrived, I saw that they were testing out camera angles for not only our monologue, but the head writer's monologue, too.

The head writer was in charge of the situation, and I could tell he was aggravated by even the sight of us.

"Let's see your monologue," he sighed, and very shortly after we started, he looked at us and the cameramen, and nodded. "Okay, we're good! We got it!" And that was that.

Doing a camera block usually takes a good hour, but when it came to blocking Tracy and me, it only took five minutes. I looked at Tracy, and said, "You know they had us come in and do this just to shut someone up."

"That was the shortest camera blocking in history," Tracy agreed.

On Saturday afternoon, we found out *again* that, yes, our monologue had been cut. Tracy and I went down to eat dinner in the cafeteria. On show nights, everyone ate between five P.M. and seven P.M. I was just going to take a bite of my BLT when the head writer's sidekick showed up and insisted that Tracy and I had to go back upstairs because Lorne wanted to see our monologue.

I put my sandwich down slowly, and he said, "Listen, if you're not ready, that's okay, but it's now or never. Otherwise, we'll just forget it." I told him we'd be happy to come do it. Tracy and I left our dinners and went back upstairs, only to see the head writer in the middle of a tantrum. He was trying to explain to Matthew Broderick how to perform his monologue, and it wasn't working at all. I looked up to see Lorne pacing back and forth, scratching his head as if to say, "Oh, Lord, I've got a problem child."

Then the head writer started pacing behind Lorne, step by step. "It's going to work!" he insisted. "I'm telling you."

"Can we just see Jim and Tracy's monologue?" Lorne finally replied, sounding fatigued. This was when I knew Lorne just wanted, ultimately, whatever was the funniest thing for the show. When we finished, Matthew said, "I love this sketch, why can't we just do it?"

Satisfied, I went back to my dressing room and shortly thereafter the head writer's sidekick wandered in and said no decisions had been made—which monologue they were going to choose was all still up in the air. And that's when it really hit me that they didn't care about the funny. All they cared about were their own egos.

"We're going to do yours for dress rehearsal," he said. "And we'll film it in front of the crowd. And then we'll see what happens."

So Tracy and I went out to do the monologue with Matthew. It crushed. The audience loved it. We improv-ed most of it. Then it came time to do my Shut-up Guy sketch in dress rehearsal, Matthew started cracking up in the middle of the sketch. When the crowd started laughing, he had a hard time getting through the sketch. As I came off the stage, the head writer grabbed me and said, "It's too bad that Matthew laughed so much during the sketch, because, honestly we don't know if it works."

I wanted to punch him. I went back to my dressing room, disillusioned. There was a knock and the head writer's sidekick came in.

"Well," he said. "We've got yours on tape, but for the live show we're going to do the other monologue. But the good thing is we have yours filmed, so we can use it on reruns if we want to."

"Why would you do that?" I asked.

"To be honest with you," he fudged, "it's because the second sketch is 'The View' and Tracy has to get through hair and makeup. Lorne's worried there's not going to be enough time between the monologue and that sketch."

I ran to Tracy's dressing room and said, "They're all going to come around here and ask if you think you can get your makeup on in time to do the monologue and the sketch. Don't cave in. Tell 'em you can do it."

"Of course," Tracy said. And his insistence helped pave the way. In the end, we got to do the monologue and it crushed. But things wouldn't be the same anymore.

* * *

Another thing that might have set the stage earlier to drive a wedge between a clique on the show and me were some flare-ups I had with Chris Kattan. Around Christmastime 1996, Rosie O'Donnell was going to host the show. I'm a big fan, so I was excited to have her on. She was really popular at the time, and I knew the ratings would be huge. I purposely saved a Pesci sketch especially for that episode, but I was going to do it as something different from the usual Pesci show. On the chalkboard in my office, I wrote down, "Pesci doing Christmas stories in front of a classroom." I was thinking it would be Pesci in a school talking to kids, saying stuff like, "Hey, you guys know about Rudolph and his red nose? Why do you think his nose was red? Because he was a rat. A snitch. His whole family was rats, he's not even a reindeer."

Chris came into my office shortly afterward, studied the chalkboard, and asked, "Pesci Christmas stories, what's that?"

"Instead of doing the normal 'Joe Pesci Show,'" I said, "I'm gonna have Pesci doing classic Christmas stories in a classroom, in front of kids. I'm saving it for when Rosie O'Donnell comes on."

"Oh, that's a great idea," he said.

Well, the week before Rosie arrived, all I remember is being in a meeting and hearing Chris's voice announce, "Al Pacino's Christmas stories," to assorted laughs. I looked up from my stack of papers in utter disbelief. My head started sweating. Lasers were shooting out of my eyes. He had snagged my idea and repurposed it as an Al Pacino sketch. Everyone was like, "Oh my God, this is a great idea." And it was picked it up—though it died in dress rehearsal and never made it to air.

I didn't confront Chris about it right away, which was probably the wrong approach. Instead, when we were rehearsing a couple days later, just before a take, I gave him a serious look, like I was really disappointed with him.

"What's the matter?" he whined. "*God.* What's going on?"

"Oh, nothing," I said.

Then he had to start all over. Just before the take, he looked at me and stopped again.

"Are you mad at me? Jeez."

"We should have a talk, actually," I said. "Let's sit down after rehearsal."

"What's bothering you?"

"Let's sit down *after* rehearsal."

"You're upset," he squealed. "Why are you upset?"

"We'll talk after rehearsal."

"Tell me *now*," he whined. "This is so distracting."

"Nah," I said. "Just rehearse and we can sit down afterward."

I kept it up for about twenty minutes and it nearly drove him insane. I wanted to see him dangle. I wanted to see the guilt come out in him. After rehearsal, when I asked Chris about it, he played dumb. "Oh, I totally forgot about that!" he said. "I'm so sorry. I didn't even think of yours! Mine's a bit different anyway, because it's Al Pacino, not Pesci." I knew he was full of crap.

Looking back, I get what happened. I understand the pressure of that place. And every time I reflect on it now, I don't find any bad feelings anymore. But at that time, we were both fighting for our lives to stay on the show. Chris annoyed me sometimes, but he was hilarious. And I loved playing his jerky older brother in the "Goth Talk" sketches. I was always really envious of what he did with that sketch. When we first started rehearsing, he told me, "Feel free to really hit me. The harder you hit me, the funnier it will be."

Then when I'd hit him, he'd stop and say, "No, you gotta really smack me in the head. They've got to *hear* it," pointing out toward where the audience would sit. I loved how seriously he took that. I guess that perfectionist attitude manifested itself in different ways for all of us. With Chris, it made him vulnerable to pranks from some of the more jaded cast members. Norm, specifically.

Whenever Norm was in a sketch, he wouldn't rehearse it properly at all. He warned us of that early on. I remember when I first got on the show, he told all of the new cast members, "Don't put me in any of your gay sketches!" So how he wound up in them, I have no idea. He had the "Update," and that's where he seemed to be happiest. So, if he did somehow wind up in your sketch—when Pamela Anderson was on in the spring of 1997, he mysteriously wound up in two or three sketches—he wouldn't bother to nail it until it was on the air.

The three of us did a *Twilight Zone* sketch where Norm had to play Rod Serling, the show's creator and emcee, who began each episode with that distinctive voice: "Imagine if you will . . ." It was Chris's only sketch that week, and he was as eager to share the stage with Pamela Anderson as Norm was.

During rehearsal all week, and into the dress rehearsal Saturday night, Chris was riding Norm about not doing the proper Rod Serling voice. "Oh my God, Norm, you're so terrible," he'd say bitchily. "Is that the way you're going to do the voice? The sketch is going to get cut! C'mon! Why don't you rehearse it the way it's going to be?" And whenever Chris was not bitching at Norm, he was flirting big-time with Pamela Anderson. "How come Jim gets to kiss you in the 'Goat Boy' sketch? I want to be able to kiss you! God, you're so hot. You're so sexy. If Tommy Lee ever breaks up with you . . ." Then he'd pause and look at Norm and start yelling at Norm again. "God, get the voice right!"

The whole time this was going on, I was shocked that Norm wasn't saying anything back. If you went after Norm, he would generally crush you with a barrage of insults. But it was almost like he was tuning Chris out.

Finally, we made it to the dress show. "Oh my God," Chris

squealed. "If this sketch doesn't get picked up, I'm going to freak out!" Again, Norm completely half-assed his lines. He knew that it would get on the air. It was a good sketch. Still, Chris didn't relax. Right before we went to air, he was still bitching at Norm. "Are you really going to use that voice, Norm? It's so terrible! I should have gotten someone else. Why are you even doing this?"

Over the PA, we heard: "One minute to airtime." Chris was still bitching at Norm, and also still trying to flirt with Pamela. He was alternating back and forth, like he was completely unhinged.

"Thirty seconds to airtime." Norm was completely oblivious and immune to Chris's scolding. I was looking over at him, as if to say, "Are you really going to let him keep badgering you? This has gone on for days!" Norm was my hero, and I couldn't stand to see him just take the abuse from whiny little Chris Kattan.

"Fifteen seconds to airtime." Just as everyone in the sketch was trying to concentrate, Norm finally spoke up, unleashing a brutal tirade. "Hey, ah, Chris, Pamela knows you're gay!" he yelled. "We *all* know you're gay. So why don't you just come out of the closet and then you wouldn't be such an angry little gay guy. Christ, you're always in everyone's business! Stop hitting on chicks!"

As soon as he finished, we all immediately heard, *"Action!"*

Then from out of nowhere, Norm perfectly captured Rod Serling's voice and began the sketch: "Imagine if you will . . ." He just nailed it. If you watch the sketch, all you see is my shoulders heaving up and down because I was laughing so hard. I couldn't get my lines out. Chris was furious. He couldn't get his lines out. It was one of the greatest things ever.

*   *   *

As I said, toward the end at *SNL* I often felt like I had no way to get anything on the show regularly, even if something killed in dress rehearsal. Things just got way too political. One of the producers, Michael Shoemaker, noticed, and one day he stopped by my office. He listened to me complain for a few minutes before he stopped me and said, "Why are you busting your ass with sketches?"

"'Cause I'd like to get on the show."

"Sure," he said. "But notice how there's an entirely different set of writers for the monologues and the 'Update'? When Sandler was here, he just completely took over the 'Update' with characters. They couldn't get him off. So, if you want to get on the show, start there. They can't touch you."

So that's where I retreated. I had great luck getting on monologues, and I found I could be creative without getting my material compromised. One of my favorites was playing Mickey the trainer from *Rocky*.

In the end, after the call from the NBC exec, I called my agent and Lorne, and I asked for my release. From my viewpoint, it wasn't going to magically get better. "You have too big a heart, Jim," Lorne said. I thought that was a little over the top. You didn't need a big heart to not want to put up with people trashing your work. But even when it was rocky, I'd gotten some irreplaceable experiences, worked with the best of the best, and created some of the show's finest moments. All in all, it was a great run while it lasted.

Chapter 15

Half Baked, Dave Chappelle, and Monk the Pooping Dog

In May of 1996, I was at a wrap party for my first season on *SNL*. It was at the skating rink in Rockefeller Center, and it was a moment when the cast really bonded and let loose. Looking back, it seems like a time when we all got along the best; maybe that was because we were all done for the season.

On this particular night, I was in a circle of drunken folks like Will Ferrell, Mark McKinney, and Tracy Morgan. I was psyched because I was coming back to the show next season, and I was happy to be among talented people who had now become my friends. I looked over and saw Dave Chappelle had shown up and that made me even happier.

Dave and I hadn't spent much time together since I got shit-canned from *Buddies*. But we quickly reconnected at the wrap party. I think he still felt kind of shitty about how the whole *Buddies* thing went down, because I remember him saying, "Don't worry, Breu Dog, one day we'll get them back, on the big screen. We'll do a movie together. That'll show 'em."

Later that summer, I was performing at Carolines in New York and Dave showed up in the greenroom after my set with a guy named Neal Brennan. Neal was the door guy when I used to play the Boston Comedy Club. He was the kid handing out flyers trying to get people into the club. He was a young guy, and he'd always wheeze, "Breuer, I got this joke for you," or "Breuer, listen to this, I got this add-on for ya."

"I want you to be in this weed movie we wrote," Dave said, pointing a thumb in Neal's direction. "I want you to play my brother Brian." He meant his real-life, happy-go-lucky stoner brother Brian. I was blown away. I had no clue that he and Neal had been collaborating.

"We're gonna have some amazing cameos in it," Dave added. "This thing is gonna blow up."

I didn't know if I believed him. Was he talking about some kind of straight-to-video spoof movie?

"When you say *movie,*" I asked, "do you mean like movie-in-actual-theaters-type movie?" I wanted clarification.

"Yeah, man," he said in his drawn-out, almost disgusted manner, like how could I be doubting the potential success of this? "*Movie* like in-the-*theaters* movie! Universal Studios wants to do this shit!"

"Okay," I said. That was all I needed to hear. "I'll do it." I hadn't even seen the script.

What was weird is that I was out pitching movies at the time. And one of them was a weed movie. I thought the times called for a great, new, adventurous Cheech and Chong. Mine was the story of me and my best friend when we were eighteen years old and smoking a lot of grass.

Now a misconception about me is that I was a real weed head at the time. Sorry, but I just look high. I have my whole life. Now, I smoked a little, but nothing close to Brian, the character I was going to play. I was never a wake-and-bake guy, but I do admit that in my last season of *Saturday Night Live* I was smoking more than I had in the past. I guess it was my way of coping with the friction there.

I wound up talking to a producer in L.A. named Bob Simonds. He'd done all the Adam Sandler movies up to that point. "Do you know Dave Chappelle?" he asked. "'Cause he was in here two weeks ago pitching a weed movie. And his is complete, and I love it and we're going with it, so you should talk to him about getting a role in it."

Still, beyond Simonds's confidence, I'd heard nothing about Universal Studios. But here was Dave, all excited, and his was the weed movie that had a shot. So I was glad he approached me because I wasn't going to try to bogart my way into his film, pardon the pun.

After that conversation, my manager Leon, who also repped Dave, sent me the script. To this day, I've never laughed harder when reading a script. I couldn't believe how well written it was. When people today tell me they like the movie, I explain that I improv-ed nothing. I only did line for line what was written, including the food-ordering scene and the killer speech. It was even Neal's idea to give Brian a hook. He came up to me during shooting and suggested Brian punctuate things by saying, "Fully, man." And all I did was perform it.

So I read the script and I didn't hear from Dave for a while, and then I heard this rumor that Christian Slater was now up for the part promised to me. Something weird was going on. Well, the weird thing turned out to be that Dave was firing our mutual manager, Leon. Everything was getting scrambled, but I really wanted to be in this thing and I didn't want to get bounced.

Then I personally called Dave and left a message. "Listen," I said. "You came and asked me to be in your movie. I said yes. But it's your movie. If you don't want me in it, I have no problem with that. It's all good, don't worry about it."

A couple of days later Bob Simonds called. "Do you like this role?" he asked.

"It's the funniest script ever," I said. "Of course."

"The role is yours," he said. And that was that. Drama over. Dave came through and held firm to his word and I was off to Toronto to shoot my first movie.

The funniest part of the whole *Half Baked* experience was that Dave brought his new dog along for the entire six-week shoot, a small Alaskan husky named Whitey. What a disaster. Dave could barely take care of himself, let alone a frisky, spiteful, undisciplined dog.

Now, I love Dave, but he is extremely forgetful. He didn't and does not care about anything. *He just doesn't care.* When we did the sitcom *Buddies,* if we had to be at a meeting or rehearsal, I would lie to him about what time it started, so he would get there even halfway on time. After a while I realized, okay, an hour's not going to cut it, I have to make it an hour and a half. His whole attitude toward everything was: "Oh, man, don't worry about it!" This is an awesome attitude for a friend to have but a really shitty one for a pet owner.

So you can see what I am getting at. Same thing on the set of *Half Baked.* No urgency about the movie. No pressure. No organization on his part. My theory is that the most artistic people are also the sloppiest. Or at least their pets are.

Case in point: I went to Toronto. Everyone in the cast was staying at this five-star hotel. It was beyond nuts. Marble floors. Soaring ceilings. Concierges everywhere. This was the place they put any star who was in town. Marilyn Manson and his creepy eyes were there. Norm MacDonald. Chris Farley. Everyone. So I walked into the lobby and there was Dave with Whitey, who was taking a shit right in the middle of it all. And Dave was just like, "My bad. My bad. I'll get it." But you know he really wasn't going to get it, and the concierges were diving on the pile like it was a live grenade. "It's okay, sir. It's okay, sir. Our pleasure."

I have no idea why Dave wanted to call this dog Whitey. I think it was partially simply because Dave wanted to be able to give something white commands. He took special glee in giving it orders:

"Whitey, sit down."

"Whitey, roll over."

"Whitey, play dead."

But at some point early during the shoot, he changed the dog's name to Monk, after the jazz pianist and composer Thelonious Monk. Dave's dad was a huge jazz buff, so it must have been some sort of tribute to name an Alaskan husky after a famous jazz musician. Who knows?

When he wasn't crapping in the lobby, Monk busied himself by trying to bite this young dreadlocked kid who drove us to the set every morning in a van. Dave would be riding, talking away to everyone, absentmindedly engaged in conversation, and the kid would be swerving and veering off the road and politely removing his bicep from Monk's mouth. Dave would scold Monk, saying, "Bad dog! Bad dog!" But it didn't do any good, and the kid didn't want to complain about it. Because ultimately Dave was the whole reason all of this was happening. The whole reason we all had jobs. So the kid would grin and bear it, and then probably drive over to the ER to get stitches after he dropped us off.

Once Monk got to the set, he'd shit in Dave's trailer. Rip it to pieces. Dave would try all different combinations to get this thing to chill out. He'd have PAs on the set walking him every fifteen minutes, feeding him, rubbing the thing behind the ears. Nothing helped. The dog had zero discipline.

So then Dave decided to leave Monk in his hotel room. Like I said earlier, Dave was disorganized. So he didn't safeguard anything. Monk proceeded to eat all of his shoes, which were all nice, rare Nikes, like vintage Air Jordans. We'd go to the mall and Dave would routinely drop five hundred or six hundred dollars on shoes and clothes. And Monk had a buffet with all of that. And he would crap all over the room. It was both funny and sad that Dave would work his ass off all day on the movie only to come home to ruined clothes and crap piles all over his room.

Across the hall from Dave's room was yet another famous person. A big, ginormous, beautiful old woman whom you might know as Florida Evans from the seventies sitcom *Good Times.* Esther Rolle was her real name, may she rest in peace.

One day I walked out of Dave's room right as she was walking out of hers. To say she wore a pained look is putting it mildly. She looked at me like I had just burned down her house and dropkicked her birthday cake into rush-hour traffic. "Are you staying in *that* room?" Her voice, as you might recall, crackled like an old 78 record.

"No, ma'am," I said. I just wanted to get back to my room. But that wasn't going to happen.

"Well, it smells like *shit* in there!" she yelled. Clearly she'd been wanting to vent for a while. Her tone was disgusted; she didn't care at all that it wasn't my room. I was guilty by association. And it was painfully obvious to her that I was a moron for even having anything to do with this foul room.

"And that damn dog is *always* barking," she said. "And I smell *marijuana*," she added in that saddened voice she used when J. J. Evans had let her down for the fourteen hundredth time. "What is going *on* in there? It is dis*graceful*. *Who* is staying in there?" I was surprised, to be honest, that she didn't slap me.

I couldn't say, "Why, it's the fine young comic actor Dave Chappelle, Ms. Rolle." She couldn't have cared less. I told her I'd ask the manager about it, and as soon as I walked away from her I started laughing. Poor Dave. This dog had managed to gross out or bite nearly everyone it came in contact with. But Dave was blind to it. He loved Monk. Treated him and loved him like he was his own kid. He made excuses for the dog constantly.

Pretty soon, all the girls from the hotel and the bellmen were walking Monk. Babysitting Monk. Trying to keep him on his best behavior, but eventually it got to the point where too many people were complaining. I found this funny, but at the same time I tried to tell Dave he had to do something. You don't wanna get sued by Florida Evans or someone else the dog annoyed. Dave was becoming stressed, too. It was like seeing a parent with an out-of-control kid who just didn't know how to discipline him. The producers of *Half Baked*, Neal Brennan, the people who ran the hotel—everyone could see that Monk was a problem. People tried to help, or at least tried to cover up the destruction, but Monk was as rabid as you can get without having rabies. Dave might as well have brought along an orangutan.

One night I was looking out the peephole of Dave's door, trying to make sure I could sneak past Florida Evans's room without incurring her wrath. Dave was sitting on the bed; Monk was lying next to him, panting quietly, satisfied, having just mangled a baseball cap.

"I think they wanna kick me out," Dave said. "I think I gotta get rid of Monk."

"Is there someone back in New York who can watch him?"

"Nah," he said. "I'll figure something out."

And then Dave got an idea. "Jim, you're gonna be proud of me," he said, patting Monk's head one day as we rode to the set in the van. "I'm sending this little guy to obedience school. Boot camp. You're gonna see some changes."

Monk went every day to obedience school for three or four weeks, and Dave was so proud of him. He would call me down to his room and show me all of the new moves and tricks Monk had learned. He'd say, "Monk, give me your paw." And the dog would do it. "Monk, lay down." And the dog would do it. No more shoes and socks got chewed up. And Dave's stress level dropped considerably. I was impressed. And yet the smell of crap still seemed to linger. It was embedded in the room somehow, but that was no big deal and it would certainly fade. Dave was so happy. He knew there was goodness in the dog. "See," he'd say after Monk did some tricks. "I told you there was nothing wrong with this dog. He has a good heart. He didn't mean to bite, he just didn't know better."

One night later on, after we were done shooting for the day, Dave was reflecting on life, the movie, and Monk. Dave was so psyched that his career was taking off.

"I want to do this like Mel Brooks," he said. "Keep writing my own stuff. Keep casting my own friends." Dave was thinking that doing movies would allow him to spend time with his dad, who was now getting older, and he was happy that Monk had been trained so well. He laughed a little bit thinking about how the dog almost got him kicked out of the hotel.

As we were talking, I looked past Dave to see Monk taking a nice big juicy logger on his pillow. Seeing Dave's face was priceless. It was like his own child had betrayed him. Monk jumped off the bed and scooted underneath it. Dave followed him. He stuck his head under the comforter and then slowly pulled back and looked up at me. Whenever I see Dave disappointed, it is the funniest thing. I don't know why.

"Man," he said disgustedly, shaking his head. "There's like forty piles of shit under this bed. On my socks. In my shoes."

All Monk was doing was going under the bed to do what he had been doing out in the open. The thing that made Dave the maddest was all the time and money down the drain.

"I just spent two thousand dollars to train this dog to be sneaky," he complained. "That's all. I paid all this money not for obedience, but just for him to be sneaky." And with that he pulled his shirt over his nose and began picking up the poop.

So sometimes you think you've solved a problem, but all you've really done is move the shit somewhere else.

I needed to figure out how I was going to play my character Brian. My niece was really into the Grateful Dead and at the time, she was living with my wife and me in New York City. I'm a metalhead, so the Grateful Dead weren't for me. I didn't know much about them at all. One day, my niece showed me a VHS box set of some Grateful Dead concerts and suggested that I might "find" Brian in there somewhere.

I sat down and watched, and on my second or third tape, I saw people going into a stadium before the show, getting frisked and patted down. There was this guy, and he's in line dancing, and he has a flower in his hand, and as he gets to the security guy and they're frisking him, he just keeps dancing. And he is still smiling. Nobody is bringing this guy down. I grabbed my wife and said, "This is Brian." No matter where this guy is in life, he's happy. He's in his own world. If he's in prison, he's happy. If he's being tortured, he's happy. No matter what, he's still got a smile on his face.

And I also took acting lessons from this teacher in Hell's Kitchen in New York City. During the shoot, I would fly down periodically, and he'd help me build tremendously on my biggest *Half Baked* scenes by really becoming Brian.

And whenever I would get back on set, having just seen my teacher, people would ask me if I was high. And I'd say no, I was just content to be alone, focusing, and staying in the Brian mind-set.

I loved everything about the whole experience of making *Half Baked.* I was excited about my trailer. It had a bedroom, a couch, a TV, a stereo, etc. To me that was the greatest thing. Craft services was unreal, too. I showed up weighing 175 pounds and when I left I weighed 195. I had no idea how it all worked.

"You want breakfast?" A guy in an apron asked on my first day on set.

"What do you have?"

"Whatever you want."

Even smoothies. One guy's job was just to make smoothies. Sometimes when I was done shooting, I wouldn't even go back to the hotel. I'd stick around the set. I loved watching scenes get made, even if I wasn't in them. Or just hanging in my trailer, rocking out to metal. I tried to get Dave to understand Metallica, but he couldn't do it. It was too crazy for him. But he got me into Biggie Smalls and Tupac.

The funniest thing is that I truly never got stoned while filming the movie. Well, almost.

Right after I finished shooting one day, a PA came up to me and handed me a little package and said, "Go enjoy yourself." On any movie you do, there's always someone on the set who eventually comes up to you and says, "I'm the whatever-you-need guy." And this was different from the craft services make-you-an-omelet guy. If you need a hooker? This guy will get you a hooker. You need a freak? He'll get you a freak. You need drugs? He'll get you drugs. He's the jack-of-all-trades; whatever you need, he can get, no questions asked. On every movie set. Sure, they're on the payroll supposedly to grip or lay down a wire, but they're really there for an entirely different purpose.

I had the next few days off from shooting, so I went into my trailer, smoked, and delivered an impromptu Metallica air jam concert to myself. I was terrifically sweaty. A PA girl came and knocked on the door. In my haze, it sounded like pretend knocking. "Just a minor hallucination," I thought. I kind of laughed, because it would be really funny if someone was really at my door. I kept the Metallica pumping, but that knock was growing louder. My heart rate quickened. I came back to earth as best I could and got a little nervous and paranoid. In a panic, I opened the windows, started fanning my hands near them, hid the weed, and sprayed some Glade air freshener. I thought this might make the knocking go away. It didn't. In my mind, chaos was unfolding. I found a couple of mints, popped them in my mouth, and opened the door.

"Hey, Jim," the PA girl said. "This sucks, but the producers are asking if you can go and film one more scene tonight."

"Uh. Um. Scene?"

"I know you're done," she said. "They want to call and ask you personally and apologize."

The PA girl left, and sure enough, my phone rang. Producer Bob Simonds was on the line explaining that Clarence Williams, the guy who played Sampson, was leaving the set. He was fed up. He wanted out and he wanted to be done tonight. Could I please do my last scene with him, so he could be on his way?

So I went to go do the scene, and this is why I freaked out: There was this makeup lady, Inga. She was in her fifties and sort of a motherly type to me. She had those instincts, you know? I made my way nervously over to the set, still high as a kite, as there was no time to sit in a chair in the makeup room; we were going to shoot this thing, send Clarence on his way, and wrap it up for the night. And Inga was just going to do my makeup really fast as I stood there, two feet away from the whole production.

She started staring at me. I was still sweating from the Metallica jam session. Then she looked right into my face and said, "Are you all right?" And that sent me *beyond* paranoia.

"Yeah," I said. "I'm just thinking about my lines."

"Well, you don't look all right."

That was all I needed to hear. Clarence was having a temper tantrum. They were all going to find out that I was high. I was not going to be able to do my lines. And I was going to get fired. I truly thought I was going to get fired from doing a weed movie just for smoking weed. And meanwhile, everyone on the set was probably blasted out of their minds. I was having a major internal meltdown. I started sweating more. Inga couldn't get the makeup right because of it, and I had to keep assuring her I was fine. Finally she threw her hands up, and I went to the set.

Before they started shooting the scene, Tamra Davis, the director, explained to me that Clarence was supposed to fall down on this X, and I was supposed to step over him and say, "Sucks to be you, man." So simple even a guy who is baked could do it, right?

The first time Clarence fell down he didn't land on the X. Or maybe it was my own perception playing tricks on me. So I did what they told me to do, the best that I could. As high as I was, I stepped over where Clarence landed and tried to make it look seamless. I was moving in slow motion. It felt like it took about forty-five minutes. My own voice in my ears sounded like I was some underwater creature. "Suuuuckkkkksssss toooooo bbbeeeeeee youuuuuuuu, mmmmmaaaaaan!" The world stopped spinning. I started hyperventilating. I convinced myself that I forgot how to breathe properly. The director, Tamra Davis, in a please-tell-me-we-got-this voice, asked, "Did we get this?"

The camera guy leaned over to her and said, "Nope."

Then Clarence stood up and yelled, "Well, I landed on *my* mark." That jarred about half of the high right out of me. And, you know, everyone was scared of him, so we had to do it all over again. And again. And again.

Clarence missed his mark three or four more times. Eventually, people were so bummed with Clarence that my fears of being found out dissipated.

In case you were wondering, I last saw Dave a couple years back at the Aspen Comedy Festival. It was long after his whole trip to Africa and all that jazz. I really felt for him at that time, and I called him and left a message saying I was willing to help him out if I could in any way. He called back and let me know that he appreciated it. In Aspen, he was a little weary of all that surrounded him. My only advice to him was that he should spend time with his kids and enjoy his family. He's one of the few guys who are such big talents that they can disappear from the public for years and then come back and pick right back up. And maybe that's what he's doing now.

Chapter 16

Birth of Gabrielle

Tracy Morgan used to tell me, "You know, you should have children, Jim. God wants you to have children, and he's gonna show up in all kinds of mysterious shapes and forms, and you may never know when he's here, but I can tell you now, one of those shapes is a baby." Tracy Morgan is crazy but he's also usually right.

In 1998, Dee and I decided to start a family. We didn't know and didn't want to know the baby's gender, but I'd been having visions of a girl who looked like a little version of my wife since forever, even before we were married. A cute, smiley-eyed girl with pigtails. Once Dee was pregnant we just prayed for a healthy baby, and if it wasn't a healthy baby we prayed for the strength to raise a child with whatever complications it might have.

If we were having a boy, he'd be named Bill, after Dee's grand-father. But we had zero names chosen for girls. I thought a little girl would be an "angel" so we hunted around for some variation on that. Just not Angela or Angelica, though. Too Italian.

When Dee was seven months along she suggested "Gabrielle."

"I've heard of Gabriella, but not Gabrielle," I said. "That sounds kinda Irish to me."

"Nope," Dee said. "Like the Archangel Gabriel, the messenger of good news."

"You know," I said, "I'm not even sure I know what an archangel is. I'm not so into that name."

The clock kept ticking and with about two weeks before Dee was due to go into labor, we'd settled on Jaquelin. It was a pretty name to us, but it had no real meaning. We were living in Manhattan at the time, and our routine was that we'd walk into Central Park on nice days, lay down a blanket, and just talk and snuggle. Our lives were going to drastically change forever, so this was a nice chance to chill and bond.

One day in the park, Dee said, "Have you ever given any more thought to *Gabrielle?*"

"No," I said.

Dee took a nap, and as I watched some kids playing in the distance, I started testing it out. "Gabrielle, come here." "Ladies and gentlemen, Gabrielle Breuer." "Don't touch that, Gabrielle." "I love you, Gabrielle." I still wasn't convinced. A while later, Dee woke up, and we folded the blanket and began walking home.

As we exited the park on the West Side, near the Sheep Meadow, a goofy-looking guy approached us. He didn't feel threatening, but I didn't know what to make of him. Dee's belly was protruding, obviously, and he came right up to it and said, "You're holding a little angel in there!"

"Thanks," we both said, smiling and walking carefully away from the man. He followed us, all smiles, and said, "It's a girl, isn't it?" Before we could answer, he said, "It's a girl and she is a little angel."

I began to get angry. I wanted to get home, not tell a stranger about our unborn child's gender.

"It is a little girl, right?" he asked us again.

"We don't know what it is," I said. "But thank you."

"I'm telling you," he said. "It is a girl, and she's an angel. Do you have a name picked out?"

"We don't know if it's a boy or a girl," I said again. "We have names picked out for both."

Out of the blue, this nutty man said, "How about Gabrielle? That's a beautiful name for your little angel girl. There you go."

The hairs on my ass stood straight on end, and time froze. Dee squeezed my hand. We stood there, numb.

Call it whatever you want, joke about a homeless guy naming our kid, but I still get goose bumps.

If only Gabrielle's birth had had a little of that magic. For one thing, Gabrielle was stuck. When Dee began to go into labor in our apartment, she really was in pain. She screamed that the baby was coming out of her ass. I'd never seen her in so much pain, so I brought her to the hospital. They stuck her in a room, and she sent me immediately to the nurse's desk and told me to ask for her doctor ASAP.

"My wife's in a lot of pain," I told this ginormous West Indian nurse.

"Of course she's in a lot of pain," the woman said dismissively. "She's pregnant. I called the doctor and when she come, she come."

I walked back to Dee's room. Another nurse examined Dee and said we should go home for the time being because Dee was only dilated two centimeters. They gave her some painkillers, which Dee took. Soon thereafter she was tripping and falling all over our apartment. I freaked out and brought her back to the hospital at three thirty A.M. In the end my wife was in labor for nineteen hours, and she was cursing so much that truck drivers were stopping by to take notes.

Her doctor finally came in.

"This woman needs an epidural!" the ob-gyn said.

"No sh—," Dee started to say through gritted teeth.

They gave Dee her epidural. Her swearing ceased, or at least tapered off. But her temperature started to rise, all the way to 105 degrees. Dee was violently shaking in the bed from the fever. Five more people in pastel-colored scrubs arrived. I was freaked out about our baby.

"Is this normal?" I yelled.

"Well," one older, calm doctor said, "you do see some reactions like this to the epidural from time to time."

By now, her teeth were chattering like a child's out in the freezing cold.

"We need to get this baby out right now," her ob-gyn said. Nurses brought in ice packs and began rubbing them all over her body. Another doctor told me to leave the room. I thought fleetingly of lying on the blanket in Central Park. Things weren't supposed to turn out this way.

"No way!" I said, grabbing on to Dee's bed. I refused to leave the room. I really thought she was going to die. All these images of her dying and the baby being born were flashing through my head. My life and my marriage were going to be over—the mother of my unborn child was going to die. I got a migraine and started throwing up all over the place.

"We're going to have to do a C-section," a doctor said.

"Is there anything else you can try?" I asked in between bouts of vomiting.

They decided to try suction cups. The doctors began sticking them in Dee, trying to get the baby out that way, and it wasn't working. They brought in all of the C-section instruments and started prepping for it. Trays were being wheeled this way and that. The nurses were still rubbing Dee down with ice packs. The fetal monitor began beeping loudly. What else could go wrong?

"This baby's heart is beating way too fast," a nurse said quickly and matter-of-factly.

"Sweetheart," a nurse said to Dee, "you're gonna have to try to push this baby out now, otherwise we will have to cut you open, hon. I'm sorry."

"Don't cut me," Dee said, gripping the bedsheets with both hands. She was soaking wet and shivering. "I think I can push the baby out." I had no idea where she found the calm and the strength, but Dee started pushing to the point where it looked like her head was going to pop off her neck, and Gabrielle soon came out. She was tiny, all gray, and I thought she was stillborn. She was covered in goo and did not cry. She seemed lifeless.

The doctors raced around doing everything they could to help the baby, sucking fluids out of her mouth and nose. And all of a sudden Gabrielle started crying. I breathed a sigh of relief and stuck my hands out to hold her.

"You can't touch her yet, Dad," one of the nurses said. "We've got to take her into intensive care."

I moved to block the doorway. "You're not going anywhere," I said, "until the mother gets to hold her." Dee'd just delivered an Olympic-caliber performance. This was bonkers.

"I just want to hold my baby," Dee said wearily, raising her head up off of her pillow.

"Sorry, sweetie," her doctor said sympathetically. "You're just going to have to wait a little bit."

As the doctor was saying that, I plucked Gabrielle out of a nurse's arms before anyone knew it and placed her in Dee's arms. Dee cried silently while looking at our little miracle. I leaned over, and Dee handed her to me, and I just held her for a minute, taking her in.

"What's her name?" one of the nurses said softly.

"I think we *have* to call her Gabrielle," I said. They took her into the ICU, which is the worst feeling in the entire world. Your wife has the baby, they take her away, and you're both sitting there helpless.

In the end, we were lucky, and she was 100 percent healthy. In the years to come my wife would give birth to two more beautiful baby girls. Those deliveries were comparatively easy. Maybe because we had them in New Jersey.

Chapter 17

Saving Steve-O

During the summer of 2002, my nephew Steve-O (no relation to the *Jackass* character) was getting out of the hoosegow down in Florida. Dee and I sat down and debated whether or not we'd want to take him in. Actually, it wasn't much of a debate. We'd taken in family members who'd needed help in the past, and Steve-O was family, and he was going to need a lot of help.

Dee and I had two daughters by now, Gabrielle and Kelsey, and we knew that Steve-O had a lot of issues. At twenty-four, he was coming out of a five-year prison sentence, so it was clear that he wasn't going to just move in with us for three months until he found an apartment, then be all better. This was a commitment, probably a couple years of dealing with the kid. Was I licensed? Not professionally. But I was a blood relative—one of the few who hadn't thrown in the towel on the guy yet.

Steve-O's mom is my half sister Patti, or as we call her, Hurricane

Patti. He'd spent his whole life in Florida, and I didn't want him going back home to his mom's place to fall into old patterns. That would be just asking for trouble. The kid grew up with no direction. He told us that his dad was into heroin and had bailed on him when he was a boy, so he got into spray-painting property, stealing bikes and VCRs, selling dime bags, and racking up a juvenile rap sheet.

Patti has a great heart, but she's ape wild. They lived around the corner from my parents' place in Clearwater. Occasionally I'd pop my head in to see if I could stop the bleeding. A typical conversation:

> **Me:** Patti, why are there three bikes in your garage?
>
> **Patti:** [defensively] Steve found them all in the garbage. Sad, isn't it? Some kids would toss out perfectly fine functioning bikes.

When I was filming *Buddies*, I brought my parents out to L.A. to check it out and Patti was supposed to watch their house while they were gone. Every day Steve-O and his knucklehead friends would go and party at my mom and dad's house, and one day, they took my parents' car out for a joyride and smashed it up. My parents came back to Florida to find a wrecked car and a trashed house.

It all caught up with Steve-O when he and some friends broke into a warehouse. They were high, and they started a brush fire inside. The thing got out of control and burned down the whole warehouse. Since he already had a rap sheet, it was like, "Boom. Show's over. You're gone." And he went to prison for five years.

Steve-O served his time, and then no one was in his corner. The whole family knew Steve-O was getting out, but no one in Florida was going to give him a fair shot. I thought Jersey might be better for him. I couldn't turn my back on him.

He arrived in our driveway in New Jersey, thinking he was just going to be visiting for a few days. He got out of the cab smoking a Marlboro Red, wearing a white tank top that revealed all of his tattoos.

"Hey, Jim," he said halfheartedly. He was slouching, throwing off really punky body language. My first thought was that I was really going to have to break this stallion. He didn't know he was getting a chance, but my plan was to take him on my comedy tour and have him be a roadie. He'd be stuck on a bus for six weeks with me and my bandmates.

A typical situation would go like this: A customer would ask how much a Breuer T-shirt cost. And he would snidely say, "Can't you read the sign?" Then the customer would turn and walk away. He was obsessed with proving people wrong or being short and negative with my fans who wanted to give him money. I was like, "Dude, you're not getting it." So pretty soon we took him off of interfacing with the general public and had him just loading and unloading the truck.

When we got back to New Jersey, I noticed that it was probably almost too quiet around our house for him at night. He was jumpy, up all night with insomnia. Jail had worn on him. He'd be outside smoking and pacing for a couple hours each night. He wasn't used to the freedom, and it took a while before he felt free and protected. When he talked about being in jail, we'd never bug him about bad stuff that may have happened. Like a war veteran, he'd only share the lighter, funnier stories of his experience.

Once we'd been home for a while, I laid down the ground rules. "Go find a job," I said. "After a while, you're going to have to pay rent."

He would just say, "I can't because . . ." It was a real favorite of his. Then he'd list these insurmountable excuses. "I need a ride to get a job," he'd say.

"Ask for one then," I said. "If you want to hunt for work, we're happy to help you. But I may die tomorrow, Steve-O. And if that happens, you've got nobody. I'm trying to teach you things you can use out there."

So he ended up getting a job at the Gap, and just being out in society was helping him achieve his potential. Soon, we helped him find his own car, after much consternation from him about not being able to get the best one on the lot.

"Take the car that costs four hundred bucks," I said. "Don't bite off more than you can chew. Take pride in what you have. It'll be your car; you worked your ass off for it, and you earned it."

As soon as he started making a little money, he'd disappear on the weekends with some local punks. I didn't like where it was leading. I could see him around them, how he'd act, and he'd use the fact that he'd been to prison as a status thing around them.

"Dude, do you really want to be known as the guy in Chester, New Jersey, who brags about having been in prison?" I'd say.

Then he'd pout. I've got to be honest here and say that there were times when I threw chairs at this kid.

Dodging flying chairs might have worked a little, but what really turned him into the great human being he is today was being around my kids. One day one of the girls came up to him and said, "I love you, Uncle Stevie." He left the room and cried. The kids would use him like a rented toy. They would play-fight with him and he would willingly hurl himself down a flight of stairs, just to make them smile.

He opened himself up and got to appreciate things he'd missed in his turbulent childhood. He'd never seen snow before. He was blown away by that. He and I began to take hikes in the mornings and have real conversations, just talking about faith and family. He was fascinated that I was on TV and in movies but that I was driving a Ford Escort. I told him he was going to be the glue to this whole family one day. Some of the best moments of my life were on those walks. All this stuff softened his heart.

Everyone around town began to call him "Uncle Stevie." And once that caught on a whole different kid came out of him. The more time we spent with him, the more we realized he was just misguided.

There was no evil in him. He loved to help the girls with their home-work. That made him feel really proud. He ended up staying with us for almost six years off and on. He's now married and, believe it or not, the head of security at a major department store in New York City.

It wasn't just Steve-O who benefited from moving in with us. I loved his company, and seeing him get things figured out really in-spired me. Today I do a lot of work with Daytop of New Jersey, which is an organization that helps out kids who are mixed up in drugs. I know it's a cliché, but charity really is its own reward.

I knew at some point, Steve-O would start a family of his own, and perhaps one day he'd have to be the anchor of this family, so I wanted to show him what it's all about. How to play and enjoy one another and enjoy life. At the end of the day, all you have is family. And little did I know what was just around the corner in my own marriage.

Chapter 18

Life in the Jersey Burbs

The year was 2004. Dee and I were living in Chester, New Jersey. Gabi was five, our second daughter was two. We were helping Steve-O out. On the surface, things were pretty cool. Big yard, couple acres. Beautiful neighborhood. This was Happytown. Dreamland. There were deer in the yard—baby ones with spots on them. There were families. And highly organized PTAs. Kids out there got the best education. (Taxes up the pooper, too.)

But Dee was not happy. Looking back, I realize she probably had postpartum depression after the birth of our second daughter, Kelsey. But maybe it went even deeper than that and just took a while to surface. This was stuff I had no clue about. We'd met down in Florida when she was seventeen or eighteen years old and I'd never seen this darkness in her. She was always bubbly, full of sunshine, a great laugher, and fun to play off of. And that was the girl I married.

And now I had no idea what was going on. Trouble between us began to percolate around my tenure on *Saturday Night Live*. It was a great but intense experience, and it put her through the wringer, and

I wasn't sensitive to that. Back then, when we were out, she was no longer Dee, she was just Jim Breuer's wife. I remember we would go out to dinner and I wanted to be recognized. It felt good to me at the time. And if someone did recognize me, I would purposely sit up, like, "Yes, I am that goat on television. That's me." I'd just bask in that.

To compensate, Dee began to wear the most gorgeous outfits. True fact: Hands down, Dee has the best butt ever. So she'd get dressed up and come to *Saturday Night Live,* and then she'd wait in my room for the show to end. And of course there'd be ten or fifteen other people sitting right there with her. After the show, I'd come in and blow right by her. "There's the singer from Blues Traveler!" "Here's the producer of that huge movie!" Occasionally, I'd stop to mumble, "Oh, hi, Dee, how ya doing?"

She always had my back before I had achieved anything, and I was paying her back by acting like a douche. But as time passed and I left the show, I outgrew my douchiness. We started a family and I thought things were fine between us. But when she gave birth to Kelsey in 2002, something snapped. She was beyond unhappy.

That was a major whoa. I could not understand that whatsoever.

At that time, I was going out on the road and doing stand-up. I had enough money to relax for a while, so I took the summers off with my family. I would play tiger with the girls for hours. I was a tiger that my Gabrielle had captured. Kelsey was in charge of training me. But I was wild. I would take them both down and start pretending to maul them. My older one would have to get a stick and beat me. It was a wholesome family game. But I digress.

Then this whole fear thing came into play. "I can't go on the road. I can't leave Dee alone with these kids when she is feeling that low." So I had to stop touring. I had to be around the house. And then everything was a fight. If we went on a date, it would inevitably end with a speech from Dee about what sucks about me.

Finally, I said, "Let's get help."

So Dee agreed to start seeing a therapist. That went rather shit-tily. So then she went to a "positive thinking" retreat called the Forum. (It seemed a bit like brainwashing to me.) Came back like a zombie. She changed her diet. Didn't help. She didn't take any meds, but she tried a ton of different vitamins. She was doing everything she possibly could to figure it out. None of it worked. We'd think that it would be working for a month or two, she'd say she felt so much better, and then whammo—it would just turn right back around.

We had two wonderful daughters and plenty of money. What the hell was she so mad about? Because it didn't make sense to me, I couldn't come up with a solution. Our life was just her saying, "I'm miserable and you suck." If I cheated, if I was a drunk, or if I was verbally abusive, I could understand it. But I wasn't doing any of that stuff. Once I started facing what was going on between us, I was torn up and scared. I thought things actually might not work out for us.

Praying has always worked for me. And I was praying my balls off about Dee and me and our family. I didn't have an upbringing in any faith, but I'd found a way to God. I guess you would call him the Christian God, but I don't think of it like that at all. I don't read the Bible, and I never have. I don't know any of the commandments. But I have a few rules for myself that I think are in keeping with the Bible.

Religion is a purity thing to me. If you look at Jesus, He would never charge you, He would never ask you for money. He would never give advice with the idea of wanting anything back. I tell people, don't get fooled into thinking that the guys in the robes and collars have all the answers or any more power than you do. Someone once said that God is a phenomenal product, but the people who sell him are thieves. I agree. So I pray in my car, in my garage, in my backyard, wherever I am. I ask the questions and God always points me in the right direction. Now, whether I listen to him or not is a whole other question. I casually brought this up to Dee one afternoon at home.

"Do you ever pray?" I asked.

"I'm not going to *effin'* pray."

That's how that went. She wanted physical proof of God's existence, and I would say that the physical proof was right in front of her in the form of kids.

"That's not proof!" she'd exclaim.

I began to look for my own apartment. I found a simple little two-bedroom place not far from our house. It was on the main street in Chester, right above a mom-and-pop restaurant. I told the landlord I would take it and be back the next morning with the deposit.

My plan was to move out of our house for at least a year, or however long it took Dee to get her head together and find peace. I'd come home every day to play with the kids, help put them to bed, and then leave. Dee hated me, and I just wanted to give her time to think and be alone. I wanted no other women. I just wanted calm. I was confident that with some space, we could figure things out. If finding some other guy was what made her happy, I would even be okay with that (although of course I would be devastated).

I never considered telling Dee to move out. She wanted a big house, kids, and a yard, and now she had it. I wasn't going to be the guy who kicked her when she was down. I was just going to leave her alone. I could survive in an outhouse, so I wasn't worried about living in some apartment.

I jumped in my car the next morning, ran a couple of errands, and showed up at the apartment a couple hours late. I knocked on the door. No answer. I peeked in the restaurant window. Didn't see the owner. Knocked again on the door. Finally, the guy drove up and got out of his car. "I'm back," I said. "And I've got the deposit for you."

"Hey," he said, looking somewhat pained. "Tell ya what. I'm really sorry, but I had to let the place go. A guy came by this morning and really wanted it."

And that was that.

Part of me was secretly happy, but I really questioned God's motivation. Did he want me to tough it out a little longer at home? What was that about? I felt like I was already at the end of my rope. I was really puzzled. I drove home. By the way, I hadn't told my wife any of these plans, but when I walked in the living room, she was in a chair, weeping without making any noise, inconsolable.

"Dee, are you all right?" I asked. I thought maybe she had found out I wanted to move out. Or maybe it was just another rotten day.

"I followed a stranger home today," she said, looking up at me, fighting back more tears.

My heart started pounding.

"You what?!" I asked. Her eyes were all swollen. I was freaking out.

"The woman from the coffee shop," she said.

"What woman?" Dee would routinely go to this little coffee shop every morning in downtown Chester.

"The older one," she explained. Dee knew a woman who worked there, but just barely. "She brought me into her house." I felt sick to my stomach. I had no idea where this was going but I knew it wasn't going to be good.

"Why did you go to her house?" I asked.

"I don't know," she said, still crying. This was like some awful riddle that would probably end with a few squad cars showing up.

"You don't know why you went to her house?"

"Well, she wanted to talk," she said with a little bit more composure.

"Keep going," I said.

"She was there," Dee said. "And her husband was there, too."

Ugh. This was going from bad to worse.

Dee continued. "And we prayed together."

"What do you mean you prayed?" I asked.

"They dropped to their knees," she said.

"What? Then what happened?"

"And then I just left," she said.

"This is ridiculous!" I exclaimed. "What on earth are you talking about?"

It turns out the couple were born-again Christians. Dee started talking to the woman at the coffee shop, and for a long time she had been begging Dee to come home with her and pray about our marriage. This turned out to be the day that Dee followed through. Dee explained that she literally could not stop herself from going to the woman's house, even though she was sure that praying was horseshit and would do no good. But when the couple actually got down on their knees in front of her and prayed, Dee was so moved that she began crying.

And that was the beginning. Soon enough she was asking me, "Have you ever read the Bible?"

Here I had a wife who had been far more cynical about faith than I was but was now waking me up for church and taking me to see Christian rock bands. I didn't even mind the music—I would try to shake my ass a little or nod my head—but then in between every song one of the guys would start preaching and moaning, and I was like, "Hey, wasn't this a concert?" It was tiresome.

And then after two or three months of intensity, it balanced out. Dee would go off to little meetings or church and come home and want to talk. She'd say, "This Christian lady is actually not very Christian, and this other one is very judgmental. And I don't really appreciate that."

I'd be like, "Yeah, well now you see there's a little bit of a balance. You don't have to be like, 'We're Christian and we hate gays and abortion clinics need to be bombed.'"

And she grew into it. And we fixed it ourselves. The fights with things getting thrown around the house stopped. If I walked you through my house, you'd see a gallery of stuff that is now repaired but was once broken: tables, dishes, vases, and my marriage itself.

Chapter 19

Partying Like a Rock Star

I realized that as I get closer to the end of this book, if I'm not 100 percent honest about myself, I won't have achieved what I set out to do. I've told true stories about myself, my wife, my parents, relatives, and other comedians. Now I need to tell some more truth about me.

One day in 2004, I think (it's a little foggy), after Steve-O had been living with us for a while, and Dee and I had been going through our struggles, I was playing tiger with Gabrielle. I was way into it. Then she stopped playing and looked at me funny.

"Your eyes are really red, Daddy," she said.

I know she had no clue what I'd been up to—smoking pot—but she was studying me really hard. That moment smashed me like a brick, because I had distinct memories of playing with my own parents when I was four or five years old. And I didn't want Gabrielle later in life to remember playing with her dad and suddenly realize that her dad had been high. I never want my kids to grow up thinking I needed to be high to play with them or engage with them.

I had always been a pretty light toker, especially for someone who's kind of famous. But in the early 2000s my marijuana use really escalated. When I was out touring then, all anyone wanted to do was get high with me—the guy from *Half Baked*. Yup, get baked and talk about aliens and life on the other side. To me that was better than sitting alone in a hotel room, missing my family. It was an even trade.

And even though I talked about helping socially rehabilitate Steve-O, he'd smoke up right along with me. Dee would sometimes say, "You can't be a role model *and* hang with your nephew like that." But I felt like pot was the only thing that would get him talking. We would hang and go out on an awesome hike into the wilderness for hours. And I'd let him vent and talk about his past and just listen to him. So weed did help. The problem was that it became a habit and a crutch.

I never thought I'd be the person to say this, but anyone who says pot is not addictive is out of their mind. To me, *anything* is addictive. I found myself starting to abuse it at the end of my run on *Saturday Night Live*. I used it to numb my aggravation and frustration at how I was being used on the show. I used it to numb any situation. When I'd get a horrifying migraine, I always thought pot was the answer. And when you find yourself planning your day around a substance, then you've got a problem.

By 2003 or so I found myself planning out my smoking, and that's when I knew I had a problem. I'd stop for months or weeks and go back. By early 2007, I finally quit. I'd also be a liar if I said I didn't think about it a lot even today. That just illustrates that I really was addicted to it. I know now that I have to stay away from the stuff.

Things were a lot clearer without weed. I didn't feel like I needed to save the world. I didn't think everything was a conspiracy. In 2007, I was itching to go back to doing stand-up and I had to remind myself that before *SNL* I was killing it on the stand-up circuit and pot had nothing to do with it. I was already funny without it. Dee was super supportive of my attempts and efforts. "You're creative and funny," she'd say. "Do you really want to say that's what helps you create?"

For me, and the direction I am headed now, the best feeling was starting to tour in 2008, because it was a weedless environment, and it reassured me that I didn't need anything to make myself funny. It gave me so much confidence. And for the record, Steve-O quit smoking it, too.

I still like to go out and spend time with rock stars—back in the old days Lars Ulrich from Metallica and I used to tear it up. We once moshed for two hours to System of a Down with my band on our tour bus, destroying a $3,000 sound system in the process.

But ultimately I was just not cut out to be a heavy partier. Lars also has a place in New York, and one night in the late nineties, we had plans to go out rabble-rousing after I did a gig. We hopped in a cab together to go down to Greenwich Village to the club where I was scheduled to perform, and I immediately noticed a knapsack in the backseat. I unzipped it and discovered it was full of books belonging to some NYU student. My nieces and nephews are in school, so I know how expensive books are. I planned to hang on to it, get the kid's address, and give it back to him the next day. That was the only right thing to do in that situation. When I announced that to Lars, he looked at me like I'd suggested we carry around a forty-five-pound pontoon anchor all night. When we got to the club, and he saw I was going to bring the knapsack along with me, he really lost it.

"Dude, do you mean to tell me you're getting out of this cab with the knapsack?" he said, perturbed.

"Yeah," I said, leaning forward to pay the cabby. "Why? Does it bother you?"

"Yes!" he said. We hopped out of the cab. "We're going to have to keep an eye on this stupid thing all night. All because some kid was irresponsible with his possessions."

"Everyone makes mistakes," I said. "He's going to want them back."

"Exactly," Lars said as I slung the bag over my shoulder and walked into the club. "And this is the kind of mistake that will teach him to be more careful with his shit! It's a valuable lesson. If anything, you can be proud to be a part of that."

"Don't worry about the backpack," I said. "Just keep it out of your mind, and I'll handle it." I did my set. We walked down the street and wound up at a little bar, and made our way up to order a couple of beers. It didn't take long for Metallica fans to trickle up to Lars to say hello and shake his hand. Another fan, a young guy, approached and noticed Lars was smoking.

"Hey, man," the kid said. From the look on Lars's face, I knew right off the bat that he didn't like being addressed in such a familiar way. "I like your band. Is it possible to bum a cigarette from you?"

"Seriously?" Lars asked caustically. "In what universe do you decide to go out for the night knowing that you will want to smoke but not having any cigarettes in your possession? Do you just plan on the goodwill of others?"

The kid's eyes widened.

"Do you know how hard I worked to be able to afford cigarettes when I want them? They're not just something I feel like sprinkling all over town, like the friggin' pied piper."

With that, Lars angrily rose, grabbed the knapsack, and left the bar. I followed him and when he made it outside, he launched the knapsack deep into the sky. It flipped end over end until it landed across the street, right at the feet of a pretty young girl. The force of the books split the bag wide open and they scattered in different directions—through puddles, under cars, everywhere.

"F—k it!" Lars yelled. He then walked against a red light, through oncoming traffic at Sixth Avenue, climbing up on top of fenders, trunks, hoods, and windshields of moving cars. "F&^* it!" he yelled again. "Are we going to party, Breuer?! Are we?"

I waited until it was safe to cross the street and caught up with him. He led me to a super-tiny, dark, exclusive bar, where nearly every major movie star and musician was hanging out: Matt Damon, Ben Affleck, Dave Matthews, one of the Backstreet Boys, etc. By then, it was two A.M. He was raging, but I had to make it all the way back to the middle of New Jersey. I had a drink and then I tried to sneak out the door.

"Breuer," Lars called out to me. "Where the hell are you going?"

"I'm pretty wiped out," I said.

"Unbelievable," he moaned. "You're a complete pussy. Only a pussy goes home at this time."

I nodded to him, as if to say, "You're right." There was no sense angering him any further. It was a long time before he'd call me again. I felt like shit about that destroyed backpack. Being a wild and crazy partier just wasn't for me.

Chapter 20

Getting Sirius

In 2005, I started thinking a lot about establishing a sort of home base. Somewhere I could still tell funny stories but not have to make everything a bit, or hop on an airplane or bus every other day. More and more it seemed like radio was the place to do that.

One of the reasons I wanted to get into radio was because I didn't want to be on the road a lot while my kids were little. Another big part of it was that I wanted the time and space to start presenting a different side of me. Since *Half Baked* I'd a had a lot of fun (too much fun maybe) doing tours, playing decent-sized venues with my friends Jimmy and Larry playing in a live band behind me. I felt like that pushed the boundaries of comedy. I'd also taken on something else I hadn't done since community college—landing a variety of roles in some smaller movies. But on radio I felt like I could sprawl out and give some depth and context to the crazy tales that comprised my life. I could show off who I was beyond just doing punch lines. I knew that standard radio relied on a formula and was filled with ratings pressure. It was serendipity that satellite radio had just sprung up and was exploring all kinds of new formats. I put feelers out to the two providers, XM and Sirius, and a talent executive at Sirius got back to me right away.

"What kind of show do you want to do?" he asked enthusiastically.

"I want to put my friends and parents on the air," I explained. "Like the ultimate backyard hangout. Beyond that I have no idea. I'll tell you what I *don't* want. I don't want to talk about what everyone else is talking about. I don't want to do anything involving news or politics or current events."

"Sounds awesome," he said. "Why don't you come in and meet some producers, and we'll make a demo. A mock show. You can see how you like doing it, and we can do the same."

So I went in and just told them some Jefferson Avenue stories—bickering with the Catholic kids, stealing my bike back from the grubby hoodlum family down the street, and listening to another neighbor kid insult the Jews across the street, stuff like that. I also gave them a couple of *Saturday Night Live* behind-the-scenes stories. I just kind of winged it. I'd done Howard Stern's show, *Opie and Anthony*, *Bob and Tom*, and local radio whenever I toured, so I had a bit of radio experience, although I'd never hosted anything. But I was comfortable with it right from the start.

They gave it a listen and liked it. And it was a go, and I could call the shots. I wanted to wade into radio and stay close to my wife and young daughters, so for the first couple of months we just did Friday nights. After that, the people at Sirius came back and said, "Let's go five days a week." It was working so well that I was inclined to agree, but then I got a phone call.

It was Opie, from *The Opie and Anthony Show*. I'd been on their show when they were on the air in New York City and syndicated pretty much everywhere else. They'd been bounced from their last gig, at WNEW, after their show encouraged people around New York City to have sex in public places and one couple got busted hooking up in St. Patrick's Cathedral.

"Don't say anything to anyone, Jim," Opie said. "But we're about to sign a deal with XM, and we want you to be part of it." I wasn't exactly certain their MO aligned with the direction I wanted to go, but I knew that they'd have a huge following. Once again potential fame started pulling me away from my instincts. He gave me the number of a talent guy at XM who was putting their show together, so I called him and left a message. A few days went by and he never called me back. I called again, and still nothing. In the meantime, Sirius called, saying, "Hey, do you want to go every day or not?" They had no idea what the holdup was.

I took a couple of days and came back with, "Monday through Thursday, two hours a day, in the four-to-six drive time on the East Coast, and then repeated again from seven to nine, so it's on during drive time on the West Coast."

Again, the Sirius response was, "Okay. Great." I even named a new dollar figure, and they didn't balk for a second. And just when I was ready to sign, I got another call from Opie.

"I think I gotta do the Sirius thing," I told him.

"C'mon, man," he said. "Don't you trust us? Just hang on and you'll be part of our team here." So, just to hedge my bets, I called the XM talent guy again. He still had never called me.

"Great to hear from you," he said, like I'd been the one playing hard to get. "It would be nice to have you come on board, but I think we're locked up budget-wise for the year. When we get up and running, then things will open up, and we can maybe bring you in."

"If it's about money," I said, "I can take significantly less." It was a boneheaded thing to toss out there, and it went against what I really wanted to do, which was cultivate my own audience. Instead I tried to hitch my star to Opie and Anthony. But the XM guy went into hiding again. It made me wonder how much (or how little) power Opie and Anthony were going to have at XM.

In the end, I called Sirius and said, "Let's go for it." I let Opie know and he said he understood. In fact, I do go on their show every once in a while to tell stories, even today. My show became *Breuer Unleashed*, a five-days-a-week gig (I relented on taking Fridays off— later I'd do them from home). And I quickly developed a following that showed up to hear me. It wasn't long before Howard Stern came to Sirius and brought millions of listeners. That certainly didn't hurt.

Breuer Unleashed was a great place to be creative. We did comedy covers, where comedians performed their favorite comedians' bits. We'd redo scenes from famous movies, using impressionists as all the stars. We had another bit called "Dysfunctional Family Poker," where instead of cards, you played with people's dysfunctional family stories. Pete Correale was an adept, funny sidekick, and my childhood friends Jimmy and Larry created original music every day in competition with each other, having listeners vote on songs they wrote. They loved to squabble like an old married couple—especially over who was stealing the other's MySpace friends. We had musicians from Alice in Chains to Charlie Daniels to Metallica show up in the studio, and comedians like Jerry Seinfeld and Chris Rock.

In the spring of 2007, my situation at Sirius began to shift a bit. That was precipitated by an interview with Bill Cosby. He was going to be a guest on my show, and his people asked for a preinterview. I was given his home phone number and as I dialed it, I had major butterflies in my stomach. I was totally nervous. I hadn't been this anxious since I met Joe Pesci. A Spanish-sounding lady answered. I explained who I was and she said she'd get him. I waited on the end of the line for a long time, there was a rustling, and the next thing I heard was his distinctive voice.

"Yuuussss, hullo. This is Bill Cosby."

"Hi, Mr. Cosby, this is Jim Breuer."

"Ya know," he said, kick-starting the whole conversation without my even tossing him a question or offering up any chitchat about the weather, "I was in California, at an airport, and this little nine-year-old white boy came up to me and started reciting an old, old routine of mine—one he would not have known without a little digging. And I sat there, listened, and thought, 'Wow, the writing!' You see, I came from an era where none of us planned on being comedians. We were going to be scholars. We were all going off to write or study things. Take George Carlin, for instance. He's not only one of the most brilliant writers of our time, he's one of the most brilliant minds."

"I agree," I said. "I think writing is very important. Did you want me to know anything in particular for tomorrow?" I wasn't trying to rush him, I just wanted to be accommodating.

"Yes," he said, then paused for quite a while. "I want tomorrow to *not* be a situation where I come on the air and you say, 'Hey, how the f—k are you doing, man!' And 'F—k this!' and 'F—k that!' I want your audience and your listeners to be inspired."

My mind was now blown. I had never heard Bill Cosby drop the F-bomb. It was really strange. I didn't welcome a lot of my guests with profanity, but maybe this was a general rule he had, not one aimed specifically at me.

"That's what I want, too," I said.

"Have you read any of my books?"

"No, sir." I hadn't and I knew that being dishonest in an attempt to flatter the guy would only backfire.

"I'm going to give you the number of my guy," he said, and then he broke into that classic, you're-going-to-learn-a-lesson Cosby staccato. "And. He's. Gonna. Send. You. A. Chapter. Out. Of. One. Of. Them. Called. 'The. Day. I. Left. Show. Business.'"

So I got the chapter and read it. In it, Cosby wrote how when he first started doing stand-up comedy, he was offered a lot of money to play a certain club, and he did it, but then he realized he hated himself for it because he had to play to an audience that he didn't feel at all connected to. And one day, he finally said, "I'm never going to do this again." It was not worth the money to be something he was not. But I wondered why he wanted me to read that. Did he sense that I was feeling myself in a similar situation?

As soon as Cosby and I were on the radio together, he asked, "Did you read what I asked you to read?" I was freaked out.

"Oh yeah," I said.

"And what did you get out of it?" he asked.

"Ohhh, my God," I laughed. It was such a heavy situation. "I found it *perfect* for the time I'm at in my life."

"Aha!" he said. He continued in the classic Cosby way, when he knows he's right or has at least touched a nerve. "Ummmm-hmmmm!"

"And—"

"Mmmmm-hmmm!" he said in his *gotcha* tone.

"Ah—"

"Hmmmmmmmm!" He continued on, playing with me. I'm not sure how he knew what an impact it had on me, but maybe the preinterview was really a preinterview of *me*. Who knows? When an icon comes and talks to you like that, you listen. Cosby and I talked for about an hour more, on the air, and that was really the first step of me accepting and going full-blown into the family comedy world. I knew it would be hard work. I knew it would mean distancing myself from what people expected of me, and I knew I'd have to go out on the road and reestablish myself, doing all-new material that was family friendly. And I knew I'd have to put it all out there in a real way, all my faults and my history, and be me and be honest so that no one could accuse me of being a hypocrite: "You're Mr. Family Man now; what about when you used to talk about smoking marijuana? What about when you used to talk about getting drunk?"

My response to all that would simply be "You've got all sides of me now. I'm not hiding anything."

There's a big group of people who think I am Brian from *Half Baked*. There's such a cult around that movie. When I toured, stoners would come up to me and say, "You're my idol." I'd be polite to them, but in my head I'd think, "I'm not your idol. That character's your idol. If I was your idol, then you'd have kids and morals and be way into your family."

My kids were also getting older, and they had started to ask, "Can I listen to your comedy? Can I watch your videos?" That made me think about what I was putting out there. Not that I ever did any material that was so offensive, but a bell went off and made me realize that I have eyes on me, and a bit of responsibility. I always did characters and goofed around for them and all the kids in the neighborhood. It would be cool if they could actually watch me work without censoring anything.

When I made my decision to scale back on *Breuer Unleashed* and just do Fridays, my cohost Pete was the most bummed out of anyone. There's still some weirdness, I think, today. But I had to move on. And the real wake-up call for me came when I first went back on the road. I couldn't sell many tickets. My radio show was doing great, but I wasn't able to leverage my listener base into ticket sales for my show. That meant I'd have to get out on the road that much more. It was tough to reconcile busting my ass five days a week without seeing these people in the crowd when I went out to do shows.

But Sirius and my new family-friendly direction have rewarded me in all kinds of ways. One day my sister picked up a call at the office and said to me, "Kevin James is on the line."

I had to ask her, "*The* Kevin James?"

I'd known Kevin back when we were both stand-ups out of Long Island, but it had been a while. It turns out he'd seen the direction I was taking and liked it. He came on my Sirius show to talk about *Paul*

Blart: Mall Cop, and at some point I said, "You should do voice-over films, because the voices you do are amazing."

"Funny you should say that," he said. "I wanna talk to you about something, later on."

When we finished the show, he told me he was working on a family film with a lot of voice-over roles for animal characters called *The Zookeeper.* It sounded great. We kept in touch and eventually he asked me if I wanted a part in the movie. It had a pretty intense cast—Stallone, Sandler, Cher, Judd Apatow. Of course I wanted in, but I knew not to hold my breath. Kevin could have the best intentions, but there were any number of ways it could be derailed.

"If it happens, that would be great," I said. "I appreciate you thinking of me." And lo and behold, it came together. I believe that if you're doing the right things and being true to yourself, good things will happen.

Chapter 21

Dad Moves In

Dad and Mom moved back north from Florida seven years ago after he'd had a couple of strokes. It just got to be too hectic to be that far way when they needed help. Now they live about a mile away from Dee and me and the kids. Over the past few years Dad has been in my life more than ever before. Most of the time it is great. But not always.

One day not long ago Dad and I were coming back from some comedy gigs. Our airplane had landed at Newark and was taxiing up to our gate. Out the window, we'd hear the jet engines start wheezing again and then we'd move a few more feet. It wasn't enjoyable, but it wasn't the worst thing anyone has gone through on an airplane.

Still, the dead air in the cabin was as thick as cream cheese. Everyone was a little sweaty. The stewardesses were sluggish and cranky in their jump seats. Their hairspray had long since stopped working. I looked around and every seat-back pocket was stuffed with crinkled newspapers and crumpled Dasani bottles. Some kid across from us had ground orange Cheez-Its into every surface. Throughout it all, my dad was a soldier. At age eighty-seven I would have been seriously cranky.

I first got the idea to bring Dad on the road a couple of years ago on the Breuniversity Tour, and we did the whole thing on a private bus, which was a little easier than getting him through major airports in a wheelchair. On the bus, we made our own schedule. If we were twenty-five minutes behind, or wanted to pull off at a truck stop for some beef jerky or a new deck of cards, no one cared. When we fly, though, from the minute we try to wheel through the security checkpoint, we're always working against the clock—on someone else's time. And it's stressful.

But there was none of that to worry about now. We were home. The plane kept inching along, and then Dad turned to me and whispered, "I gotta shit."

"Well," I said, "that's good, because we're only about thirty yards from the gate. Just chill, Dad." The guy often needs help in the bathroom at his age, and I've learned to avoid airplane toilets if at all possible. First there's the smell, then there's the turbulence, then there's the fact that once you have two adult men confined inside an airplane bathroom—one of whom can't move very well—it can get ugly in a hurry.

The plane stalled out on the tarmac for another minute or two. It wasn't long before I smelled something majorly foul. I slowly craned my neck in his direction.

"Dad?"

No response. He looked straight ahead, hands folded innocently in his lap.

"Dad?" I asked again. "Did you, uh, holy cow, I'm getting a waft of something over here."

"What?" he said crankily. "I'm holding it. I'm holding it, jerk."

"No, you're not," I said. "Unless you count holding it in your underwear as holding it."

Miraculously, there was a baby two rows behind us, and my immediate reaction was to look back at the family repeatedly, raising my eyebrows in a way that put the blame squarely on them.

Dad had crapped himself before, but never in a confined environment. My plan was to let everyone else get off the plane before we made our move. All I could think about was people stuck behind us, looking at the giant crap stains on Dad's pants and getting a good whiff of it, too. I didn't want to put the other passengers through that. And I didn't want to put Dad through it. I had a horrible vision of something nasty rolling out of Dad's pant leg onto the aisle and then getting tracked all over the place by those little suitcase wheels and people's shoes. It would have been a nightmare. It could have potentially polluted all of Newark airport as people fanned out in different directions.

So when the plane emptied, I went down the aisle first. Dad waited in his seat. I pulled a wheelchair right up to the doorway, went back onto the plane, and walked him gingerly right to that wheelchair, and once he was in it, we made a beeline for the Continental Presidents Club.

Once we were in the bathroom, I pulled Dad's pants down. It looked like someone had stuffed pudding all up and down his back. The smell was so foul I started dry heaving immediately. As I sat retching loudly, travelers flocked in and out. I was extremely lucky that I'd had the foresight to pack an extra outfit for Dad in my carry-on bag just in case anything happened. I cleaned him up and threw his old clothes right in the garbage. I feel bad about doing that to the Continental Presidents Club, but I figure I've racked up enough miles with them that we're square. When I was done, Dad was sitting, in clean clothes, in his wheelchair. He looked down at the floor sheepishly and said, "I didn't mean to do this. I didn't mean it."

"Of course you didn't mean it," I said. No one puts that in their planner: *Wake up. Have breakfast. Drink OJ. Read the paper. Get dressed. Get on the plane. Crap myself. Have my son bring me into the bathroom stall, wipe my ass, clean me up.*

"I guess you're not taking me on any more trips," he said, looking up at me.

"I'm taking you on more trips, Dad," I said. "I'm just going to make sure you don't eat for two days before we go."

*   *   *

The best compliment I hear after a show nowadays is when someone comes up to me and says, "I started watching your videos and I reconnected with my dad."

If I can be a player in this game and bring humor to it, I want to do it. I want to use it as a forum. Is it tragic my dad craps his pants in a crowded airport when we have fourteen minutes to make our connecting flight? Yes. Definitely. It's also funny.

There are a lot of people in my predicament, and we've been brought up not knowing how to take care of our parents as they get older. No one wants to face it. My generation and even the baby boomers have traditionally been like: "I'm really smart and I make lots of money and that money will buy my health and my parents' health. When they slow down, I'll stick them in a nice nursing home." To me, senior citizens are just like kids. They don't want to be stuck in a facility. They want to socialize and feel valuable, not degraded. They want human contact. Which is how I got to where I am with my parents today.

Growing up, I was close with my dad, but he wasn't a huge communicator. He was always just there, like a tree. My attitude was: "I'm safe as long as that tree is there." My mom was way more conversational and direct with me, asking about school and girlfriends. I bet my dad would have a hard time naming even one of my friends. But he was always there, which was more than enough. I knew what he felt for me.

When I first started doing stand-up and was traveling all over and I still lived with him, he'd show his love by making sure my car was fit to drive long distances. I'd be out doing something and come home and instead of Dad saying, "I love you," he'd say, "The oil's changed and the car is all clean."

Once in Florida we were out at a comedy club and I went outside to talk to a chick, and when I came back in, there was a crowd around him. I thought, "Oh my God, here we go. Something happened."

As I got closer, people were all staring at him and laughing their asses off. One guy turned around and said to me, "Can I hire him for a night? He's *killing* right now." So every once in a while, he knows how to rip apart a room. He wouldn't always show that off though.

He's a hard guy to get to understand, but overall, I know his behavior. And when Dad turned eighty, I knew he wasn't doing well, not just physically, but emotionally and spiritually to boot. He'd experienced some small strokes, which definitely did not help things, and as a result, he wasn't allowed to drive his car anymore. But it was parked in his garage in Florida and he was fine with that. And whenever we came to visit him, he'd always say, "Hey, use our car. It's got no miles on it." And I'd drive him around in it, but after a while, without even asking him, my mom gave his car away to one of her kids. And I think that triggered something right there, and he shut the whole world off. We moved them up near us, and by and large he still wasn't participating in the world. He liked to do jigsaw puzzles or read the newspaper and do the Jumble, or take a walk, or just go outside and get some fresh air. Now he wouldn't do any of it, and he wouldn't shower or shave. He'd just sleep for hours.

And my mom isn't so helpful with him. Her idea of tenderness is "Here, let me get you breakfast, and I'll also get you a napkin because you're a slob." They wear on each other. She's great with her grandkids but really bizarre when it comes to dealing with him. I think it's partly because she's still very mobile and he slows her down. She's the same age as him. She must look at him and fear that's where she's headed. At her age, a lot of the care he needs is beyond what she can do. And there's nothing wrong with that.

So I started bringing Dad on the road with me. He did six straight weeks on the bus with me on a tour of colleges called the Breuniversity Tour. The schedule, the pace of it, and all the new faces every day stimulated him, and some of his old wit and personality returned. On that tour I filmed a documentary about me, my dad, and aging called *More Than Me*, which ended up getting the attention of the Elder Aging Services of California. They had me out to screen the film at one of their seminars to a room full of the elderly and their caregivers.

Once the Breuniversity Tour ended, and I was doing one-off gigs, I couldn't always bring Dad because it just wasn't cost-effective. I have to pay for his flight, his hotel room, and all of his meals. So I'd take him about half the time. When I'd leave him, I'd come back and see that he was further behind. Withdrawing. Sleeping all day.

So with Dee's blessing, over the past year, we started having Dad stay with us for a couple of weeks at a time. When he was first staying with us, he'd come in a room, look at me, and ask, "Should I sit here?"

"Sit where you want," I'd say.

"Should I go in the kitchen?"

"Go where you want, Dad," I'd say, laughing. "I'm not going to tell you where to go."

I think my mom had some stern rules for him. But being around the kids and a house full of activity helps keep him fresh, and it actually takes some stress off of my mom. He still doesn't ever want to get too deep with me. Everything is an Abbot and Costello routine. He prefers not to make sense much of the time anymore. On the road, when I'd check with him to see if he had any money, he'd often respond, "No, but I think I know a plan to make some."

"Really?" I'd ask. "How?"

"I'm going to buy some pigs," he'd say confidently.

"Oh, then we can have a petting farm?" I'd ask. "What are we going to feed them?"

"I don't know."

"Well, how much do we charge, Dad?"

"Fifty bucks a head."

"Wow!" I'd say. "Do you think people will come?"

Then we'd be off for twenty minutes of gibberish. He'd tell me he walked to a flea market in Paris to buy scarves.

There are times when Dad's staying with us, and I'll pull up to see an ambulance in front of our house. They're there all the time, because Dad will have episodes where he has trouble breathing or just completely zones out. If I'm around, I usually don't call them, because I've just been around the symptoms long enough that I've got a pretty good hunch if we really need medical help. But I wonder what I'll do when he needs more help than the paramedics can provide. What if he needs to be put in a hospital? Do I want that? He's had a full life. Maybe it would be better to just let him die in my arms.

Every time Dad passes out they want to ship him to the hospital. I did it enough times; they stick him full of needles and tests and keep him there for observation. Hospitals are overrated. They're great if you have to have surgery. They're great if you need that emergency care. But if you're old, do they really need to keep you there for two weeks? Here's what's wrong with him: He's eighty-seven years old. He's *going.*

But in the meantime, the kids get to play with him. He gets to sit out on the back deck and watch me mow the lawn. If I'm cooking, I'll make him chop up some basil. I don't have to tell the guy I love him because I'm sure he knows it.

Epilogue

RV Tour

Last summer, I was going to be touring a lot, and I decided to try something different. If I was going to go on the road, doing family comedy, I was going to take my family with me. Not for some puny little weekend jaunt. For the whole thing. And we weren't going to fly. We were going to spend a real American summer together. In an RV. My kids are growing up way too fast to be apart from them for such long stretches. Little milestones go by—something simple like the fact that even my littlest, Dorianne, who's five, can swim now— and you step back and hope you're not taking any of it for granted. Also there's this: My oldest, Gabrielle, is eleven and on the verge of entering that whole texting and IM-ing universe, and that really freaks me out.

So the tour dates were all in place, and my plan was to rent the smallest, most navigable RV ever, get them all to pile in it, and along the way we'd hit campsites, barbecues, water slides, amusement parks, and truck stops. I would have even brought my parents, but my mom is so wedded to her routine that she'd have driven us crazy on the road. I'd get a baseball hat that says CAPTAIN or ADMIRAL on it and those little sunglasses things that people attach to the front of their regular glasses—and I don't even wear regular glasses. This was going to be the best summer ever, filled with Breuer-style togetherness.

My wife and kids bought into the idea immediately. After a few clicks on the RV rental Web site I wound up looking at one I thought I could handle.

"You've gotta be crazy," my wife said, looking over my shoulder. "We'll smother each other in there. We've got to get a bigger one."

I clicked another. To be honest, I was petrified of driving a really huge RV, but I didn't want anyone to know.

"That one's also way too small, Jim," Dee said. "It'll get so claustrophobic in there, we'll kill each other."

"We may not have to rent an RV for that to happen," I said, starting to lose my cool.

I clicked on another. A beautiful, manageable twenty-five-footer. Nice sandalwood interior. Entertainment console. Kitchenette. GPS. Seat coverings that were resistant to pudding, glue, finger paint, nacho cheese, and marker stains.

"Let's pick this," I said. It was settled. This was the RV in which we'd see the country and bond.

The first hour we were on the road, I realized I just loved the thing. I loved the idea of never having to stop to pee or eat. With all the females in this vehicle, it could have taken three days to travel 108 miles. Having an RV meant we wouldn't be stopping. It sank in that we were really going to be traveling the USA in an RV.

Dee was in a great mood. Happy to be taking her family on a journey. I wondered how long it would last when the reality that the girls were seated just three feet behind her kicked in. They were doing their best to open every bag of chips on board, along with all the rest of the groceries we'd purchased, then spilling them onto the floor, where they'd get crunched to tiny pieces and slide all over the place. They'd also begun their chorus: "She's sitting next to me." "She's against me." "Don't touch me." "She called me poopy." "She's staring at me." "Can I have some chips?" "I can't find them." "She ate a chip out of my bag." "That's my water!" "She took my seat."

A glance at the GPS told me that we'd made it only about forty miles from home. We were still in New Jersey, and our first campsite was all the way across Pennsylvania, located about an hour from Pittsburgh, the site of my first show.

But as the day wore on, a quiet calm settled over the RV, the kids napped, and looking out at the open road—I was now camped in the passing lane, getting cocky, flashing my brights and blowing past slowpokes—I fleetingly wondered why I'd ever chosen to travel any other way.

Until I realized that Western Pennsylvania was a long ways away. I was bored out of my mind, looking at the speedometer, the GPS, and the clock over and over again. I just wanted to set up camp and unwind. By the time we pulled off of I-80 onto the bumpy little county highway that we thought would lead us to the campground, it was dusk. It was getting a lot harder to see anything and we didn't have any backup instructions; we were just going on full-blown GPS.

"Does it matter that the GPS keeps saying to turn right, Dee?" I asked.

"The GPS knows what it's doing, Jim," she said.

"Then how come there's nowhere to turn right?" I said.

"I have no clue," Dee said. "Maybe I'll try using my cell phone, we've gotta be really close by now.

"I have no bars," Dee said, holding up her cell phone.

Concern was now spreading slowly across my face. "Oh, man," I said. "The GPS isn't working either. Without the GPS, we really don't know where the campsite is," I said through gritted teeth. "Didn't you have, like, a *paper* map of the area? And," I said, continuing to freak out, "I guess it's not like we can *call* anyone for directions!" I scowled, Dee scowled.

But a quick glance back at the kids confirmed that they weren't concerned with being just a little bit lost. They'd woken fully from their naps and were playing their Nintendo DS games, happily and obliviously eating Cheetos and Doritos. The road became bumpier and more winding, and with every pothole we hit all of the pans and the oven rattled like the whole RV was going to fall apart.

And it was getting darker outside.

That was probably for the best at this point. Because, outside of the RV windows, we didn't see many houses, and the ones we did see were not ones where you'd stop for directions. The residents were either missing teeth, not wearing shirts, or hanging out with pit bulls who were chewing on old tires—probably from RVs that had run out of gas nearby and been ritually dismantled. Then the road twisted more and driving became more stressful, because I didn't know how much leeway I had if another car was coming at me.

If we kept driving in one direction, I figured, we had to hit a main road where someone could offer us directions. I was pretty confident that there were people in Pennsylvania who have teeth, who live in cities, and who get to them by driving on a main road. We kept driving for twenty more minutes. There were no main roads.

"I'm just going to pull over," I said finally. I'm not one of those guys who won't ask for help. Even when the neighborhood is sketchy. "Next person I see, we'll stop."

"Oh, man," Dee said, sighing. "Don't ask any of these people. Don't let them know we're lost!" The kids kept munching their snacks.

At that point, just turning around and going back to the interstate wasn't even an option. We'd deviated from the straight-line plan and made a bunch of turns, and it's not like we could just turn the GPS on and make our way back.

"I'm serious," I explained. "The next reasonable-looking place I see, I'm going to stop in and ask for directions. And just maybe, I will make it back to this RV without an axe in my head."

Finally, we happened upon what I think was a motel or gas station or wood shop. The lights were on, and I thought I saw an old woman in the doorway, and I thought I saw an office. The Bates Motel had an office, too, but I was willing to take my chances.

I pulled in on the mystery business's gravel driveway. There was no sound but the engine of the RV and the slow, gentle churn of rubber tires across the pebbles. Oh, and also the clanging of all those pots, pans, dishes, forks, knives, spoons, Crock-Pots, melon ballers, ice cream scoops, and pie tins that my family members had packed, all stacked in the RV's kitchen. I broke the silence.

"They're closed!" I exclaimed, pointing at the rickety houselike structure. "No one here is going to help us."

"I see an old lady there!" Dee said. "Grow a pair and ask her the way outta here."

I saw her move, shuffling slowly toward our headlights.

I threw the RV into park. The GPS had safely brought us hundreds of miles. And now this wise old woman was going to take us the last furlongs. I hopped out of the cab. The old woman approached. I looked back and saw my family's faces huddled under the dome light, still chewing their snacks.

"Ma'am," I said politely, "I'm looking for a campsite. . . ."

I could see from her body language—a scratch at the crotch region of her tattered housecoat—that she'd obviously fielded this one before. "Make a left out of the parking lot," she explained politely. "And it's three and a half miles down the road, on your left . . ."

I could hear cheers now coming from the RV. The old woman looked at me and nodded at the RV. We were going to go camping! Or RVing. You know what I mean.

We made it to our campsite and pulled into our spot. This was the only one left and it was right next to the toilets. And when you go to one of these places (a campsite, not toilets) you have to back into your spot. I had never driven the RV more than three feet in reverse before, and it took me about a half hour to do a mediocre job of parking. By the time we got in place, a sizable crowd had gathered. And the girls were yelling that they wanted to finally get out of the RV.

"I wanna ride my Spider-Man bike!" Dorianne said. "I'm just going to jump out, okay? We're already in the parking lot!"

"Where are the vending machines?" Kelsey asked.

"I'm getting out first, 'cause I'm oldest!" Gabrielle fired back. Then they all raced to the door, pushing and grabbing at each other.

"It's too dark for bikes," I explained. "We're just going to chill out and get some fresh air."

At first I thought being close to the toilets would be a great thing due to the convenience. But people were going in and out of them 24/7. And when all the parents went to sleep for the night, guess where the teenagers' dope-smoking and booze-guzzling hangout was? And then there was the smell: a permanent, heavy, *bathroomy* odor.

At about three A.M. the no-good kids all cleared out because it started pouring. It rained all night long and all through the next day. So the girls didn't get to ride their bikes. We didn't get to hike. No one went in the lake. We were all stuck in the RV. Just like the day before. It was like *The Shining,* only everyone was Jack Nicholson.

We eventually decided that we should just move on to the next campsite. First, though, we had a little chore to complete: a dump of the RV's sewage tank. In the rain. This is exactly what it sounds like. There's a meter in the RV that tells you when you need to get rid of all of the poop and nasty water you're lugging around. And by that time, it was redlining. I waffled about doing it myself for a second, before Dee happily took the reins. "I'll do it," she said. "Because this is one job you just can't do halfway. If anyone screws this up, our trip is going to be ruined." She was basically saying that she didn't trust me not to half-ass it, and I was fine with her logic.

When you rent an RV, in order to suck all the crap out of your ride, you have to hook up a hose, kick a little motor on, and send it all into a receptacle at your local campsite. Guys in rock bands on tour buses often have a rule against dropping loads on the road. I have no idea why or how they decided on this rule—maybe they're trying to flush the wrong kind of stuff—because we were assured RV toilets never backfire or plug up, and ours didn't thankfully. You just really want to make sure when you're emptying it that the hose is attached correctly and the valves are all synced up, otherwise you will be in a world of trouble.

As I sat there watching Dee sync it all up perfectly, I had a moment of realization. I'd been on TV, met my idols, and lived a life beyond my most ambitious dreams. And there I was in the rain, in the middle of nowhere, watching my wife pump shit out of an RV. And I was happier than I'd ever been before.

Acknowledgments

I owe major thanks to my sister Dorene, who had the unenviable job of typing out this book. As I would hand her pages and pages of unreadable scribbles, she would laugh, get pissed, cry, and then laugh again. Most of all, she encouraged me to keep going. She has been a guardian angel, fiercely protecting me and my family from the showbiz vultures. I love her beyond words.

Special thanks go out to my cowriter, Jeff Johnson, who spent many nights Skyping with me as our kids and wives juggled their lives for us. I was not looking forward to having a writer go through my stuff, but Jeff made this the best experience possible. He caught every emotion and made my own writing more like me. Jeff, you knocked it out of the park.

A huge thank-you to Eric and Steve at FarmHaus Studios. They have been tremendous in bringing to life every vision I have—from Web sites to videos to posters to social media stuff. Without these guys I would not be able to do what I do. Hands down, these guys are my saviors. They are amazingly talented at what they do, and I've been blessed to have them work with me. Beyond that, I count them both as friends and role models; having them around makes my life so much better.

A special thanks to my manager, Judi Brown-Marmel. She really and truly gets it. And she busts her rear end to get the real Jim Breuer out there! I trust her and believe in her. A big thanks, also, to Robert Hartmann and the entire group at Levity Entertainment for helping me start this all with *Let's Clear the Air.* That show was just the beginning; thanks to all their hard work.

Thank you to Peter McGuigan, who saw the potential of this book from the very beginning. He has kept this thing on track the whole way through. He's the best literary agent out there.

And, of course, I have to thank Bill Shinker, Patrick Mulligan, Lisa Johnson, Lindsay Gordon, Dick Heffernan, and everyone—and I mean EVERYONE!—at Gotham Books and Penguin. This has been exciting from the moment I walked into their office to meet them. What a great group. This company believes in my passion, and has done everything to show me they stand behind this book. And that's all anyone can ask for.

Thanks to everyone who takes time to read this. I hope you laugh your ass off, perhaps get a reality check, and most important, just be entertained. Because entertaining you all is my job, and it's what makes me truly happy.

Special thanks to Jimmy Sciacca, Larry Schneidmuller, Pete Correale, and Phil Collura for being the best "brothers" anyone could ever pray for in a lifetime. These are my go-to guys in life.

And last but not least, a special thanks to Jimmy in Boston, Rooney, Pocono Bob, Terrance, Rob and Brian from Jersey, Lindsey and her family, "Blue collar in the house," all the Regulators, and the list goes on to every fan who has supported me, trusted me, listened to me, and has come out to see me again and again. You guys are what it's all about.